POWER, PRIME MINISTERS AND THE PRESS

POWER, PRIME MINISTERS AND THE PRESS

The Battle for Truth
on Parliament Hill

ROBERT LEWIS

DUNDURN
TORONTO

Cover image: istock.com/MBCheatham
Printer: Webcom

Library and Archives Canada Cataloguing in Publication

Lewis, Robert, 1943-, author
        Power, prime ministers and the press : the battle for truth on Parliament
Hill / Robert Lewis.

Includes bibliographical references and index.
Issued in print and electronic formats.
ISBN 978-1-4597-4264-2 (softcover).--ISBN 978-1-4597-4265-9 (PDF).--
ISBN 978-1-4597-4266-6 (EPUB)

        1. Canada. Parliament. House of Commons--Reporters and reporting.
2. Journalism--Objectivity--Canada. 3. Press and politics--Canada. I. Title.

PN4751.L48 2018   070.4'49320971   C2018-904102-1
                                                     C2018-904103-X

1   2   3   4   5   22   21   20   19   18

Conseil des Arts du Canada   Canada Council for the Arts   Canada   ONTARIO ARTS COUNCIL CONSEIL DES ARTS DE L'ONTARIO an Ontario government agency un organisme du gouvernement de l'Ontario

We acknowledge the support of the **Canada Council for the Arts**, which last year invested $153 million to bring the arts to Canadians throughout the country, and the **Ontario Arts Council** for our publishing program. We also acknowledge the financial support of the **Government of Ontario**, through the **Ontario Book Publishing Tax Credit** and the **Ontario Media Development Corporation**, and the **Government of Canada**.

Nous remercions le **Conseil des arts du Canada** de son soutien. L'an dernier, le Conseil a investi 153 millions de dollars pour mettre de l'art dans la vie des Canadiennes et des Canadiens de tout le pays.

Care has been taken to trace the ownership of copyright material used in this book. The author and the publisher welcome any information enabling them to rectify any references or credits in subsequent editions.
— *J. Kirk Howard, President*

The publisher is not responsible for websites or their content unless they are owned by the publisher.

Printed and bound in Canada.

VISIT US AT

 dundurn.com | @dundurnpress | dundurnpress | dundurnpress

Dundurn
3 Church Street, Suite 500
Toronto, Ontario, Canada
M5E 1M2

To Sally, my rock for the ages

For Aiden, Elise, Ruby, and Charlie
Our hopes for the future

CONTENTS

NEW BOY ON THE HILL

The day I arrived for work in the Parliamentary Press Gallery, February 15, 1965, was a grand occasion. It was not about me, an unknown, fresh-faced twenty-two-year-old reporter, who had landed at the train station the day before with all my worldly possessions in a green steamer trunk. The excitement was about the new Canadian flag snapping in the clear, chill air atop the Gothic Revival Peace Tower, the stylized eleven-point red maple leaf proclaiming a new day. It went up for the first time amid prayers and much hope. Prime Minister Lester Pearson, who had led the divisive battle to replace the Red Ensign as Canada's national flag, intoned: "God bless our flag, and God bless Canada." Governor General Georges Vanier told a cheering crowd of ten thousand: "I appeal to all Canadians to set aside pettiness, selfishness, and intolerance where they may exist, and to cultivate a spirit of brotherhood and mutual confidence."

What I witnessed unfolding inside the building over the remaining months of the twenty-sixth Parliament — and beyond — gave new meaning to the words *pettiness*, *selfishness*, and *intolerance*. For me, it was a rude awakening. From one day to the next, crisis gave way to chaos. Personal name-calling and allegations of scandal reverberated through the halls, whether it was a federal worker accused of being a Russian spy or a mysterious East German woman admitting she had a relationship with a Cabinet minister. Someone set off a bomb in the washroom adjacent to the prime minister's office, killing himself but no one else. Aides to the prime minister were accused of consorting with the Mafia, and one went to jail for accepting a bribe. Cabinet ministers left in disgrace, seemingly almost as fast as they arrived. The many judicial commissions of inquiry became a growth industry for lawyers and consultants. Even from a distance of fifty years, it was truly one of the most bitter periods in Canadian parliamentary history, embracing the bloody downfall of Progressive Conservative leader John Diefenbaker, scandals and allegations that tainted the reputations of Cabinet ministers on both sides of the House, and the unhappy end of Lester Pearson's political career. It also got me on page 1 most days.

It was truly a wonderful time for a journalist to claim a front-row seat to watch Canadian history unfold, with all its imperfections — and in all its glory. Indeed, amid the many crises — manufactured and real — came some lasting legislation that endures today: the Canada Pension Plan, medicare, reform of immigration rules, the Canada Assistance Plan, and the Pearsonian concept of official bilingualism. And throughout, there was the leitmotif of Canada's past and present, the ebb and flow of nationalism in Quebec, and the federation's struggle to respond. Then came the rise of two promising leaders, Robert Stanfield for the Conservatives and Pierre Trudeau for the Liberals. And, boy, did we watch *him*.

I was proud and pleased as I walked up Parliament Hill into the expansive embrace of the West and East Blocks, up the marble steps under the Peace Tower. Ever since I put up my hand and volunteered to work on a class newspaper in grade five, I had wanted to be a journalist. In school I applied myself more in the newsroom than the classroom. Some of the relatives of my university classmates in Montreal were prominent politicians and were chronicled in my local morning paper, the Montreal *Gazette*.

The news fed my interest in the big issues of the day, especially the nascent Quebec separatist movement. Marcel Chaput, a one-time federal civil servant who launched the militant Rassemblement pour l'Indépendance Nationale, came to campus to speak.

I landed my first job mainly because my "clips" included a report in my school paper, the *Loyola News*, on a speech about Quebec nationalism by Walter O'Hearn. The distinguished executive editor of the *Montreal Star* — O'Hearn lived until 1979 — hired me as a summer police desker at fifty dollars a week. In the early weeks I monitored a police radio — in the two official languages, French and static — retyped incoming bureau cables, and called bereaved families for pictures of their deceased loved ones. Then, moving to "nights," I got the keys to the company car and covered speeches and press conferences, and chased fire engines. Assigned to run film back to the office from a subway cave-in, I saw my first accident fatality, a crumpled, gruesome sight I will never forget. After nine months I was assigned to cover Ottawa and took my first walk up Parliament Hill as a reporter.

I identified myself to the guard and made my own way, unescorted, to Rooms 340 to 350 North, the fabled National Press Gallery where, for almost a century, the "greats of journalism" had filed their reports. What

Don Newlands/KlixPix, *Maclean's*

Slumming in the corridor annex before the fire marshal closed it down. Lubor Zink, right: as journalism goes, so goes democracy.

I found was a space just one trash can short of a slum neighbourhood. The parliamentary bureau of the *Montreal Star* was actually just an alcove off the main hallway leading to the Commons and Senate chambers. The cubicle, today a series of enclosed phone booths, was exactly one hundred paces to our press box–like gallery overlooking the floor of the House of Commons to the west, and twenty-five strides to the Senate press gallery in the other direction.

The cramped quarters contained four battered typewriters and wooden desks that groaned under the piles of newspapers, budgets, public accounts, and Hansards. Empty beer bottles, a heel of stale Scotch in a glass, cigarette butts, ashes, discarded typewritten sheets, and dustballs provided the ambience for the tap-tap-tapping coming from Jean-Pierre Fournier of *Le Devoir* in the next cubicle. Announcements from the desk clerk blared over the speakers: "Bruce Phillips, call on line one." It mattered not that the Dominion Fire Marshal had condemned the premises or that the speaker of the House had threatened to close the hallway and remove us from Rooms 340 to 350 North. We refused to go and give up our special access to the Commons and Senate galleries, to their respective lobbies, and to the men and women who debated and passed legislation for a nation on the cusp of its one hundredth birthday. But in 1966, after months of negotiations between Public Works and the gallery executive, the speaker ruled that the hallway had to be cleared, and most bureaus moved off the Hill to the Norlite Building across the way on Wellington Street, now the National Press Building.

What did matter, I learned, was what went on in the gallery and in newsrooms across the country. Democracy and debate flourish on the free flow of information. Journalism is an essential tool in the process. In the motto of the Canadian Journalism Foundation, "As journalism goes, so goes democracy." That idea is amplified in a quotation from Lord Byron's *Don Juan* chiselled in stone on the mantelpiece of the press gallery lounge on Parliament Hill:

> But words are things, and a small drop of ink,
> Falling, like dew, upon a thought produces
> That which makes thousands, perhaps millions think.

For the first ninety years, members of the gallery largely churned out the party line for their chosen party. That sycophantic era came to an abrupt end in 1956 when the majority of gallery members rebelled at the Liberal government's arrogant shutdown of debate during a funding crisis. The first wave of university graduates, including those from the new journalism schools, also moved onto the Hill in the early 1960s, bringing more rigour to the coverage of government. Then, in the 1970s, Watergate opened the floodgates and everyone wanted to be an investigative journalist.

Still, in the winter of 1965, I felt as if I had walked onto the movie set of *The Front Page* and I was the innocent among seasoned veterans. My new colleagues, as they told me later when we became friends, were astonished that they had asked for relief and head office had dispatched a child labourer as the third hand. When June Callwood's piece in *Maclean's* about the press gallery appeared in April 1965, I was proud to see a picture of me walking outside our corridor encampment, but I was such a newbie that the caption identified only the reporter with his back to the camera.

It was a quick learning experience. Journalism on Parliament Hill was intimate and intense. John Turner, the dashing MP from Montreal, would drop by our enclosure to chat with bureau chief W.A. "Bill" Wilson, one of the gallery opinion leaders. Tom Kent, Lester Pearson's policy guru, would wander around, chatting with columnists and senior reporters. Along the west wall, reporters from the Montreal *Gazette*, *Ottawa Journal*, and *Toronto Telegram* could be observed trading notes on stories and sometimes actually sharing carbon copies of their typed pieces ("swapping blacks," in the jargon of the day).

The main action centred on question period, which in those days began at 2:30 p.m. Those of us working for evening papers ("Whatzat?" you ask) would make a mad dash from the Commons to the bank of phones to meet midafternoon deadlines. For overnight stories, we would hand our typed articles to CN-CP telegraph staffers at a desk at the front of the room, who would shove the copy into a pneumatic tube and send it downtown for dispatch by teletype.

I also discovered something else about covering politics in the hot house: there are moments of searing brute emotion and tragedy that make the heart stop. Such was the case on the evening of Monday, November 14, 1966, when a jeering crowd of Progressive Conservatives rejected John Diefenbaker's appeal for support at the party's annual meeting in the ballroom of the Château Laurier hotel.

"Is this a Conservative meeting?" he demanded.

"Yes!" came the roar from his detractors.

From a spot to the right of the stage, I could see tears in the old chieftain's eyes.

There had been similar emotion on the floor of the House of Commons on the night of June 29, 1965, when Prime Minister Pearson told a hushed House that he had accepted the resignation of his justice minister, Guy Favreau. He was the leading francophone in Cabinet, a decent man brought down by ceaseless hectoring by the Conservatives, his own flaws, and Pearson's unwillingness to protect him after he mishandled allegations that Liberal staff members were involved in influence peddling. (The other thing I remember about that Tuesday night was that I was supposed to have dinner with the vivacious and comely Sally O'Neill, a visitor from Montreal. Fortunately, she waited for me.)

Two years later I had a similar experience of high drama covering Charles de Gaulle as the French president addressed a crowd outside city hall in Montreal. As he uttered the famous "*Vive le Québec libre*," my spirits sank as a crescendo of voices rose in a fierce nationalistic cheer. And there, to my right, was a colleague from the press gallery in Ottawa, a francophone friend, joining the rapturous chorus, tears of joy streaming down his cheeks.

In later years I learned another lesson: the disappointments that inevitably follow the triumphs of our political leaders. Many undertook historic nation-building exercises: the transcontinental railway (Macdonald), the national broadcaster (R.B. Bennett), the St. Lawrence Seaway (St. Laurent), the Trans-Canada Highway (Diefenbaker), the maple leaf flag (Pearson), the Charter of Rights (Trudeau), and free trade (Mulroney). Yet all the leaders had fatal flaws that led to their demise, whether through scandal, self-inflicted wounds, or regional disaffection.

In Ottawa I worked the noon-to-close shift (no overtime pay). It was a time when reporters actually sat covering the debates of the House of Commons into the night. We even ventured into the Senate gallery from time to time — and members of the government caucus there, pleased that we paid them the courtesy, often became good sources. It was the way a boy from Quebec's Eastern Townships learned about freight rates in the West and the cod fishery off Newfoundland. In the reading room we could peruse the papers from across the country, and we could do research in the nearby Library of Parliament. We interviewed MPs in the private members' lobbies of the House and got to know them as individuals and sources. On some afternoons after question period, John Diefenbaker, by then an embittered, defrocked leader, would hold court in the members' lobby about the good old days. By evening, not a few bottles of bootleg booze from the gallery's "blind pig" got cracked in MPs' offices, the Maritimers the most ebullient about their rum and Coke. On many nights in the sixties, walking back to my bachelor apartment from the Hill, I had the sense that I had been in touch with all of Canada that day.

For francophones, however, Ottawa was no idyll on the Rideau in the 1960s and '70s. A kind of two solitudes often marked relationships between the French and English journalists. When Rimouski-born Luc Lavoie turned up in September 1976 to work as a broadcast news reporter for La Presse Canadienne, he spoke no English and discovered that "Ottawa was in fact an English-speaking city." He listened to nothing but English TV and radio and read only English papers, teaching himself by dint of persistence to become functionally bilingual in two months. He was delighted to be in the company of so many outstanding French-speaking colleagues, among them Madeleine Poulin, Jean Bédard, Gilbert Bringué, Lise Bissonnette, Denis Lord, Marcel Pépin, Jean Pelletier, Gilles Paquin, and the dean of them all, Jean-Marc Poliquin. In his lively 2018 memoir, *En Première Ligne,* about his years as a reporter and senior adviser to Brian Mulroney and Pierre Karl Péladeau, Lavoie described a close gallery tribe, "most of whom adhered to the sovereignist agenda." For many, René Lévesque's Parti Québécois victory in 1976 "was a kind of revenge — a very modest one when you think about it — for the defeat of the Plains of Abraham." In contrast, many anglophone journalists on the Hill, the *Globe*'s André Picard once observed, adopted more of a "Team Canada, rah, rah" approach to national unity.

Whatever the language, it was an era of journalistic entitlement. Even though getting free railway passes from CN and CP and free letter franking had ended by the time I arrived, there were myriad other perks and privileges:

subsidized gourmet meals and good company in the Parliamentary Dining Room, cheap breakfasts — and the latest gossip — in the West Block cafeteria, twenty-five-cent shoe shines in the barber shop, and free stationery. (That was a throwback to the 1900s when one of the correspondents' perks was "the trunk" — a leather-bound case with forty dollars' worth of stationery.) In the sixties our care and feeding extended to free parking on the Hill. One hot issue arose when tourists began taking the free spots assigned to gallery members and the RCMP started ticketing us for parking outside the lines in our allotted spots. The gallery filed a formal complaint with Justice Minister Lionel Chevrier, no less, who ruled that the Mounties "will not henceforth ticket a press gallery member's car if it is within area No. 60 no matter in what manner it is parked." So there.

The real pampering came from the stewards responsible for the "blind pig." Beers were twenty-five cents, chilled in an old Coke machine, and shots of gin or rye were fifty cents, delivered to your desk. (Scotch cost a whole seventy-five cents.) The boss was Bob Carisse, whose father had been the gallery's chief clerk in the 1930s. Carisse also supplied the booze at the annual black-tie press gallery dinner, a highlight of the political year when politicians, bureaucrats, and reporters gathered for an evening of irreverent off-the-record speeches, skits, and two-fisted drinking. The bar tab for the May 7, 1966, dinner was $1,108.71 (about $8,000 today), consisting of sixty-seven bottles of rye, seventy-three bottles of Scotch, twenty-five of gin and twelve of rum, plus twenty-four cases of beer. The hard-liquor crowd gargled only seven bottles of red wine.

That was the dinner when the gallery skits focused on Gerda Munsinger, the sultry East German escort, and the scandal about her meetings with two of Diefenbaker's Cabinet ministers, Pierre Sévigny in Defence and George Hees in Trade. The gallery paid an artist $144 for a large painting of Gerda, sprawled on a sofa, that graced the entrance to the dinner. The good-humoured Hees, never one to waste a good line, looked up as he passed beneath the painting and said to his host, "Got the eyes wrong."

In those days, the gallery dinner was a raucous, ribald affair. Pamela Wallin, then a new Hill reporter for the *Toronto Star,* recalled her astonishment at viewing a prominent columnist and a female Liberal minister emerging together, dishevelled, from a hotel washroom during a pre-dinner cocktail party. Author Rod McQueen, then a senior adviser to

Joe Clark, reports that in the mid-1970s two reporters, Peter Meerburg of the Halifax *Chronicle Herald* and Iain Hunter of the *Ottawa Citizen*, caused a sensation at the post-dinner reception when they streaked back and forth naked through the Hall of Honour directly beneath the Peace Tower.

Doug Fisher, the New Democratic Party (NDP) MP turned columnist, once jocularly dismissed gallery members as "lushes, drunks and incompetents." At times the disapprobation was not wide of the mark. An official report in 1964 by the chief of Protective Services, describing an after-hours incident in the press gallery lounge, makes the point:

> Mr. Dewar said that at approximately 8:30 p.m. Mr. Murphy emptied a jug of ice water over him, and, in a joking manner, Dewar chased Murphy down the north corridor, 3rd floor, towards the General Gallery, east entrance [of the House of Commons]. Evidently Mr. Murphy did not realize he was so close to the end wall, for upon looking over his shoulder to see how close Mr. Dewar was, crashed into the stone wall injuring his right leg.

There was more:

> Upon being taken back to the Press Room, Mr. N. DePoe contacted Mr. Murphy's doctor, namely Dr. Roche, and received instructions to put Mr. Murphy in an ambulance and the doctor would meet him at the Emergency Ward of the Civic Hospital. However, Mr. Murphy refused to get into the ambulance, stating that he had an experience with an ambulance in the past and would die before he ever got into another one. The ambulance was then sent back. Mr. DePoe then called the doctor again, also Mrs. Murphy. They both arrived in the building before 11 p.m.

Needless to say, the evening did not end well for Mr. Murphy. Nor the next morning.

You can't make this stuff up.

"Hey, hey, it's the first of May, outdoor lovin' starts today!" With that, reporter Jim Munson jumped off the bus with a woman and headed for a grove off the Gatineau Parkway, just south of the speaker's summer retreat where the annual cocktail party for Ottawa dignitaries — and inked-stained wretches — took place. When an RCMP officer approached the couple, *in flagrante delicto*, Munson calmly informed the cop that the lady was his wife, Ginette.

"I was wearing a little white dress," Ginette recalled, with a twinkle in her eye.

"Yeah," added Munson, "that's why we were in the bushes."

With a chuckle, Ginette added: "I had folded the dress neatly and laid it on my red shoes in the grass."

Munson explained: "I'm a very spontaneous person. It just seemed in the moment of love to be the right thing to do."

In December 2017 the Munsons celebrated their fiftieth anniversary on a trip to Manhattan with their two grown sons.

From his salad days, the boisterous Munson, a self-described "corridor commando," is also remembered for a shoving match during a scrum with Pierre Trudeau, for pouring a beer over Brian Mulroney's head during an argument at a press gallery dinner, and for lighting up a joint as he sat next to the commissioner of the RCMP at a gallery dinner. Ultimately, his peers elected him president of the press gallery. He had a distinguished TV career with CTV on the Hill and as a foreign correspondent, and later served as press secretary to Prime Minister Jean Chrétien before his appointment to the Senate, where he is an ardent proponent of the rights of people with disabilities.

To be sure, the Ottawa press gallery was an old boys' club, with an emphasis on *old*. When columnist Chantal Hébert came to the gallery in 1977 as a twenty-three-year-old, she felt "like I suddenly had landed in my parents' living room." Women were not allowed in as members until 1924. Even as late as 1966 they could not attend the annual gallery dinner or be members of the unofficial Hill watering hole, the National Press Club.

Gail Scott, one of the well-educated young women who entered the business in the late 1960s and rose to be anchor of CTV's *Canada AM*, noted that "alcohol abuse was rampant, overt and covert sexual harassment was rampant.... We put up with an awful lot of garbage." One year, in an effort to send up the male chauvinism, she hosted the gallery dinner wearing a bikini.

Christine Hearn, who was twenty-six when she arrived on the Hill in 1975 as a reporter for BCTV, recalled: "The sexism was so ordinary and pervasive that you didn't even think about it. There was no point in picking a fight about any of it. If you stopped to worry about it, you'd never get your job done."

Hearn avoided overt sexual harassment, but Kathryn Young was not so fortunate. She was a twenty-four-year-old Canadian Press (CP) reporter, just out of journalism school in 1984, when she was assaulted during an after-hours drink in her apartment with Michel Gratton, press secretary to Prime Minister Mulroney. "He just leapt on top of me," she told CBC Radio's *As It Happens* in 2014. "He ripped my shirt open and had his hands down my shirt." After she yelled, "No! No!" Gratton stood up and went home.

Young did not go to the police and told only a few intimates. But several months later, when Young heard MPs in the Commons — and male colleagues beside her in the gallery — snickering about allegations that Gratton had propositioned her gallery colleague Judy Morrison, she went public. Both women received an apology from Gratton, who died in 2011, but both felt their careers began to ebb after being branded as troublemakers in the male-dominated environs of the Hill. Carol Off, host of *As It Happens*, reprised the incidents in the *Globe and Mail* at the height of the 2018 #MeToo movement, recounting her own disturbing memory: being groped by a senior member of Mulroney's Cabinet while she was a young gallery reporter in 1987. At the time, gallery colleagues told Off to keep quiet about the matter. In a haunting warning, one man cautioned: "Remember what happened to Judy Morrison." She is best remembered as the accomplished host of CBC Radio's Saturday morning show *The House*, and went on to a successful career as a businesswoman who became active in local politics and several volunteer youth organizations.

Back in the mid-1960s, there was a changing of the guard in the gallery as retirements by veterans gave way to a wave of new faces. Among the departures were Arthur Blakely of the Montreal *Gazette* and Peter Dempson of the *Toronto Telegram* ("the *Tely*"). Among the newcomers were Geoffrey Stevens of the *Globe and Mail* and his colleague Norman Webster, both destined for the top two jobs at the paper; Martin Goodman of the *Toronto Star*, later president of Torstar Corporation; former NDP MP Doug Fisher, columnist for the *Toronto Telegram;* and Fraser Kelly, the *Tely*'s new correspondent, who later ruled supper-hour news in Toronto for CTV and CBC. Other newbies destined for high-profile careers joined that year: Bruce Phillips as a correspondent for Southam News, later CTV's face in Ottawa; Frances Russell, United Press International, who later became the *Winnipeg Tribune*'s influential Ottawa columnist; and Jean-V. Dufresne of *Le Devoir.*

The pace of growth was so dramatic that when young Cape Bretoner Linden MacIntyre arrived for the Halifax *Chronicle Herald*, bureau chief Eric Dennis had to appeal for an earpiece for simultaneous translation in the Commons. The tight-fisted sergeant-at-arms had decreed that the number of supplied devices already exceeded the number of members. In a letter to the gallery, the sergeant-at-arms had warned sternly that the gallery had been issued "a total of 163 ear pieces, which is considerably in excess of your membership. On replacements, we simply give you new instruments for damaged ones."

Print ruled the day. There were protests about the CBC bureau acquiring its own telephone, an echo of the opposition broadcast reporters faced when they had applied for accreditation in the late 1950s. Even in 1965, with the exception of Norman DePoe of the CBC and Jean-Marc Poliquin of Radio-Canada, newspapers — and the ubiquitous CP staffers — were the dominant forces. Blair Fraser of *Maclean's*, the *Toronto Star*'s Peter C. Newman, W.A. Wilson of the *Montreal Star*, Anthony Westell of the *Globe*, Charles Lynch of Southam, and Amédée Gaudreault of *Le Soleil* were among the veterans who set the agenda for the nation — as well as for a new generation of reporters who had the good fortune to become their proteges.

It was always thus. From the earliest days, the veterans looked after the newcomers. I was fortunate to have two gentlemen mentors, the veteran

Bill Wilson, whose sources were amazing and impeccable, and Jim Stewart, one of the finest reporters and most generous colleagues with whom I ever worked. The very first time I flew in an airplane was after Bill arranged for me to go with Prime Minister Pearson on his private government Viscount propeller plane up to his Algoma East riding, heady stuff for a sheltered young man in his early twenties.

Many of us came to Ottawa from police and courthouse beats, which often proved useful, or from a provincial legislative press gallery. A few of us would go on to become editors and publishers or TV anchors, more became ministerial advisers or lobbyists, a few made Cabinet minister in their own right, at least one became head of the Parliamentary Library (Alfred D. DeCelles had also been editor of both *Le Journal de Québec* and *La Minerve*), one made governor general (Radio-Canada's Roméo LeBlanc), and one even rose to the heavenly heights as thirteenth Anglican bishop of Quebec (Bruce Myers). Arthur Ford, a member of the gallery in the early 1900s and later an editor of the *London Free Press,* called the gallery "a postgraduate school for newspapermen." A 1969 government task force on government information concluded: "The Gallery is unquestionably the most important instrument of political communication in the country." That was then.

By today's standards the means were decidedly rudimentary. Even when I went back to the gallery in 1975 — by then the CN-CP telegraph desk had been shuttered and the corridor slum had been cleared — there was no 24/7 news cycle. *Newsworld*, Canada's first cable news network, did not take to the CBC airwaves until 1989. There was no internet and there were no Sunday papers. We filed our Ottawa stories to *Maclean's* in Toronto on a fax machine, one page at a time, or by CN-CP wire if we were on the road. On the campaign trail there was a Runyonesque air to the proceedings. Fraser Kelly, then a young reporter with the *Toronto Telegram,* recalled returning to his room after a wild party in St. John's in 1965 and getting an anxious call from his desk demanding to know where his report was on Pearson's speech. Fraser, who had filed his account already, said: "I had to sit down on the edge of my bed and, sort of through a fog, dictate the whole story on the spot. It turned out that the wire agent had gone to the party too and hadn't filed any of the stories." The next day the *Telegram* not only received another copy of Kelly's story courtesy of the wire agent, but the menu from the banquet and some stories meant for other papers.

For my part, *Time* magazine came calling in 1967 — mainly because of the exposure I enjoyed in the *Star* — and I moved to Montreal as its bureau chief. I had a dream assignment covering Expo 67, but politics was never far from mind. I was in Quebec City when the Liberal Party forced René Lévesque from its ranks and launched him on the way to his independence party (shades of Marcel Chaput); I covered the leadership campaigns of Robert Stanfield and Pierre Trudeau.

Stanfield was always more approachable than Trudeau. One night after a well-oiled Tory leadership reception at Expo 67, my wife and I shared a taxi with a very relaxed Robert Stanfield and his wife, Mary, as the putative Tory leader proceeded to give us a hilarious tour of Montreal in his distinctive French.

I also enjoyed two later stints in the press gallery: from 1969 to 1970 with *Time* magazine and, from 1975 to 1982, as bureau chief with *Maclean's*. Those years embraced the coming of Pierre Trudeau — and, briefly, his going, during the Joe Clark interregnum — and the re-emergence of John Turner, this time as Liberal leader. As for the others, from Chrétien to Martin, through Mulroney, Campbell, and Harper, I was an interested observer with periodic direct contacts as managing editor and editor-in-chief at *Maclean's*. I once encountered Justin Trudeau, but he was just a lively eight-year-old off-the-record kid in his father's entourage at the G7 Summit in Venice, feeding pigeons in Piazza San Marco.

By the late 1970s everything changed. The gallery became more diverse as women assumed their place on the national scene. The gallery executive regularly protested against the efforts of the Pearson and Trudeau governments to limit access — a theme that is as old as Confederation. The old cozy relationships gave way to more confrontation. Broadcast reporters on the Hill and a live TV feed from the House of Commons took over the agenda. In the decades ahead, reporters would tweet or blog their stories or file from BlackBerrys and iPhones.

That in turn ushered in new approaches to news management. No longer did the quiet background briefings for reporters and off-the-record chats predominate; now TV and radio demanded on-camera speakers for their "clips," and those became the new normal — whether they conveyed reality or otherwise. Reporters could skip attending House sessions and watch them from their offices live. Parliament became defined by clips from question period and the scrums outside the Commons. The apparatus for feeding and watering the media grew at a much faster rate than the number of journalists on Parliament Hill, to the point that reporters are now outgunned by civil servants, public relations specialists, and lobbyists for special interests (who tend to dominate the talk shows as well). Many journalists face constant deadlines, filing for websites, tweeting, blogging, and shooting video. "You watch people doing so much with so little," Jim Munson observes. "That doesn't serve journalism well."

By the early 2000s the governing Conservatives were even shooting and posting their own video reports online, and the prime minister rarely entertained questions from reporters, often delivering major policy statements away from Ottawa before partisan audiences. A deep freeze descended on the public service. Public relations specialists controlled by the prime minister's office approved any and all communication — usually via email.

Ostensibly, that all changed on October 19, 2015, the day Canadians went to the polls and massively rejected the mean-spirited Harper government and elected Justin Trudeau and his "sunny ways" team of newbies. On media relations, Trudeau did all the obvious stuff, putting distance

In the scrum: Peter Mansbridge (left foreground) and Jean Rivard of CKAC (front).

between himself and the Harperites. He released Cabinet ministers to scrum with reporters and allowed senior officials to do backgrounders. But even today, when the House is in session, adults in the corridors of Parliament Hill are still supplicants, beseeching ministers from behind rope barriers for morsels that will make a snippet in their reports.

In the early years, Trudeau seemed to be everywhere, from Davos to La Loche, from Washington to Beijing, making speeches, doing interviews, posing for selfies. For the first time in years, a prime minister returned to the National Press Theatre to face reporters. Time would tell if his "sunny ways" represented a real change in media relations that would prevail during a major crisis. Was Trudeau the real deal?

The initial indications were that not much had really changed. He broke several election promises. Liberals in the ranks who dared criticize government policies were relegated to their own Elba on the Rideau. And while Trudeau was highly visible, he rarely sat for a full-on inquiry by the press gallery. He did launch a revolutionary attempt to give power and dignity back to Indigenous Peoples, and although many problems remain, this could stand as a historic legacy. One of Trudeau's biggest early challenges was the fallout from his controversial decision to take over the construction of the Trans Mountain Pipeline from Alberta to the coast. But the Justin Trudeau reign has been as scripted as any that has gone before — sometimes to excess, as when he paraded around India with his family, dressed in colourful outfits. He has even adopted some tricks from the Harper playbook: using omnibus bills to introduce unrelated changes to laws, denying cost information to the independent parliamentary budget officer, and flouting rules on conflict of interest and party donations. Someday down the road, another generation of reporters in the press gallery will tell the nation how that all worked out for Justin Trudeau. They always have.

———

I still harken back to my days as a young reporter on the Hill. February 16, 1965, belonged to the promise of the future — well, at least to my first assignment: covering a reference to the committee on privileges and elections. In its own small way, the case spoke volumes for what had gone before — and what was to come. Gilles Grégoire, the fiery deputy leader of the Créditiste Party, a rump of Quebec nationalists who often supported the minority Liberals, had been arrested on the Hill for ignoring two outstanding traffic warrants. Grégoire had refused to accept the warrants because they were not "officially" issued in French. He claimed he had been manhandled by three RCMP officers and called the RCMP commissioner "public enemy number one" of all French Canadians. The government's House leader actually supported Grégoire's right to a hearing. MPs of all parties, said George McIlraith, must be allowed to attend to their parliamentary duties freely. "It is clear," he added, "that the service of Parliament is paramount to all other claims."

And there it was in a nutshell: language rights, an RCMP controversy, and a brouhaha in the Commons, themes that resonate even today. There would be bigger issues and battles to come, bigger stories to cover, a world of wonders to discover. For now, February 17 was a day of immense pride for a young reporter, a sense of arrival in the big league of his chosen career. The headline on the left-hand column of the *Montreal Star* on page 28 was a modest signpost:

COMMITTEE GETS MP'S PROTEST
BY ROBERT LEWIS
OF THE STAR'S OTTAWA BUREAU

Those were the days.

Part I

DAYS OF YORE

Chapter 1

IN THE BEGINNING

On Wednesday, November 6, 1867, official Ottawa was abuzz with excitement. A nineteen-gun salute from the Ottawa Field Battery greeted Viscount Charles Stanley Monck, the forty-eight-year-old governor general, as he arrived to preside over the first session of the new nation's Parliament. After the formalities of swearing in MPs and the Cabinet ended, Sir John A. Macdonald, the fifty-three-year-old prime minister picked by Monck for the role, moved the appointment of the first speaker of the House. Seconding the motion was Macdonald's seatmate, Sir George-Étienne Cartier. Then, Joseph Dufresne, the Quebec Conservative MP from Montcalm, rose in his seat and, addressing the House in French, protested the election of Honourable James Cockburn of Northumberland West. In the words of the Toronto *Globe* the next day, Dufresne complained, "the gentleman could not speak the French language. He thought it was to be regretted that, at the inauguration of the new system, greater respect was not shown to Lower Canada in this matter. He looked upon this as a matter of national feeling." Without further discussion, the House then went about its business in English. Along with the report, the *Globe*, a partisan Liberal outlet in its day, used an adjacent column in the November 7 paper to condemn Macdonald for using the speaker's office as a reward for a loyal but unpromising follower.

So much for a smooth start for the first Parliament.

The *Globe* report was significant: it affirmed the vital role of the press gallery in national affairs, since there were no official records of debates

— known as Hansard — until 1875. Indeed, the Parliamentary Press Gallery is as old as Confederation. While the great fire of 1916 that razed the Parliament Buildings destroyed most of the official records, the first volume of the House of Commons Journals mentions the "reporters' room." In 1872 the *Canadian Illustrated News* carried artist Edward Jump's sketch of the press gallery in the Commons. In fact, pre-Confederation reporters covering the Parliament of Upper Canada actually worked out of the still-under-construction Parliament Buildings in 1866 — an anniversary the press gallery marked with the publication of a retrospective, *Sharp Wits & Busy Pens*, in May 2016.

The tradition of covering legislatures dates back to the colonial days. John Bushell published the first issue of his *Halifax Gazette* in 1752. Quebec's pioneering paper, *La Gazette*, appeared in 1764. Journalists had reported on political debates in Quebec City since 1792 and established La Tribune de la Presse Québécoise on November 18, 1871. Étienne Parent, the young intellectual who was the guiding spirit of the *nationaliste* paper *Le Canadien*, later served as a senior Cabinet official for the Province of Canada, moving as the seat of government shifted among Kingston, Montreal, Toronto, and Quebec City between 1843 and 1859 — and submitting

Sketch of Reporters' Gallery, 1872, from the *Canadian Illustrated News*.

occasional articles to his paper. Other pre-Confederation journalists led the fight for press freedoms and reform. William Lyon Mackenzie, destined to mount the Upper Canada Rebellion against the Family Compact, wrote in his *Colonial Advocate*: "Wherever the press is not free, the people are poor, abject, degraded slaves."

Halifax editor Joseph Howe of the *Novascotian*, George Brown of the *Globe*, and Parent were among the influential journalists who later played strong, controversial political roles in shaping Canada. Of the ninety-eight-member Province of Canada delegation attending the Charlottetown Conference in 1864, twenty-three were journalists. As educator George Grant observed in 1828, referring to Howe's activities, "At this time in the history of the world, it was almost impossible to be an editor without being a politician also."

And how the members of the press gallery could play politics. Thomas White Jr., called "the Father of the Gallery" by the *Canadian Illustrated News* in 1875, bought the *Hamilton Spectator* and the *Gazette* in Montreal before getting elected and becoming Macdonald's influential minister of the interior. Henri Bourassa left Laurier's Cabinet and founded *Le Devoir* in Montreal, later turning over direction of the paper to a gallery veteran, Georges Pelletier. In the 1900s, two English giants of journalism — friendly with the party in power — graduated from the press gallery to become editors of powerful newspapers: John Willison of the *Globe* in Toronto and John Dafoe of the *Free Press* in Winnipeg. In almost a direct line, Dafoe's figurative descendants over the decades continued the close association and influence with Liberal governments, including Grant Dexter of the *Winnipeg Free Press*, Bruce Hutchison of the *Vancouver Sun*, and Blair Fraser of *Maclean's*. For the Conservatives, there was the irrepressible Grattan O'Leary, who rose from poverty in the Gaspé to the editorship of the *Ottawa Journal* and was a confidant of three Tory leaders. In an era when there was no Twitter, Snapchat, or email, these men wrote diaries and exchanged letters with leaders and each other, providing a trove of archival material for historians about their thinking and their actions.

From all of that, we know that early press gallery members were a highly partisan lot. Indeed, the seating plan mirrored the one on the floor of the Commons below. *London Free Press* editor Arthur Ford, who covered his first Parliament in 1907 for the former *Winnipeg Telegram*, recalled in his memoir, *As the World Wags On*: "When I first went to the capital, the Liberals were in power and sat, of course, to the right of the Speaker. The representatives of the Liberal press sat in the press gallery also to the right." When the Conservatives won the 1911 election, the Tory reporters swapped with the Liberals and moved over to the speaker's right. So-called independent journalists were relegated to the cheap seats.

Until Laurier's time, governments ladled out information — even including election calls — as patronage only to their friends in the gallery, the "ministerial press," as they were known. Willison, who started in Ottawa in 1886 as a correspondent for the Liberal-leaning *Globe*, complained about his pro-Tory rivals having access to official documents before they were tabled in Parliament. "Their dispatches would be in the telegraph office before less favoured rivals could examine the reports," he wrote in *Reminiscences, Political*, and *Personal*, his 1919 autobiography. "It was one way a grateful ministry paid newspapers for their support."

And what support. Ford recalled that one of his freelance gigs was filing to the Fredericton *Gleaner*, then owned by a rabid Conservative, James Crocket. Prime Minister Borden had just finished outlining his proposals for the controversial naval assistance bill to provide England with cash. Wilfrid Laurier's response was highly anticipated, given the opposition in his party ranks and the anti-Imperial furor in Quebec. Laurier happened to follow Sir Douglas Hazen, a Conservative Cabinet minister who was a close friend of owner Crocket. When Ford asked his Halifax desk how much copy they wanted on Laurier, the response came back: "Ignore Laurier entirely. Send Hazen verbatim."

That was the way it was, mainly because the parties owned the major papers. Macdonald invested his own money in repeated newspaper ventures that supported Conservative policies, including the *Mail* and then the *Empire* in Toronto. So did Laurier, who worked to assure the welfare of Liberal-leaning papers. At one point Laurier learned of a plot by Conservative friends of Macdonald to acquire the pro-Liberal *La Presse* so they could malign Laurier in the 1910 election. Laurier persuaded the Canadian Pacific Railway (CPR) to back out of the acquisition and then leaned on two of his railway friends to buy *La Presse* out from under the conspirators. Laurier did attempt to change the channel on access by offering off-the-record sessions with reporters from Conservative as well as Liberal papers. Revealingly, a *Globe* Ottawa correspondent protested, urging Laurier to maintain the previous practice of partisan publicity. He did not — on the advice of the reporter's boss, Laurier's friend Willison.

From the beginning, journalists were active players in the government of the day, forming an intricate interlocking directorship between press and politicians. One season they might work in the press gallery, another time they would be in Cabinet or the back room. Quebec journalists would bounce between federal and provincial politics and the gallery. White, a respected parliamentary reporter, got Macdonald's backing in his takeover of the *Hamilton Spectator*. Later White and his brother Richard bought the *Gazette* in Montreal and turned it into the leading Conservative voice in the new country — helping Macdonald to secure his hold on Quebec. From that base, Thomas White won election to Parliament and became known for his prodigious work as Macdonald's confidant and, until his death from pneumonia in 1888, possible successor.

Likewise, lawyer-turned-journalist Ernest Pacaud encouraged Wilfrid Laurier to get into politics in 1874. Laurier, in turn, designated his friend as editor of *L'Électeur*, the newspaper the prime minister established with his wealthy friends as a counterpoint to *Le Canadien*, then run by Conservative journalist/ideologue Joseph-Israël Tarte. Tarte later became Laurier's public works minister. In 1896 Tarte and fellow Liberal MP Henri Bourassa were the federal negotiators in the compromise settlement of the Manitoba Schools Question, allowing limited access to French-language education.

In the beginning, reporters would travel to Ottawa for the sessions, returning home after three or four months. In the dusty old lumber town, liquor flowed with the political gossip at the legendary Russell House on the corner of Sparks and Elgin Streets, which predated the Château Laurier as a favourite lodging for the "sessionals" who could afford it. Stained-glass versions of provincial coats of arms graced a dome over the opulent rotunda. Liveried servants discreetly worked the dining room to the dulcet strains of the house orchestra.

Paul Bilkey, the *Toronto Telegram* correspondent at the turn of the twentieth century, noted in his memoir: "It used to be said that the Dominion was governed more from the lobbies and rooms of the Russell House than from the ministerial offices or from the House of Commons."

Journalist Augustus Bridle assured female readers of the *Canadian Magazine*, "Here you are more likely to discover the man you want than almost anywhere else in Ottawa, except up at Parliament." Indeed, the Russell was the temporary abode of senior politicians and bureaucrats, including Laurier, who penned letters from his bed-sitting room to his beloved mistress, Émilie Lavergne. Lesser mortals settled into cramped rooming houses with no running water.

But even for the governing class, the capital of the new dominion, Queen Victoria's geographical compromise between Upper and Lower Canada, offered few comforts. Goldwin Smith, the snobbish British historian and journalist, dismissed the place as "a subarctic lumber village transformed by royal mandate into a political cockpit." There was mud everywhere in the spring. In winter, Arctic blasts blew into poorly insulated homes and ice coated wooden sidewalks. In her telling period look at post-Confederation Ottawa, journalist Sandra Gwyn wrote: "Stinking piles of garbage and 'night soil' accrued behind houses all winter, to be hauled away in April, and dumped on the river ice."

In the summer, there was little relief from oppressive heat, and the lack of running water made the stench from toilets unbearable. For the political class and their followers in the press contingent, elegant balls at Government House and elaborate house parties staged by the gentry provided some respite. The revelling often continued until dawn. But, as Gwyn put it:

> Even at the most elegant parties, the air was dank with the smell of stale perspiration. Teeth, even in rosebud mouths, were frequently snaggled and discoloured. The roads were full of mud and manure; the wooden sidewalks covered with clots of spittle, tobacco juice or worse.*

To be sure, there was violence and menace. In the wee hours of April 7, 1868, Prime Minister Macdonald heard a visitor outside his house shouting that Thomas D'Arcy McGee, the journalist and passionate representative of Montreal Irish in Parliament, had been fatally shot. The planks outside the boarding house where McGee stayed were stained with his blood. The

---

* Sandra Gywnn, *The Private Capital: Ambition and Love in the Age of Macdonald and Laurier* (Toronto: HarperCollins, 1989), 49.

owner of the house was Queen's Printer George Desbarats; he erected a plaque in McGee's honour outside his nearby printing shop. Nine months after McGee's assassination, a fire burned Desbarats's shop to the ground. Too discouraged to rebuild, he moved his family to Montreal and launched the *Canadian Illustrated News.* According to his great-grandson, the late journalist and journalism professor Peter Desbarats, family folklore had it that Fenian rebels, upset by McGee's constant warnings about their violent ways, torched the place in revenge for Desbarats' support.

Still, there was an untroubled intimacy to life in the capital. Edmund Meredith, the prominent journalist turned public servant, regularly received morning instructions from his minister when he walked past his front door on his way to work. Guglielmo Marconi, in town to lobby for federal funding of his wireless station in Cape Breton, caused a stir one day when he strolled through the lobby of the Russell. All the MPs and senators were housed in common offices in the Centre Block, within hailing distance of the press gallery. The *Globe*'s M.O. Hammond, a Willison appointment, met with Laurier for a private chat shortly after he reported for duty in the press gallery in 1903. Later when news reached Ottawa that England had failed to secure a good deal for Canada in the Alaska boundary talks, Hammond went around to Laurier's office and found the prime minister "on his knees on the floor studying a map. He was very indignant at the decision and said it was 'a damned injustice' and 'utterly indefensible.'"

According to Dalhousie historian P.B. Waite, the newly opened House of Commons was dark, hot, and stuffy, the oxygen depleted by flickering gaslights. The 211 members sat in green leather chairs, seven rows on either side. There was a members' basement restaurant and an unofficial bar that specialized in rum drinks (the specialty in the Senate bar was sherry). Waite wrote, "It was not uncommon for half the MPs to be under the weather when the house adjourned at midnight." Waite adds that MPs habitually ignored proceedings. During a speech by Tory Guillaume Amyot in the great debate about Riel's hanging, the Tory-leaning *Montreal Star* revealed that six Liberals were asleep, nine were reading papers, four were writing, six were talking — and only nineteen were listening.* It was an early example of "gotcha journalism."

---

* P.B. Waite, *The Man from Halifax: Sir John Thompson, Prime Minister* (Toronto: University of Toronto Press, 1985), 160.

Until the introduction of Hansard in 1875, parliamentary correspondents produced long reports of debates that many newspapers ran verbatim, but anonymously. It was not unusual for the *Globe* to carry a full-page report of three or four thousand words. Journalist Kennedy Crone wrote, "In those earlier days, a Press Gallery member was, of necessity, a fast shorthand writer, and often little else." An article on the tiny press gallery in the *Canadian Illustrated News* of 1875 gushed, "We owe the boon to the sharp wits and busy pens of these twenty reporters."

The quick ones also made extra money on the side recording committee hearings. Hammond of the *Globe*, who boasted that he could take down 138 words per minute, supplemented his salary by a princely eight hundred dollars in 1905 — enough to take his wife to the World's Fair in St. Louis. In the *Canadian Liberal* journal, Robin Adair observed: "The speeches were taken down in short hand without colour or comment, and dispatched by post to the newspapers, there being no telegraph. Such 'editorializing' as there was existed in the headline of the story and the scathing editorial page comment which frequently paralleled it."

But the bias came in the selection. In his memoir, journalist Ford asserted: "A Conservative paper covered the speeches of its leaders and more or less ignored the speeches of the Liberals and vice versa. Reports were biased and unfair." Waite oversaw the Centennial Year publication of the 1867–74 debates — a collation of the clippings of debate reports from the Conservative *Ottawa Times* and the Reform *Globe* (available online at Parliament's historical debates site). His major disappointment was the poor quality of the transcription of French speeches; he concluded, "If an MP wanted to make any substantial impression at all on Parliament or public, he had to speak in English."

As documented by historian Allan Levine, in either language the insults flew, but often with more wit than is evident among today's practitioners. In 1878 the Tory-leaning Halifax *Morning Herald*'s editor, Martin Griffin, described his encounter with Liberal prime minister Alexander Mackenzie at a Government House ball: "Mr. MacKenzie [*sic*] was present, disguised as a gentleman." Later he dismissed a group of Liberals as "a motley collection of office seekers, looking around for free lunches and cheap whiskey and sadly in need of both."

Although George Brown had joined Macdonald and the other Fathers to bring about the new Confederation, his *Globe* was a fierce foe of the prime minister. After a raucous night of debate in 1878, under the headline "The Disgraceful Scene at Ottawa," the paper led off disingenuously in its April 16 edition: "We take no pleasure in saying what may be regarded as harsh things." The report added:

> To say that Sir John A. Macdonald was on Friday night somewhat under the influence of liquor would be a grossly inadequate representation of the fact. He was simply drunk in the plain ordinary sense of the word. As the night wore on he became still more so, and from 6 to 8 on Saturday morning he was, to quote the conventional language usually employed on such occasions, 'thoroughly laid out,' and had to be hidden away by his friends, if not in shame at least in pity, and as an absolutely prudential proceeding.

Given all the attacks from Brown and the *Globe*, Macdonald once famously parried that Canadians "would prefer to have Sir John A. drunk than George Brown sober." And they did, defeating Brown on his only run for the new Parliament and electing Macdonald five times with a majority government, for a total of almost nineteen years.

There was plenty of news to cover. Macdonald, as the leading Father of Confederation, had fought for, and achieved, a remarkable federation of former colonies, with strong central powers within a British parliamentary system. In six elections between 1872 and 1891, the people defeated Macdonald only once, after the epic scandal surrounding the Pacific Railway. He had defied both U.S. and British predictions — and some wishful hoping — that the new nation would fail. Instead, with a singular focus on independence for Canada, and not a little old-fashioned patronage, Macdonald wooed the colonies of Prince Edward Island and British Columbia into Confederation, to join New Brunswick, Nova Scotia, and the former Canada West and Canada East. He established the concept of a professional civil service. The Intercolonial Railway, a precursor of the Canadian National Railway (CNR), opened between Quebec and Halifax.

Despite the graft and corruption that brought him down in 1874, he launched the building of the CPR to the West, and then extended Canada's embrace to the vast stretches of British-controlled Rupert's Land and created the North-Western Territory. He battled against implacable forces, ranging from his own binge drinking to the confrontations between Quebec and the rest of Canada over the treatment of the Métis, who had taken up arms to protect their land and tribal rights from the new arrivals, and to protest the hanging of Louis Riel. One blot that surfaced more than a century later was the Macdonald government's creation of the infamous residential schools for Indigenous children. And throughout, there was the issue that would never die — trade reciprocity with the Americans versus Macdonald's National Policy of tariff protection for Canadian industry.

Along the way, members of the Parliamentary Press Gallery shared the vision of nation building, if not always the means. At the end, even his harsh critic Willison described Macdonald as "a great man who with all his faults loved Canada and served Canada with singular fidelity and remarkable ability." On an afternoon in May 1891, when word that Sir John was slipping away reached the press gallery, according to *Globe* correspondent A.J. Magurn, the telegraph company set up a machine with an operator in a shed adjoining Earnscliffe, the prime minister's official residence. "All thought of the correspondents was concentrated on Earnscliffe, and bulletins were sent out every hour," Magurn recalled. One unnamed — and misguided — newspaper asked its correspondent to get a photo inside the guarded room where the prime minister lay dying. Today reporters call it "the death watch."

Chapter 2

DAFOE AND WILLISON: THE GODFATHERS

John Wesley Dafoe and John Stephen Willison were the dominant English journalists of their era. Both were rural Ontario farm boys, both were school dropouts, both turned to journalism as teenagers, and both became powerful newspaper editors in the early 1930s after serving in the Parliamentary Press Gallery — where they became partisan Liberals through and through.

Dafoe arrived in Ottawa in 1885 amid the first reports of the North-West Rebellion. Led by Louis Riel on behalf of the Métis, the rebellion was staged to try to protect ancestral rights and halt the advance of the railway and white settlement by forming a militia and provisional government. Willison arrived the next year as the great debate over hanging Riel was in full throttle.

———

"I was born under a favourable star," Dafoe once observed. And so he was, professionally, joining the *Montreal Star* as a six-dollar-a-week junior of seventeen. Newspapers in those days afforded able young men with little formal education an opportunity to become important members of society. In the early days, clean-shaven and dressed in his four-button jacket, with covered buttons and matching waistcoat, he looked every inch the aspiring executive. A bright, ambitious youth, he took full advantage of the opportunities as he moved from job to job in Montreal, Ottawa, and Winnipeg, finally settling in as editor of the *Free Press* in Winnipeg. There, for his last forty years, he had a powerful influence on prime ministers Laurier, Borden, and Mackenzie King on issues ranging from free trade to conscription.

Dafoe was nineteen on his first day in Ottawa. He recalled: "I walked directly over to the press gallery and got there just in time to hear [Public Works Minister] Sir Hector Langevin announce the outbreak of the rebellion and the slaughter of the police and settlers by the insurgents." Initially, he agreed with the Macdonald government's decision to punish Riel by hanging. But during the great debate the next year about Riel's sentence, he listened in awe to the oratory of Liberal leader Edward Blake: "I went up that stairway perhaps not much interested in politics, and I came down a fighting Grit." Blake, he added, "swept me off my feet."

He also was much taken by the young Wilfrid Laurier, whom he had befriended during their frequent encounters in the Parliamentary Library. Years later, Dafoe recalled seeing Laurier in action before a crowd of fifty thousand in Montreal, six days after Riel's hanging: "Addressing a vast meeting on the Champ de Mars in Montréal he made the famous remark that if he had been living on the banks of the Saskatchewan in the spring of 1885 he would himself have shouldered his musket." Later, watching Laurier wade into crowds in Ontario to defend his policies, Dafoe observed: "His complete fearlessness in facing hostile audiences, and the power of his eloquence, gave him a position in the Liberal Party and in public regard that made his selection as leader inevitable when Blake, following the defeat of 1887, threw up his hands."

Willison's parliamentary reporting career also was forged in the embers of the Riel crisis. By the time he arrived in the press gallery in 1886, Riel was dead and the fires of English-French enmity burned across the new nation. In his heart, he believed that Canada was, and should be, an English country. He opposed expanding bilingual education services in Ontario and Manitoba.

But Willison, schooled by Laurier, worried about the rise of Quebec nationalism caused by Riel's hanging and anti-French and anti-Catholic sentiments bubbling in Orange Ontario in response. And he observed first-hand the hard English-French split in the House of Commons when Liberal leader Blake condemned Macdonald for executing a man many felt was mentally ill and had been provoked by the government. Siding with the Métis leader was not a popular position with two dozen Ontario Liberal MPs. They voted with Macdonald's Tories to defeat a censure motion, while French-Canadian Tories voted with Liberal Blake.

What most impressed Willison was the thoughtful but spirited intervention in the Riel debate of the forty-five-year-old member from Drummond-Arthabaska, Wilfrid Laurier. He spoke eloquently for two hours. In those days, before the great fire of 1916, the press gallery in the Commons swung low over the speaker's chair, close to the floor. The drama was palpable. At times there was such a hush that members could hear the ticking of the parliamentary clock. Laurier accused Macdonald of contempt for the Métis and blamed him for causing the North-West Rebellion. "We cannot make a nation of this new country by shedding blood," he declared, "but by extending mercy and charity for all political offences." Historian Richard Clippingdale concludes in his sweeping biography: "Willison refused to be outraged, as many an Ontario Protestant was, by Laurier's position on Riel's execution." Still, Blake's humiliation by his rebel caucus members was the beginning of the end. Macdonald held on to power, winning a majority in the 1887 election.

———————

Willison came from humble beginnings. He was born in rural Ontario to a Conservative family in the farming hamlet of Hills Green near Lake Huron on November 9, 1856. Having failed to make a go of farming the land, his father took whatever employment he could find — blacksmith, stonemason, woodsman. John, who quit school at fifteen, developed Liberal sympathies as a sixteen-year-old farm labourer, working for neighbours of an uncle near Oshawa. His employer, a Reform-Liberal, subscribed to George Brown's *Globe,* and there the young Willison read the accounts of the Pacific Scandal in 1873 and Macdonald's defeat later that year.

Willison doubtless devoured the reports that surfaced about what Macdonald biographer Richard Gwyn termed "the best-known telegram in Canadian history" — Macdonald's secret request to railway magnate Hugh Allan for more funds to fuel his election coffers: "I must have another ten thousand. Will be the last time of calling. Do not fail me. Answer today." The charge of corruption — linking Allan's payments to a government promise that his company would get the commission to build the railway to the Pacific — aired first in the House of Commons when prominent Eastern Townships Liberal MP Lucius Huntington proposed a motion of non-confidence on April 2, 1873. Later, the *Globe* not only gleefully reported the telegram, but on July 18, 1873, stacked eighteen separate headlines atop a page 1 report, complete with exclamation marks, among them:

THE PACIFIC SCANDAL!
ASTOUNDING REVELATIONS!
MACDONALD AND CARTIER
TAKE MONEY FROM ALLEN

Below them was a detailed report on an agreement between Macdonald and the railway for a series of payments, written as a "Dear Sir" letter from one of the executives involved. It was likely the day that turned Willison into a Liberal.

One of his early jobs was as a store clerk in Tiverton on the Lake Huron shore. In his off-hours he took in local political debates, submitted articles to local newspapers — and met the love of his life, Rachel Turner, who would bear him twin boys and preside over a loving family life. He finally landed a job as a typesetter at the *London Advertiser*, owned by John Cameron, a man who mentored several prominent journalists. When Cameron moved to the *Globe* as editor and general manager, Willison went with him.

He had a rapid rise. At twenty-seven he was assigned to cover the Ontario legislature and Liberal premier Oliver Mowat. He became an active member of the Young Men's Liberal Club. In June 1885 John and Rachel married. The next year, after he had covered three legislative sessions, the *Globe* sent him to Ottawa. His mandate was to study

Parliament and to cultivate the same "working relationship" with Ottawa Liberals that he had developed covering Mowat, that is to say, worshipful. As Willison recalled candidly in his 1919 memoir: "It was petty and trivial and partisan…. It was of the atmosphere of the legislature in those days one worshipped his political idols; blasphemed the enemy and rejoiced."

In Ottawa he easily slipped into the role of a partisan. When Sir Charles Tupper, the legendary Father of Confederation and powerhouse in Macdonald's Cabinet, invited Willison to dinner — the only invitation he ever received from a Tory — the young reporter hesitated. "I telegraphed to the *The Globe*," he revealed, "and was assured that acceptance would not be treated as a betrayal of the [Liberal] Opposition."

Watching Laurier in the Riel debate and getting to know him socially had a lasting impact on Willison. He was a tall, dark, bearded man, with a studious mien and an inquiring mind. A new Tory journalist friend in the gallery, Arthur Colquhoun, described him as "a good talker, although prone to a rather irritating tendency to believe the Liberal Party always right." At times that was difficult for Willison, especially when it came to the rights of French Canadians.

That issue dogged Laurier and Willison for the next decade. It first came to a head in 1888 when nationalist Quebec premier Honoré Mercier awarded the Catholic Church four hundred thousand dollars to compensate for properties the Society of Jesus had lost in the British conquest. The so-called Jesuits' Estates Act ignited an unholy uproar in English Canada. MPs demanded that the act be disallowed because it favoured the Catholic church. Prime Minister Macdonald and Laurier both rejected a disallowance motion in the Commons, fearing the further fanning of nationalist flames in Quebec. Interestingly, Willison did not take an active part in the debate, except to note that "to the bulk of Protestants" it was "an exasperating" piece of legislation. When the *Globe* opposed the Liberal policy on the issue, Willison wrote to Laurier assuring him of his continued loyalty.

That summer, Laurier invited Willison to be his guest in Arthabaskaville, the bucolic seat of his law practice northeast of Montreal in Quebec's rolling Eastern Townships. There, they had long talks about policy and their mutual love of English literature. After Laurier lamented the hostility directed at him by Ontario, Willison arranged for the Quebecer to speak in Toronto at the Horticultural Pavilion in what is known today as Allan Gardens. It was a fiery session with plenty of heckling. Willison wrote later that Laurier "prevailed and never again in Ontario did the Liberal leader find an audience unwilling to receive his message...."

In their frequent meetings, Willison tutored Laurier on the ways in which he, a Catholic French Canadian, could become presentable to Orange Anglo-Ontarians. From Laurier, Willison, a son of the British Empire, learned the necessity of accommodating Quebec nationalism, much as it disturbed him. He also became a strong advocate of free trade and Laurier's campaign for "unrestricted reciprocity" with the United States.

As time went by, Willison became even more lyrical in his appreciation of Laurier as a leader who would share "a bright and brilliant place" in the Liberal pantheon. After Laurier thanked Willison for his coverage of an Ontario tour, the young reporter wrote to him: "I do not have to assure you that any service I can do you either as an individual or as a journalist will be very, very cheerfully rendered" — words underlined by Willison for emphasis. Laurier reciprocated. On June 19, 1890, Willison became editor of the *Globe*, with an important recommendation from Laurier. He was only thirty-three — an astonishing rise for the son of a blacksmith who grew up in a log house and did not finish high school. But politics was in his blood and he could write like the breeze.

One of Willison's singular acts on Laurier's behalf shortly after he became editor marked him forever as a backroom politician as much as a journalist. With the election of 1891 looming, Willison received from Blake the draft of an eight-page letter addressed to the president of Blake's West Durham constituency association, denouncing Laurier's reciprocity plank and signalling his intention to resign from the Liberal caucus. Willison recognized that the letter from a party icon denouncing Laurier's key plank would be a devastating blow to the leader's campaign. He consulted a newsroom colleague who urged him to publish the letter. But Willison recalled: "I pointed out that if we did so the Liberal party would be overwhelmed in the election." Willison then went off to talk to the publisher and the *Globe* directors. They said the letter had to be published, since Blake would insist.

But Willison decided to stall publication. He made a direct appeal to Blake "to maintain silence until Mr. Laurier could be consulted." Blake was furious. He warned if the *Globe* did not publish the letter, it would appear in the rival *Mail*. He also denounced the decision by Laurier to call a convention of Ontario Liberals without consulting him. Willison said he would contact Laurier. Blake agreed to hear Laurier's response. Laurier came to Toronto, where Blake agreed to postpone publication of the letter until after the election. In return, Laurier cancelled the Ontario convention. Loyal to the end, Willison wrote: "I saw Laurier shortly after his interview with Blake, but much of what was said cannot be disclosed." He wrote that in 1919, twenty-eight years after the crisis of the West Durham letter. It *can* be reported that Borden won the "reciprocity election."

Willison initially was at odds with Laurier on one of the other defining issues of the era — the abolition of separate schools in Manitoba. He saw it as a matter of provincial rights, not justice for a minority. The constitutional guarantee for a largely Catholic, francophone constituency was part of the resolution of the Red River Rebellion when Manitoba was created in 1870. Laurier refrained from announcing his position, while the issue roiled the fractured Conservative ranks as the 1896 election approached. The *Globe* editor urged Laurier to oppose the government's so-called remedial legislation that would force Manitoba to reinstitute francophone rights. "I do not want to preach to you," he wrote Laurier, "but I cannot refrain from telling you that if you can avoid any declaration in favour of remedial legislation it will be an enormous advantage in Ontario."

The Liberal leader, under intense pressure from Quebec nationalists at home, was furious and accused the *Globe* of acting as though "the whole of Canada is composed of one province." Willison's *Globe* eventually fell in line with Laurier's plan for a compromise: no remedial action, but limited instruction in French where warranted. Laurier won the election of 1896 and successfully negotiated what he called a "sunny way" compromise with Manitoba — borrowing the phrase from an Aesop fable.

Willison did break firmly with the Liberal Party and Laurier near the end of his stint as *Globe* editor. Progressive movements were growing across the continent, and muckraking journalism in the United States began

John S. Willison, 1913: lyrical in his appreciation of Laurier.

exposing the abuses of concentrated power. Besides, newspapers could no longer survive on party funds alone and needed to attract readers and advertisers with solid journalism. Willison decided that he had had enough of party journalism — or at least Liberal Party journalism. In a speech to the Political Science Club of Toronto in 1899 he said it was the "mission" of the press to serve "the plain unorganized and unsubsidized people."

By this point, Willison had joined the elite in his own right, as Richard Clippingdale documents in *The Power of the Pen: The Politics, Nationalism, and Influence of Sir John Willison*. He took up lawn bowling and joined the prestigious York Club. Rachel was active in community organizations. After being groomed at Upper Canada College and the University of Toronto, their twin sons, Walter and Bill, went into journalism. In 1900 Willison *père* became a Fellow of the Royal Society and president of the Canadian Press Association, a lobby group of owners and publishers. At the National Club in Toronto in January 1913, Toronto's elite turned out to fete Willison for his recently announced knighthood.

As editor, Willison appointed bright, able *Globe* reporters to the Parliamentary Press Gallery, with instructions to give full, impartial coverage to both parties. However, as complaints from Liberals mounted, Willison hit back. In a 1901 letter to Clifford Sifton, Laurier's powerful interior minister — and owner of the *Free Press* in Winnipeg — he stated: "Personally I resent the assumption of every Liberal politician that I am his hired man." Willison eventually resigned from the *Globe* and, after time out to write a favourable biography of Laurier, in 1903 he became editor of Joseph Wesley Flavelle's new Toronto *Evening News*. For the next dozen years, the paper faithfully supported the Conservatives.

Willison's new opposition to Laurier's Liberals became apparent when the schools issue arose again in 1904. Laurier, determined to affirm francophone rights, introduced legislation guaranteeing separate Catholic schools upon the creation of two new provinces in the expanse of the North-West Territories between Manitoba and the Rockies. The Catholic minority in Saskatchewan and Alberta — and Catholic Quebec — welcomed the move, but influential forces around Laurier did not. His most powerful minister, Clifford Sifton, favoured non-denominational schools and resigned from the Cabinet. Willison, too, was appalled. His *Evening News* denounced the government. In a private letter to Laurier, he expressed his "profound regret that we should be separated on the issue," and added with a telling remark that, while "I have all this respect for the natural race sentiment of French Canadians, no man could be more strenuously opposed to clerical interference in State affairs." Even after a Cabinet crisis forced Laurier to soften the provisions, Willison was not mollified. He joined Conservative leader Borden in denouncing the Autonomy Act. The Liberals were about to discover that their free ride with Willison and other friends in the press was over; and that their other significant booster, John Dafoe, was about to go the same way.

———————

Dafoe, like Willison, was a product of modest surroundings. He was born in a log cabin in the bush on March 8, 1866, near the Ottawa Valley town of Combermere. His father was a struggling homesteader who supplemented the meagre family income as a lumberjack in winter, occasionally taking John logging. But the boy was not to the fields or forests born. He was a reader and, at thirteen, he went away for schooling in nearby Arnprior. At fifteen he left and started teaching kids almost his own age at Bark Lake, a new settlement near home. He also was reading European history and the works of radical British reformers, and moving away from the family's Orange Tory roots and devotion to Sir John A. Macdonald.

Looking for another challenge, he answered an ad for a junior editor at Hugh Graham's *Family Herald and Weekly Star* in Montreal. There, his career in journalism began in 1883. After only a year in Montreal, during which he broke several stories, the paper sent him to Ottawa as parliamentary correspondent.

By 1885, after only one year in the gallery and a brief overlap with Willison, Dafoe was on the move, this time down from the Hill to become editor of a new Ottawa newspaper, the *Evening Journal*, at the improbable age of nineteen. Realizing that he was beyond his depth, Dafoe resigned the editorship after only five months and prepared to set his sails for New York.

An offer of a job as a "mere reporter" for the *Free Press* drew him to Winnipeg in 1886 to make a new start. Assigned to the provincial press gallery, he covered two major national issues that grew out of local politics: protests against the Macdonald government's use of federal powers to prevent the building of a second transcontinental railway that Manitobans demanded for exports to the United States; and the elimination of separate schools. Before the issues were resolved, Dafoe found himself back in Montreal, this time as editor of the Liberal *Montreal Herald*, encouraged by Laurier to take the job. But the paper foundered in difficult financial seas and Dafoe returned to Conservative Hugh Graham's empire as editor of the *Family Herald and Weekly Star*, with instructions that he could not write about politics. Still, with Graham's forbearance, Dafoe was "soon in the thick of the Liberal campaign" in the election of 1896. As he recalled in his 1943 remarks: "I do not think any of my experiences in later campaigns ever quite matched the night of June 23, 1896, when we were able to figure out before midnight a definite Liberal majority."

During the campaign, Laurier's political opponents denounced him as a traitor to his race for not backing Conservative legislation restoring separate schools in Manitoba. Knowing the bitter reaction that would cause in English Canada, Laurier favoured a negotiated settlement, a position Dafoe also supported. A document read in all Quebec churches warned Catholics to vote only for candidates who supported a remedial law. One prelate said it would be "a mortal sin" not to obey the bishops; another priest declared, "Choose the bishops or Barabbas Laurier."

For Dafoe, the eight years in Montreal were pleasant and fulfilling. He had started a family with his young wife, Alice Parmalee of Waterloo, Quebec, whom he had met when she worked for the federal government in Ottawa. The weekly was thriving, with a strong national circulation, and he had returned to publishing non-fiction articles. But in 1901 Dafoe, then thirty-five, accepted Sifton's call to become editor of the *Manitoba Free Press* (the forerunner of the *Winnipeg Free Press*). "I do not think we can afford to let you work for the Tories any longer," he told Dafoe. Sifton advised skeptical lieutenants in Manitoba that Dafoe had earned the respect of eastern Liberals "notwithstanding the fact that he has been for many years on the *Montreal Star*." Dafoe concluded, "I had landed the very position I had often dreamed of occupying, for I had found after my return to Montreal that I had given my heart to the West."

Dafoe arrived by train in Winnipeg with Alice and their six children (a seventh was born in Winnipeg). Once ensconced at the *Free Press*, Dafoe worked long hours and tackled the big issues. But he was devoted and playful with his children and later his grandchildren. "He had lots of time for us," recalled Christopher Dafoe in a biography of his grandfather. "There was the famous occasion when he was supposed to be attending a very important meeting to decide the future of the *Free Press* and he suddenly remembered he was taking us to the circus, so the meeting was cancelled." Most days, he held court at the comfortable Manitoba Club with an elite circle of politicians and businessmen that became known as the "Sanhedrin" — after the high court of Jewish elders in ancient Judea.

Dafoe was a strong Canadian nationalist who resented the country's dependency on the British Privy Council for important judicial decisions, including the Manitoba Schools Question. He opposed the British-American settlement of the Alaska boundary in 1903 because he felt the mother country had giving the shop away. He vividly denounced attempts at appeasing Hitler in 1938. An internationalist, he was a big supporter of the League of Nations. As a hawkish free trader, he used the columns of the *Free Press* to support Laurier's reciprocity election plank in 1911, even though Sifton, now out of Cabinet, was so determinedly opposed that he led the campaign against Laurier.

———————

While free trader Dafoe backed Laurier from his post at the *Evening News,* Willison — now a protectionist — actively worked against the government's trade agreement with Washington in 1911. With Sifton's help, Willison organized the so-called Toronto Eighteen to oppose the elimination of protective tariffs. This was a powerful group of Toronto Liberal business leaders — among them department store owner J.C. Eaton, biscuit maker R.J. Christie, and senior executives of Manufacturers Life and the Dominion Bank. Willison travelled to Ottawa as their advocate. Their anti-reciprocity manifesto closely resembled Willison's editorials on the subject, and Conservative leader Borden embraced it. Facing a filibuster, Laurier called a September election. Borden recruited Willison to write his party's platform. The Conservatives won the election. Later, Borden bestowed a knighthood on Willison.

As the decade unfolded, the *Evening News* faced increasing financial challenges. Weary of the struggle, Willison quit the paper and began writing full-time for the *Times* of London, a role that Wilfrid Laurier helped secure for him.

But then came the Conscription Crisis. Laurier's position on the issue lost him the support of both Willison and Dafoe, as Laurier refused to join Borden in the Union coalition. Dafoe turned the *Free Press* into the voice of the Union government, backing Borden's call for conscription. He was convinced, like Willison, that Laurier had become too preoccupied with Quebec and the anti-conscription attitudes of the crusading Henri Bourassa and his *Le Devoir*. Sifton, again, was one of Borden's key advisers. Willison became publicity director for the Unionists and coordinated the speakers' bureau and a propaganda effort that, according to historian Mason Wade, "constantly linked Laurier, Bourassa, and Quebec, and roused ethnic feeling against French Canada." Dafoe meanwhile joined Joe Atkinson of the *Toronto Star* in dispatching cables to the troops abroad, urging a vote for the Union government. Borden won re-election and dangled the promise of a Senate seat before Willison, but that never happened.

That disappointment paled beside the much greater loss that Willison suffered at the time. In September 1916 he and Rachel were devastated when their son Bill was killed in fierce fighting as the Canadian Corps routed the Germans near Courcelette. The death notice appeared in the *Evening News* the same day as the report of that victory — the battlefield story from France was written, improbably, by Bill's brother, Walter.

After the war came a changing of the guard, with William Lyon Mackenzie King taking over from the weary Wilfrid Laurier and Arthur Meighen replacing Borden as prime minister. Willison became a major force in Toronto business and professional circles: chair of the Ontario commission on unemployment, head of a provincial committee on housing, a member of the Ontario royal commission on universities, a trustee of Queen's University, a governor of the University of Toronto, and head of several finance corporations.

On the personal front, Willison suffered another loss when his beloved Rachel succumbed to pneumonia in 1925. Following Rachel's death, Willison married Marjory MacMurchy, an old journalist friend who had worked with him at the *Globe*, the *Evening News*, and *Willison's Monthly*, the public-affairs magazine he and Walter founded in June 1925 that became a forerunner of *Canadian Forum*.

Looking back on his journalism career in his memoir, he was proud of what today seems like modest accomplishments: "that reports should be accurate" and that Conservative readers of the *Globe* should not have "to go elsewhere for the speeches of their leaders." He added: "In time, the commercial and political wisdom of fair and full reports of public meetings was established … [and] that, I believe, was my best contribution to Canadian journalism."

In 1927 he entered Toronto General Hospital where doctors diagnosed him with cancer. He died on May 27, at age seventy.

Meanwhile, in Winnipeg, Dafoe and Sifton had agreed that the Liberals represented the best interests of the West, and they helped engineer the victory of William Lyon Mackenzie King in 1921. When war came in 1939, the *Free Press* backed King all the way, Dafoe correctly previewing the menace to come. Writing in the *Queen's Quarterly* in 1935, he declared, "the comfortable theory that Canada is remote from the centre of world affairs and is therefore protected by distance and the sea no longer holds." As for outright support of the Liberals, Dafoe told executive editor George Ferguson in a private memo that "unless something is done that we simply cannot stand our business will be to go along with the government and help them out in every possible way by explanations, intelligent publicity and so forth."

He also prodded Ottawa to commit to a maximum war effort, short of conscription. And when Hitler and Chamberlain reached agreement on September 29, 1938, the *Free Press's* front page and Dafoe's editorial struck discordant notes. Page 1 headlined celebratory Canadian Press and Associated Press stories under the banner:

WAR FEAR ENDS AS POWERS AGREE
ON PROGRESSIVE CZECH CESSION
NEW BORDERS GUARANTEED

JOY UNCONFINED
EUROPE'S MILLIONS GREET
SETTLEMENT WITH ECSTASY

The headline on Dafoe's editorial in the same issue was a strident: "What's the Cheering For?"

In acerbic tones he denounced the Munich Pact and Hitler's annexation of the Sudetenland, and warned of more to come: "Austria yesterday; Czechoslovakia today: What of tomorrow and the day after?" Ferguson later explained Dafoe's vehemence: "He hated Hitler, he came to hate Chamberlain. He hated King's aloofness; he hated the America firsters and the isolationists at home." How right he was, in the end.

John Dafoe at nineteen: a new member of the gallery, 1885.

After the war, Dafoe regarded the *Free Press* as an "opposition paper," not a Liberal sheet. His editorial page overflowed with expert commentary and insight. He hired top people, three of whom became editors in their own right and legends in journalism: Grant Dexter, Bruce Hutchison, and George Ferguson. He was a founder of the Canadian Institute of International Affairs. During much of the war, Dafoe served on the benchmark Rowell-Sirois Commission on federal-provincial relations, which inspired Ottawa's active role in health and hospital care and equalization. But he still found time to lead the *Free Press* in the then-unpopular opposition to the Munich Pact and a call for aggressive participation in the war effort. The editor-in-chief was at his desk at the *Free Press* on January 8, 1944, a Saturday. He planned to finish an article the next morning at a card table in his bedroom. But, as Christopher Dafoe writes, "an aneurysm imposed his final deadline. He died in his doctor's car on the way to the hospital." John Wesley Dafoe was seventy-seven.

Like Willison, Dafoe had started out on his path having developed a strong loyalty to Wilfrid Laurier that would have blurred the lines between journalist and politician today. In the end, both editors fell out with Laurier over conscription for the First World War. This is what gave them their opening and led them to take the first halting steps in the transition that saw their papers — and Canadian journalism — begin the slow progress from blatant partisanship to relative independence and concern for the average citizen.

Chapter 3

THE BOYS' CLUB AND THE WOMEN WHO BROKE THE BAN

As Dafoe and Willison rose to national prominence in the grand age of print, their newspapers were opening their doors to the first generation of determined female reporters. The papers were in search of copy that would appeal to women readers. The women who sought employment with them were looking for an exit from the Victorian era — and were not always willing to confine their interests to the women's sections. Ottawa and the business of Parliament beckoned.

Along came Genevieve Lipsett-Skinner. By the time she arrived in Ottawa at the beginning of the Roaring Twenties, she had done it all. She began as a twenty-one-year-old cub reporter at the *Winnipeg Telegram* in 1906 after teaching school. She wrote everything from soft features for the *Sunshine Section* to exposés of the "death traps" in the city's North End slum dwellings. Away from work, her life was a whirlwind. She married businessman Robert Skinner in 1911. The next year, as a founding member of the Political Equality League, she joined fellow suffragettes Nellie McClung and Francis Beynon on stage in the play *The Women's Parliament*, which mocked the provincial government for denying the vote to women. In 1918 she became the first married woman in Manitoba to get a law degree, graduating with honours. In 1919 her marriage ended in divorce, an unusual state of affairs in those times. In

1920 she ran as a Conservative for a provincial seat in the legislature, but lost. Back at the *Telegram*, she decided it was time for a new challenge: covering Parliament.

The job went to a man. She believed he was less qualified. Outraged, she demanded an explanation. "You are a woman and you would not be admitted to membership in the Parliamentary Press Gallery," her boss replied.

As detailed in Marjory Lang's authoritative *Women Who Made the News*, Lipsett-Skinner was not deterred. She quit the *Telegram* and in 1921 headed for Ottawa, where she had connections, including such notables as Tory leader Arthur Meighen and her younger brother, Robert Lipsett, the well-connected parliamentary bureau chief for the *Montreal Star*. When he wasn't there, she sat down at his desk and filed vivid reports to papers about life behind the scenes on Parliament Hill — much of it gleaned from the time she spent entertaining politicos at the rented home she shared with her brother. With typical irreverence, in a profile of the sergeant-at-arms in the Commons, she wrote: "Colonel Bowie is practically the only man born in Ottawa who has risen by merit to a position of consequence in government service." Eventually her "string" included the leading dailies in Montreal, Toronto, Calgary, Edmonton, and Vancouver.

Still, the all-male club that controlled gallery membership would not grant her accreditation: after all, she had not been sent to Ottawa by a newspaper. That she filed regularly as a freelancer to five of them did not count. So, she appealed to the enlightened publisher of the *Vancouver Sun*, Robert Cromie, who agreed to "send" her to the gallery. On March 8, 1922, just shy of her thirty-seventh birthday, she was officially granted membership, the first female with formal accreditation. As it happened, that also was the day that Ontario MP Agnes Campbell Macphail of the Progressive Party became the first woman elected to the House of Commons. Both were the only females in their respective roles — for a long time. (A factor in Macphail's election was the Union government's introduction of the vote for women, a measure that Lipsett-Skinner strongly supported.)

The history of the Parliamentary Press Gallery is strewn with tales like Lipsett-Skinner's. Through the years the club was a bulwark standing against modernity — as were most institutions in the country. Nominally reporting to the speaker of the Commons, the gallery set its own rules, and its executive was a self-perpetuating line of white males. In addition to denying women membership, at various points the old boys rejected Jews, freelancers, magazine writers, and broadcasters. Even after admitting women, the gallery banned them from attending the annual black-tie dinner on Parliament Hill until 1967. And down the Hill, the National Press Club, the watering hole for journalists and political aides, restricted membership to males until 1970. The women of the press gallery tended to be a lonely breed until their numbers began to increase in the late 1970s. As of June 2016, of the 335 full-time members, 130 were female. But through the 1920s and 1930s, any female member tended to be the only woman. "This is a record year," wrote Kennedy Crone in 1936, "with one permanent and two temporary memberships held by women."

———————

It was not until the late nineteenth century that women began newspaper careers in significant numbers. By then, political parties were abandoning ownership of papers because the costs of producing them were draining their coffers. Amid sinking circulations, papers began folding or merging. Their push for new revenues from advertising meant they needed mass audiences to attract advertisers. The result was an outbreak of crazy contests and giveaways — portraits of famous people and free packets of garden seeds — and false circulation claims. The emerging advertising agencies and national brands also wanted to reach the household decision-makers — women. Papers introduced new features geared at attracting the kind of female readers desired by the likes of Eaton's, Simpson's, and Quaker Oats. Women's sections became standard features and a popular entry point for female journalists.

But it was not all cooking recipes and floral arrangements, as Marjory Lang's study documents. Many women journalists headed for the exit doors out of the nineteenth century and fashioned careers as investigative journalists or authors. Sara Jeannette Duncan did both. "In this Golden Age for girls," she wrote, "we ... want to do something; something more difficult than embroidered sachets, and more important than hand-painted tambourines." As a supply teacher in Brantford, Ontario, in her late teens she published her first poem in the Toronto *Globe* and her first essay in *Canada Monthly* in 1888. There, in an echo of Susanna Moodie thirty years earlier, she referred to "this very practical country" where "the aesthetic is only beginning to find an existence."

In 1884 the twenty-five-year-old Duncan persuaded John Cameron, then editor of the Toronto *Globe,* to pay for articles on the World's Industrial and Cotton Centennial Exposition in New Orleans. She also sold freelance pieces on the world's fair to the *Washington Post,* the *London Advertiser,* and the Memphis *Appeal.* That led to a job the next year as editorial writer for the *Post* in Washington and in 1886 to a breakthrough offer as a columnist at the *Globe,* the first woman to be hired on staff. In her first *Woman's World* column on September 3 she admonished the insurance industry for denying women the same coverage as men: they could not get injury disability coverage because they tended not to have any wages, and those who worked were ruled to be frailer and more susceptible to injury than men. She wrote: "There was a time when for many reasons it was deemed inadvisable to insure women. The time has gone by, and the reasons with it. A multitude of women are now in positions of responsibility and profit.... The sooner Canadian companies understand this matter fully the better it will be for them."

In the fashion of the day for female journalists, her *Woman's World* appeared under her manly pen name, Garth Grafton, although she left no doubt about her feminist views and gender. In one early column her acerbic eye focused on newspaper advice columns for women: "Our ideal selves are constantly before us, the masculine conception, that is.... Unregenerate woman must be convinced of the evil of her ways at all costs, and if the process results in her eternal welfare, a series of well-cooked dinners may surely be his reward who brings it about."

The ever-industrious Duncan also wrote under her real name for the literary periodicals the *Week* and *Canada Monthly.* In one critique she denounced the "vituperation" in debates about two hot topics — politics and temperance — that she felt were overshadowing scientific and literary subjects: "The Province of Ontario is one great camp of the Philistines.... We are still an eminently unliterary people." With that, improbably, in 1887 Duncan decamped from the *Globe* and went to work for the *Montreal Star* in the Ottawa press gallery, where politics and vituperation abounded. Barred from sitting with the guys in the press gallery of the House of Commons, she sat in the Ladies' Gallery. It was an epochal time in Canadian history: in the wake of the bitter debate about the hanging of Louis Riel, Wilfrid Laurier had become Liberal leader following Edward Blake's second defeat at the hands of Sir John A. Macdonald.

In Ottawa, Duncan became friends with the only other woman in the gallery, Eve Brodlique, who, also not a member, was covering her second session of Parliament for the *London Advertiser*. Her distinguished reportage — "telegraphic political work," as it was called in those days — gained her a wide following under her *nom de guerre,* Willice Wharton. Brodlique had

Sara Jeannette Duncan, the *Globe*'s first female staff member.

begun her career as a secretary to MP David Mills, a "Blake man." He also was the owner of the *Advertiser*, run by John Cameron, an outstanding editor who had hired Duncan (Garth Grafton) and, before that, John Willison, at the *Globe*.

From Parliament Hill Brodlique also filed freelance reports to the *Detroit Free Press*. She eventually moved to Chicago where she worked on all three of the city's dailies. The pace in Canada was too slow for her; she longed for the greater professionalism and opportunity of U.S. journalism. "The papers of the United States," Brodlique said, "seem to have been the first to discover that there is no sex in brains, and that women could be educated to an interest as wide as that enjoyed by men." By 1896, the year Laurier became prime minister, she was a staff writer in Chicago for the *Times-Herald* and president of the Chicago Women's Press Club.

After a year in the gallery, Sara Duncan also was on the move again. It was the era of yellow journalism, which often featured circulation-boosting, swashbuckling tales of derring-do travel by women, the riskier the more appealing. After resigning from the *Star*, Duncan set off on a trip around the world with fellow journalist Lily Lewis (who used the pen name Louis Lloyd). The *Star* published their exotic accounts: clinging to the cowcatcher of a train through the Rockies, visiting with geishas in Tokyo, riding a camel to the Great Pyramid, and taking a moonlight stroll to the Taj Mahal. "Plainly," wrote Lang, "their patrons believed that the reports of these two female adventurers would boost sales of their respective journals." The *Ladies' Pictorial* in London picked up a revised version of Duncan's pieces. That coup launched her career as a novelist.

While in India, Duncan met museum official and journalist Everard Cotes and later married him after he proposed to her at the Taj Mahal. Her first book, in 1890, *A Social Departure: How Orthodocia and I Went Around the World by Ourselves*, was based on the world trip. Her first major work, *A Daughter of Today*, was the first novel published under the name she used the rest of her life, Mrs. Everard Cotes. In all, she published twenty-two books, including the autobiographical *On the Other Side of the Latch,* which was set in her garden in Simla, the summer seat of India's government, where she had spent a year trying to recover from a lung infection. In 1904, critics hailed publication of *The Imperialist* as a departure in literary realism and celebrated the book, which sells to this day, as the best Canadian novel ever published.

She also continued to contribute articles to the *India Daily News* in Calcutta, where her husband was editor, and to Canadian papers such as the *Winnipeg Tribune* (a colour piece on the London social scene in 1912 appeared in the section called *Of Interest to Women*).

The couple retired to England in 1921, where Duncan, a smoker, died from a chronic lung condition at the age of sixty.

———————

Perhaps the most dramatic swashbuckler of the era was Kathleen Blake, an Irish émigré known to readers of her weekly column in the Toronto *Mail*, *Woman's Kingdom*, by the byline Kit. The column morphed into a section and Blake extended its reach to science, politics, business, and other subjects. She became celebrated as "Kit of the *Mail*." In one typically tart piece, she wrote: "I simply detest fashion and I think it is paying us women a poor compliment to imagine we cannot take an interest in the highest and the very deepest questions of the day."

A single mother, she ardently supported equal pay in her column. The anonymity of her one-name byline served as a kind of protection when some readers judged her writing to be overly vicious. After she married Dr. Theobald Coleman, she then wrote as Kit Coleman.

Although Sir John A. Macdonald was a founder and funder of the Tory *Mail*, Coleman herself had fans across the political spectrum, including Sir Wilfrid Laurier, a man she admired. She met up with Laurier on assignment at Queen Victoria's Diamond Jubilee celebrations in 1897 and continued a correspondence with him through the years. The high point of her career was when she broke free of *Woman's Kingdom* to cover the Spanish-American War in Cuba, the first woman accredited as a U.S. war correspondent — over objections from male reporters.

Although she never covered Ottawa, Kit Coleman became one of the most admired reporters in the country — and an inspiration to women from all walks of life to get involved by joining school boards, hospital committees, and other civil institutions. She was typical of the new breed of women journalists who reported on organizations and causes they embraced. In Vancouver, for example, the work of Clare Battle of the *World* united women behind efforts to secure the city's first maternity ward.

The very first woman to cover Parliament in Ottawa, by all accounts including her own, was English-born Kate S. Massiah (née Norris), whose father was publisher of the *Manchester Guardian*. In the nineteenth century it was more common for women to have roles in newspapers run by their fathers or husbands than to be hired on staff elsewhere. She began her career in journalism on a challenge from her father. When she disputed the accuracy of a *Guardian* report about a speech by Charles Dickens that they both had attended, he told her to write a better story. She handed it to the editor the next day and he published it. She said it was "my first taste of success in the writing field." She was fifteen.

In 1871, a family move brought her to Montreal where her brother, John L. Norris, was editor of the *Herald*. She worked for the paper for eight years. After her marriage to Christopher Massiah, the couple moved to Ottawa where he covered the Macdonald government from the press gallery for a Toronto paper. She served as his assistant and, in 1879, at twenty-four, became Ottawa correspondent for the *Herald*.

After her husband's death during the 1885 smallpox epidemic, she went back to Quebec where she and her brother launched the *Independent* in the village of Lachute, northwest of Montreal. A "To Whom It May Concern" note in the first issue in 1888, signed simply as "Norris & Massiah, Editors and Proprietors," proclaimed it "a business enterprise" and "not the offspring or suggestion of any clique or party."

The early issues were heavy on local news and federal and provincial politics, including long excerpts from political debates. On her death in 1936 at eighty-one, the *Gazette* saluted Massiah as "one of the last of Canada's pioneering women journalists." Two years before her death, she publicly refuted claims by other women that they had been the first female journalist or the first female newspaper proprietor. "I am just old enough," she told a Manitoba newspaper, "to want credit placed where it is due."

––––––––

A key battle for the rights of women journalists, ironically, started over a freebie — the now-discredited practice of journalists accepting favours from companies. At the turn of the century the Canadian Pacific Railway had been trundling male journalists all over the country in hopes of generating interest in passenger travel, especially to the West. But it had never extended the courtesy to any female journalists — until Margaret Graham, the young Ottawa correspondent for the *Halifax Herald*, walked into the Montreal office of CPR's publicity director George Ham in June 1904 in search of reciprocity. As detailed in Concordia journalism professor Linda Kay's book, *The Sweet Sixteen*, Graham demanded to know why no women had been invited to join the male reporters whom the CPR was taking to the world's fair in St. Louis, the so-called Louisiana Purchase Exposition. Ham challenged Graham: find a dozen women who could get assignments from their newspapers and he would personally escort them to St. Louis. Graham and her colleagues excelled in the challenge: they rounded up sixteen women, eight French and eight English, including the indomitable Kit Coleman of the *Mail*; Robertine Barry, the leading French-speaking female journalist of the day who wrote as Françoise; Katherine Hughes of the *Montreal Daily Star;* and Kate Simpson Hayes of the *Winnipeg Free Press.*

They left on June 16, 1904. Along the meandering route to St. Louis, via Detroit and Chicago and back, the women bonded. They posed for a historic picture in their finest floor-length skirts and tailored jackets with, as Kay put it, "their upswept hairdos and elaborate hats adding inches to their height." They decided to organize, and by the time they returned to Canada they had formed the Canadian Women's Press Club (CWPC). They subsequently elected the woman who had inspired the idea as the first president — Katherine Blake Coleman. The club became an important source of mentors and training for female reporters who often worked alone, or isolated, in newspapers across the country. Applicants had to demonstrate that they had worked at least twelve months for a newspaper or had been paid the going rate for ten articles by established publications — and then they served a year's probation. Lipsett-Skinner joined in 1913 and at different times headed the Winnipeg and Montreal branches.

As it attracted leading female journalists, the club's influence grew. William Lyon Mackenzie King took note of a reunion in 1906 at the Banff Springs Hotel where he was staying, and invited himself to dinner. The eligible bachelor and labour minister in the Laurier government sat beside Robertine Barry. In *The Sweet Sixteen*, Linda Kay deliciously speculates that they may have discussed their mutual interest in spirit-ualism. Barry, she noted, "consulted clairvoyants and believed in premon-itions, telepathy, spirit communication, and the power of certain objects to bring good luck."

Most of the women died young — Barry at forty-six in 1910, Coleman at fifty-one in 1915, founder Graham at fifty-four in 1924. But the club endured. One of the most loyal activists was Lipsett-Skinner, a woman who always seemed ahead of her time. As a teenager she served as a school commissioner. After her marriage she travelled to Britain and Ireland to promote opportunities for women in Canada at the behest of the Canadian government. As a CWPC member she argued that "many of the handicaps of women and children could be removed if more publicly-spirited women understood the laws as they are, and could constructively work for suitable amendments." In her reporting she was fearless. She exposed the poor con-ditions of immigrant women in Winnipeg. She waded into the controversial General Strike in Winnipeg in 1919. She raised the hackles of the Calgary Stampede when she denounced a popular rodeo wrestling event for "the appalling cruelty to the steers chosen to illustrate the prowess of the cowboys in the manly art of 'bulldogging.'"

Charter members of the Canadian Women's Press Club, 1904.

FIRST WOMAN IN OTTAWA PRESS GALLERY DEAD

Newspaperwoman Dead

Mrs. Genevieve Lipsett-Skinner Widely Known as Journalist Here

MONTREAL, Jan. 30—Former member of the parliamentary press gallery at Ottawa and one of Canada's outstanding women journalists, Mrs. Genevieve Lipsett-Skinner died in hospital here Tuesday after a lengthy illness.

The funeral will be held here Friday, burial being in Mount Royal cemetery.

Educationist, lecturer, graduate with honors in law, Mrs. Lipsett-Skinner was best known for another phase of her versatility — newspaper work. She specialized in writing about the business of government and became the first

MRS. G. LIPPSETT-SKINNER

Mrs. Lipsett-Skinner, well-known Canadian newspaperwoman, died following a long illness at Montreal, Tuesday.

Genevieve Lipsett-Skinner, a trailblazer for women.

She was also an ardent supporter of conscription in 1916, as were most CWPC members, including Nellie McClung, whose son had enlisted. That caused a split with their comrade-in-arms Francis Beynon, an ardent pacifist and feminist whose column at the influential *Grain Growers' Guide* supported the weekly's commitment to the farmers' co-operative movement.

According to Carleton professor Barbara Freeman, her "radical" politics led to her departure from the *Guide* and an angry exchange with McClung, a backer of the Borden government's conscription plan. In *Beyond Bylines: Media Workers and Women's Rights in Canada*, Freeman writes, "Beynon's story demonstrates the complex wartime connections among Prairie feminism, social gospel reformism, agrarian politics and newspaper culture."

After Genevieve Lipsett-Skinner left the press gallery in 1926, it was another decade before the next woman arrived. That may be why, even today, Evelyn Tufts is sometimes described as the first female member. In fact, the correspondent for the Halifax *Chronicle Herald* was the second woman to receive formal accreditation in the history of the gallery. And for the next decade she was the only woman.

She was no shrinking violet. As a freelancer she was the only reporter to cover the murder trial of an Inuk man in the High Arctic in 1935 that made news across North America. Later that year she was in New York for a holiday and the *Herald* asked her to cover the famous trial of the man accused of kidnapping and murdering baby Charles Lindbergh Jr. She was the only Canadian reporter there, and that landed her a full-time job with the *Herald*. By 1936 she was promoted to the Parliamentary Press Gallery where she emphasized her femininity. A photo from the archives shows her, hand on hip, dressed to the nines, wearing a giant hat with a plume as she stood in the cluttered workroom chatting with one of the boys. She was a contemporary of the titans of the day, including Grant Dexter, Bruce Hutchison, and Blair Fraser. In 1951 she represented the press gallery as an official pallbearer at the funeral of John Diefenbaker's first wife, Edna, in Saskatoon — an official role for a reporter that would be unusual today. In all, Tufts spent almost twenty years reporting from Parliament Hill, and she became the first woman honoured as a lifetime member.

As Marjory Lang observes in *Women Who Made the News*, Tufts "became obsessed with women's failure to make headway in politics, either as participants or observers like herself." As a member of the Canadian Women's Press Club, she continually bemoaned the lack of females writing about politics.

Press gallery, 1948. Evelyn Tufts of the Halifax *Chronicle Herald* talking to the *Toronto Star*'s R.K. Taylor, bemoaning the lack of women in politics.

"Apparently," she told club members in a speech in 1948, "the men pre-empt this field, as they do the press gallery. They still stick to the old cliché about a 'woman's angle' when they hand out assignments."

The next woman to get membership was Helen Brimmell. She was ninety-six when I met up with her in Ottawa in June 2016. She was a graduate of the University of Toronto, where she was deputy editor of the *Varsity* student paper ("the editor was always a man," she noted dryly). The CP wire service in those days recruited the top *Varsity* people and, after six months, CP editors sent her to Ottawa to cover women's affairs and softer news, like Government House — the governor general's comings and goings. She did not have a press gallery card. But after filling in for a male staffer covering a committee, she asked for a membership. She got it in April 1946 on condition that she *not* attend the annual gallery dinner stag. "I told them, 'It's all right with me.' I didn't want to spoil their fun." She was only the third woman accredited as a member in seventy-nine years.

Helen Brimmell, the oldest living member of the gallery, Ottawa, 2016.

The CWPC tried mightily to change the dial. In 1955, at the height of the Cold War, the club chartered a plane and took seventy-two female journalists on a news gathering trip to Europe and the Soviet Union, where an unexpected meeting with foreign minister Andrei Gromyko generated news. Membership peaked at 680 in 1968. But three years later, membership was waning as members drifted away. Some felt it had lost its focus on professional development and become a mere social club, while all but abandoning francophone journalists who were so vital to its launch. In 2004 the CWPC folded without fanfare. It lives on only in awards named after famous members given to journalists by the Ottawa-based Media Club of Canada. Now, the club has male and female members.

———————

Joyce Fairbairn's route to the press gallery was only slightly less challenging than Lipsett-Skinner's forty years earlier. When the twenty-two-year-old

Albertan reported for work on Parliament Hill for United Press International in 1962, she was the only woman in the gallery. In a recording made by Tom Earle for Parliament's oral history project, she said that for the first few weeks, Norman McLeod, her boss in the one-room office, wouldn't even speak to her because he "was initially reluctant to have a woman in that bureau." Her first big scoop that year was a bulletin reporting that the Diefenbaker government would fall. Fairbairn had done the basic legwork of asking the leader of the Quebec-based Créditiste Party, which held the balance of power, how he intended to vote later that day. He said he was going to vote against the government and cause an election.

To Fairbairn's dismay, McLeod decided that she should stay off the election campaign trail leading up to the June 18 vote. He felt, as she put it, "something awful might happen" behind the flimsy canvas curtains on the sleeping cars of the trains to "this slip of a girl." Her hopes were "dashed," said Fairbairn. Ever since graduating from the University of Alberta and getting her journalism degree at Carleton, she had wanted to be a political reporter. Prime Minister Diefenbaker and Liberal leader Pearson got wind of the issue, and "to their eternal credit, said the decision was absolutely wrong" and that she "had the same right as anyone else to cover their campaign."

At the time, the annual press gallery dinner, a black-tie affair attended by the who's who of official Ottawa, was still off-limits to Joyce and any females. She could buy tickets for male guests, but she couldn't go herself. The old boys finally lifted the ban in 1967 — after all, it was the year of Expo 67 and Judy LaMarsh, the secretary of state, was responsible for Centennial Year celebrations. CP correspondent Susan Becker noted that the women of the gallery abstained in case the vote in favour was close and women got the "blame." An influx of new male members helped to throw out the ban for good. The new breed felt that more than journalism had to change.

Fairbairn went on to a distinguished career with the FP News Service, filing regularly to six member papers: the *Winnipeg Free Press*, the *Calgary Albertan*, the *Lethbridge Herald*, the *Vancouver Sun*, the *Victoria Times*, and the *Ottawa Journal*. In 1970 she jumped to Prime Minister Pierre Trudeau's office, just in time to help organize his responses in the House to the War Measures Act. She was his senior legislative adviser for fourteen years. In

Joyce Fairbairn with the boys. Left–right: Geoff Scott, Robert Hull, Tom Earle, Lester Pearson, Ian Macdonald, Eric Dennis, Fraser MacDougall, Joyce Fairbairn, Peter Jackman, and Pierre O'Neill.

1984 Trudeau appointed her to the Senate where she became the first woman government leader. In her later years Fairbairn lost her husband, the journalist Mike Gillan, to heart disease, and in 2012 she withdrew from the Senate with a diagnosis of dementia.

———

In 1964 Rosemary Speirs, fresh from the University of Toronto, was applying for a job at CP. Over afternoon coffee and a bowl of french fries in May 2015, she recalled the response from bureau chief John Dauphinee as only an experienced reporter can:

> He said that my credentials were good and the things that
> I had done were good if I was going to come in there as a

young reporter. But he said, "I'm sorry, we don't hire little girls." I just lost my temper. I banged on his desk and said, "I am not a little girl." I think that's what he was waiting for, actually. He just sat back and laughed. He just wanted to see if I could take the newsroom, I guess. He was well to be wary. There was a protest walkout of the male news staffers the day I came in because a female was going to be in the newsroom.

Speirs worked her way up from doing stock listings and sports scores to the CP labour beat in Montreal. Occasionally she would go to Ottawa to cover what seemed like the annual postal strike. One day, she saddled up to the bar of the National Press Club to order a beer. From the other end came the bellow, "A woman touched the bar!"

Speirs explains: "I remember jumping back from the bar wondering what contagion I was supposed to have conveyed by merely touching it. The rule then was that females could not touch the bar."

In fact, the club had a males-only membership rule. The year was 1964, and the exclusion lasted until 1970 when members, finally embarrassed by public demonstrations, voted to admit women to membership. *Ottawa Journal* reporter Sandra Woods was in her early twenties and remembers picketing the Press Club with a sign reading: TYPE STORIES, NOT WOMEN. In the end, Woods never joined. Her reporter husband John Ferguson was already a member and, she said, "that was enough for one family." So it was that Susan Becker became the first woman to join the Press Club.

Speirs left CP and Montreal to join the *Star* in Toronto as a labour reporter (by then she had completed her Ph.D. in labour history). Then the paper promoted her to be the Ontario legislature bureau chief at Queen's Park. She subsequently crossed over in the same role for the *Globe*, ultimately returning to the *Star* as the Queen's Park columnist. In 1989, just in time for the free trade election, Speirs became the first female Ottawa bureau chief of the *Toronto Star*.

Like her predecessor Lipsett-Skinner, Speirs also agitated for more women to enter Canadian politics. She was a member of the Committee for 94, which aimed to have women MPs make up half of the House of Commons by 1994, and later was a co-founder of the bipartisan Equal

Voice. In 2004 she explained her motivation in a speech to interns at the Ontario legislature: "The answer, if you ever climb into the Press Gallery to look down on the floor, will be obvious. From that perspective, it is a sea of men."

In Ottawa progress came at a snail's pace. The number of women in the gallery increased dramatically, but in the House of Commons, not so much. When Speirs made her speech in 2004 there were sixty-three female MPs, 21 percent of the House. In the election of 2015 eighty-eight women were elected, or 26 percent.

Almost a century earlier Lipsett-Skinner had fought to advance the cause of women. In her twenties she convinced the Canadian Women's Press Club to create a fund to help "any infirm, ailing or needy member" who was in need of financial assistance. By 1934 Lipsett-Skinner applied to the fund herself. She died the next year. Despite a funeral attended by the Drummonds and Bronfmans of Montreal, and a spray of orchids and lilies of the valley sent by Prime Minister Mackenzie King, her estate contained only enough funds for a dinner for fellow members of the CWPC branch in Montreal. She was only forty-nine. But she had marked a trail for generations of women to come.

Part II

THE HAPPY
WARRIORS

Chapter 4

GRATTAN O'LEARY: FOREVER TORY

The year was 1911. Liberal prime minister Wilfrid Laurier's time was drawing to a close. His proposal for a Canadian navy independent of the Royal Navy ruffled the feathers of the Orange Lodge and those attached to Imperial Britain. His campaign for reciprocal trade with the United States alarmed the business establishment, which preferred protective tariffs, and those who favoured strong ties with the mother country. Conservative leader Robert Borden campaigned on the slogan "No truck or trade with the Yankees" and defeated Laurier. It was a time of big issues — perfect for a new reporter looking to tackle the big leagues.

Michael Grattan O'Leary was twenty-two years younger than John Dafoe and thirty-three years John Willison's junior, but like his illustrious predecessors he was a pup when he arrived to cover Parliament in 1911. He was twenty-three. On his first day in Ottawa he almost blew it. Instead of reporting directly to the *Ottawa Journal* office, he went up to the House of Commons and spent the afternoon listening, transfixed, to speeches by Laurier and Borden. His Ottawa career eventually spanned sixty-five years, fifty-five with the *Ottawa Journal,* twenty of those in the press gallery. As the editor and later an executive of the *Journal*, he knew prime ministers from Laurier to Pierre Trudeau. A partisan Tory, he actively worked for his close friend Arthur Meighen and for not-so-friendly John Diefenbaker, who appointed him to the Senate in 1962. But as former *Ottawa Citizen* editor Christopher Young wrote on the occasion of O'Leary's death in

1976 at eighty-eight, "He was a Tory partisan but he believed so strongly in partisan politics that he loved the Grit partisans almost as well as those of his persuasion."

A son of Gaspé Irish Catholics, he grew up poor on a farm near Percé, by the harsh gulf shore. As a boy, he recalled, he would walk three miles to the village store, "the sea wind cutting like a knife, selling eggs for ten cents a dozen, butter for fifteen cents a pound." He left school at twelve and worked in lumber yards and a brewery, and as an oiler in the engine room of a seagoing ship. In his spare time he read anything he could get his hands on. He was a character from the start. In 1909 he applied for a job at the Saint John *Standard* in New Brunswick. When the editor asked if he had any reporting experience, twenty-one-year-old O'Leary replied, "No, but I'm a good Conservative." After covering fires, courts, and the arriving ships, he applied to the *Journal* in Ottawa, which took him on for seventeen dollars a week as a press gallery reporter.

O'Leary, a slight man with a big personality, belonged to the era in Ottawa of the "happy warrior," where no quarter was spared in the heat of partisan battle, while private friendships blossomed across party lines around the whisky bottle in the club room. "I vote with the Tories but dine with the Grits," he liked to say. He loved to recall the time he asked press gallery colleague John Dafoe why he had become a Liberal, and got the response, "I simply think of all the sons of bitches in the Tory party, then I think of all the sons of bitches in the Liberal Party, and I can't help coming to the conclusion that there are more sons of bitches in the Tory party." O'Leary was very much one of the boys. He had a regular Sunday morning golf game with Liberal powerhouse C.D. Howe, once wrote a *Maclean's* piece about acing a hole at the Royal Ottawa Golf Club, and relished weekly poker games with his mates and betting on hockey games with members of the paper's sports department.

O'Leary was a powerful writer, "sometimes marked by snorting fire," in the words of an elegant, unsigned tribute the *Journal* published on his death. "It was said that he went through life with a sword in one hand and a lyre in the other." His main weapon was a battered typewriter atop a rickety wood table blackened with burn marks from his endless cigarettes. He used the two-fingered hunt-and-peck system and, recalled his friend and *Journal* colleague, I. Norman Smith, "If it didn't 'read,' he'd cross it out with a vicious tattoo on the 'x' and 'm' keys, and do the sentence again until it did." Soon O'Leary was writing several *Journal* editorials each day and contributing a regular political column to *Maclean's*.

The real fireworks of O'Leary's early days on the Hill had to do with reciprocity and Borden's election. Many Canadians, O'Leary concluded, viewed Laurier's trade policy "as a rejection of ties with the mother country" and feared that "commercial union would lead to political absorption." While O'Leary was pleased that a Tory was back in office for the first time in fifteen years — and, like him, one who parted his hair in the middle, played poker, and liked a good Scotch — the feisty journalist retained his independent view of the parade. In contrast to the mellifluous oratory of Laurier, Borden's was relentlessly lawyer-like and, said O'Leary, so painstakingly written that "his staff had to steal his fountain pen or he'd never stop correcting his speeches." In later years O'Leary angered another Tory prime minister when he wrote that Arthur Meighen was losing touch with his base. Of Meighen's successor R.B. Bennett, who loved to bully reporters and ignore advisers, O'Leary once said: "He was not above asking the opinions of others, he was only above accepting them."

In 1962 O'Leary effectively forced John Diefenbaker to appoint him to the Senate. As related by his friend Tom Van Dusen, a reporter turned Tory aide: "He told me that unless the Chief named him to the Senate in the very near future, the prime minister would lose his paper's support." Van Dusen relayed the message. After O'Leary took his seat in 1962 he immediately declared his independence from Diefenbaker: "I have not come into this chamber to turn myself into a political eunuch, and I have no intention ever of running about with those people with open minds, some of their minds so open that their brains fall out."

O'Leary admired the great speakers of his time, and he himself was one of them. But he respected the fact that Parliament was the proper forum when any of them had something important to say. "The ideas and even the words were largely their own," he wrote in his 1977 memoir, *Recollections of People, Press and Politics*. "There were no P.R. men, no second-guessers, no poll-takers…. Government had to operate on conviction or principle not on what the next poll would bring." But then, as time went on, "speech writers appeared. Radio was coming in and political figures needed help to cope with the unfamiliar medium."

As with so many good reporters who emerged from the police and court beats, O'Leary's grounding in the basics of journalism — getting it fast and accurately — served him well in his early days at the *Journal*. The paper dispatched him to New York when word first reached the desk of the sinking of the *Titanic* in the dark hours of April 15, 1912. Without New York City police credentials he could not get on to the dock where survivors were arriving. He went to the Associated Press office where an "upstanding Irishman" on the night desk gave him a pass. From dockside, he described the emotional scenes as survivors stumbled from the decks of the *Carpathia* into the waiting arms of relatives and friends, and told their gripping stories of survival. O'Leary's report contributed to such brisk sales of the *Journal* on April 19 that the paper printed a second "Extra" edition.

The other great story of the time was the fire that destroyed the Parliament Buildings. O'Leary was at a boozy dinner staged by the minister of militia, Sam Hughes, in the Château Laurier on February 13, 1916, when the blaze started in the Parliamentary Reading Room shortly after 8:00 p.m. The group ignored a visitor carrying the first warning; they were more intent on listening to an Irish visitor belting out the classic folk staple "Where the Mountains of Mourne Come Down to the Sea." An hour later the party ventured out of the hotel into a bitterly cold night and was stunned to see, in O'Leary's words, "a pall of black smoke obscuring Parliament Hill and the main tower of the Centre Block shooting great gouts of flame high into the night."

People inside clambered down ladders and leapt into snowbanks. Prime Minister Borden crawled on his hands and knees through dense smoke and "made his way hatless through the crowd from the Centre Block to his East Block office, where he watched from a window." The fire destroyed the Centre Block but spared the library. The wife of Speaker Albert Sévigny escaped through a window in her husband's office, O'Leary recounted, but two of her guests died in the fire, along with an MP and four others. A burning cigar butt in the reading room was one suspected cause — although there were conspiracy theories too about a German operative. With the building gutted, Public Works hurriedly arranged to transfer Parliament south to the Victoria Museum, quickly stripped of dinosaurs and historic relics for animals of a different nature. It was there, in a House of Commons fashioned out of an auditorium, that the great wartime debates about conscription and the Union government unfolded.

As the war approached, Borden had scrapped Laurier's plan to create a made-in-Canada navy independent of Britain and brought in his own policy of cash contributions to the British cause against Germany. He invoked closure to get approval of the Naval Aid Bill — only to see the Liberal majority in the Senate kill it. The outbreak of war in Europe had a tempering impact on the political climate. The press acceded to Borden's War Measures Act of 1914, which ushered in censorship in the name of national and Allied security.

Anti-conscription forces rioted in Montreal, while support for Union grew in English Canada during the wartime election. Publishers in English Canada rallied to the cause, including Dafoe in Winnipeg, Atkinson of the *Star* in Toronto, Graham in Montreal, and O'Leary in Ottawa. The result on December 17, 1917, was predictable: an English-French split with 153 seats for the coalition Unionists and 82 for Laurier's Liberals — 62 of them from Quebec. After the election O'Leary went to see Laurier in an attempt to confirm rumours that he would resign. He recalled: "I found Laurier stretched out on a couch in his temporary office in the Victoria Museum, strangely at home amid the artifacts and curios and reading a life of the Empress of China, to all appearances completely relaxed and oblivious to the currents of rumour and gossip swirling around his leadership." But the leader was in no mood to tell secrets.

In early 1919 the aging Laurier failed to persuade the Liberals who had deserted him for the Union to return. And his health was failing. On February 16 he suffered a cerebral hemorrhage and told his tearful wife, Zoé, "This is the end." He died the next day. In his memoir, O'Leary wrote: "With the possible exception of Macdonald, Laurier remains the greatest of our prime ministers," and that the Liberal was "the greatest" orator of all. Shortly before his death, O'Leary recalled hearing what amounted to Laurier's "last will and testament" during an address to young Liberals in London: "Remember that faith is better than doubt and love is better than hate."

When Borden retired in 1920 the government caucus turned to Portage la Prairie lawyer Arthur Meighen, cheered on by O'Leary, Arthur Ford, and other supporters in the press gallery. A transplant from Ontario, Meighen carried plenty of baggage. He had served Borden loyally in helping to organize the Union government and, as solicitor general, drafting and implementing the conscription legislation. He also brought in the anti-sedition law in the wake of the Winnipeg General Strike in 1919.

If O'Leary had a favourite among leaders, and a person who reciprocated the respect, it was Arthur Meighen. O'Leary described him as "a young man of glacial calm and sparkling intellect." The two men had been friends ever since O'Leary wrote a glowing portrait of Meighen in 1912 for the *Canadian Magazine*, "The White Hope of the Conservative Party." The next year Meighen arranged to have O'Leary seconded from the *Journal* to CP, and invited him to sail to the Imperial Conference in London with the official party. He was, in effect, Meighen's Boswell, producing a steady flow of favourable page 1 articles about Meighen's policies and performance, notably his success in promoting a process for a multilateral agreement on disarmament. In one article, under the headline "Britain Owes Gratitude to Mr. Meighen," O'Leary quoted more than three hundred words verbatim of an article praising the Tory Meighen from the *Manchester Guardian*, "the leading organ of British Liberalism," as he put it.

O'Leary also made some news of his own while attending a formal luncheon with senior correspondents and officials. "After a couple of cocktails," O'Leary wrote, he unburdened himself of an attack on "England's indifference to the real interests of the country." As exhibit one, he denounced the articles the *Times*'s Canadian correspondent, John Willison, was filing from Canada, many critical of Meighen: "All he's doing for you is writing for the *Times* what the *Times* would like to see in the *Times*. All damned nonsense." The critique worked. The next day O'Leary had an article of his own in the *Times* pushing the theme that he and Meighen had articulated during the conference: that Canada had to hold to a more independent course. O'Leary became a regular *Times* contributor.

O'Leary's support was nowhere effective enough, however, to help the Conservative Party maintain its grip on power. Indeed, its future did not look bright, and as Meighen came to power in 1920 clouds were looming. On the Prairies, John Dafoe and his *Free Press* embraced the new agrarian

Progressive Party, which was championing the sweeping calls for reform being made by western farmers opposed to high tariffs. The Liberals had a new leader in the crafty William Lyon Mackenzie King, and he had managed to persuade some Grits to leave the Union coalition, while others fled to the Progressives. Canadians were reeling from a deep postwar recession. And there were strong memories of Meighen's seminal role in the Borden government as law-and-order solicitor general and, in Quebec, as the "champion of conscription." On top of all that, the powerful Montreal establishment, led by Graham's *Star*, opposed the nationalization of the Canadian Northern and Grand Trunk Railways.

With so much against the Conservatives, it is not surprising the 1921 election resulted in the party's defeat. When the final tally was made, Meighen's coalition had been reduced to fifty seats. King's Liberals formed a minority government with 116 MPs, and Progressives held the balance of power. Meighen and seven of his ministers lost their seats.

It was to be the first of three improbable encounters between Meighen and King on the hustings. The second was on October 29, 1925, when Meighen campaigned effectively and came within seven seats of winning a majority (116 seats to 99 for the Liberals and 22 for the Progressives). In that election, O'Leary, who had agreed to stand as a Meighen candidate in the Gaspé, had his nose well and truly bloodied. Back at the *Journal* after his defeat, O'Leary was outraged as he watched King cling to power with support from the Progressives, despite the fact that Meighen's Tories had won more seats than the Liberals.

This alliance fell apart, however, when the House censured King following a scandal that erupted — at the height of Prohibition — involving bribes to customs officials to overlook bootleg liquor entering Canada. King thought he could defeat Meighen clearly this time in a new vote. As O'Leary wrote: "Fortified by his consultations with the spirits, strong in the knowledge of his dead mother's approval, King wanted an election." But Governor General Lord Byng refused King's request and instead asked Meighen to form a government. "King," an incensed O'Leary declared, "was motivated by one concern: to get back in power as soon as possible." That he did in the 1926 election, campaigning against Byng as much as Meighen. It was, said O'Leary, "diabolically clever, Machiavellian."

Meighen resigned on October 11, 1926.

Following Meighen's exit, O'Leary next tried to help Conservative R.B. Bennett, who replaced King as prime minister in 1930. In the years after his victory, Bennett's relations with the press gallery were strained. The *Toronto Star* greeted him with the headline, "Pooh Bah Is on Job at Capital." Bennett immediately barred the *Star* reporters from his office. O'Leary was among the pro-Tory reporters who kept on friendly terms with those on the "enemies list" and briefed them on the Bennett government. When the *Ottawa Journal* ran a critical editorial, Bennett refused to recognize O'Leary. Still, ever the loyalist, O'Leary advised Bennett in 1935 as he prepared his "New Deal" radio broadcasts. They were not enough to save Bennett, and in the December election King returned as prime minister — there to remain for another thirteen years.

By this time O'Leary was editor of the *Journal*. Years later, in 1957, he became president, a post he held for nine years. He chaired the Royal Commission on Publications, which recommended protection for the

Grattan O'Leary, 1957: a happy political warrior.

Canadian magazine industry. He was the proud rector of Queen's University. On the political front, the senator defended Diefenbaker when his government was falling apart in 1962. But, in the end, impatient with Dief's egotism and indecision, he spoke out against his chief at a party meeting and became one of Robert Stanfield's early backers in 1967. In his memoirs, O'Leary declared: "I never felt any gratitude to the prime minister who appointed me. I did not say, 'You can have my conscience if you will send me to the Senate.'" True to his word to the end, O'Leary also said: "The job of the press is to protest, to expose, to oppose."

Chapter 5

GRANT DEXTER: FOREVER GRIT

The first report reached the empty newsroom of the *Manitoba Free Press* late Tuesday evening, July 29, 1913: A herd of elephants had escaped and was stampeding through the circus grounds during a furious summer electrical storm in Winnipeg. Grant Dexter, the seventeen-year-old copy boy, was the only person available, or sober, so he went off to cover his first story. "At 1 o'clock this morning," Dexter wrote, "Aubrey Street presented a strange spectacle. Elephants were wandering up and down the streets, priceless show horses were standing with their backs turned to the storm and men were running everywhere trying to herd the animals into their proper places."

The writing was unremarkable and, although it provided lurid details of smashed tents and men wielding pitchforks against the beasts, the article ran the next day on page 24 of the twenty-six-page edition. But when editor John W. Dafoe came in to work that day, he inquired approvingly, "Who did that story?" He was pleased to learn that it was the work of the teenager he had hired the year before when, as he recalled much later, "a tall, slim youngster came in and struck me for a job. I liked his looks, and when I found he was the son of a man whom I had known twenty years before I took him in." Dexter, he said, "was sent to the file room, which was, so to speak, our detention place until we decided what to do with its inmates."

Young Dexter soon broke out. In quick order he won promotion to cub reporter, and then police, court, and city hall reporter. After war service with the Royal Strathcona Horse, he was sent to the press gallery of the Manitoba legislature. By 1924 he had the paper's top reporting job, political correspondent in Ottawa. He was only twenty-six. But Alexander Grant Dexter was also the emissary of the most powerful editor in Canada. He continued in that role, serving as Dafoe's eyes and ears on capital events for twenty years. His private memos to his boss — "the Chief," he called him — were often more revealing than his dispatches for the paper. In the process he became part of the small, elite Liberal establishment of politicians, bureaucrats, and "pressmen" that ruled Canada from William Lyon Mackenzie King to Lester B. Pearson.

Like so many of his illustrious press gallery predecessors — Willison, Dafoe, O'Leary — Dexter came from humble roots and had little formal education. His father, Henry Dexter, abandoned the family and left town after his law practice fell apart in the real estate crash of the 1890s. Grant's mother struggled to make ends meet for her five children. They lived for a while in Hamilton, Ontario, where Grant completed his first year of high school. After the family returned to Manitoba to live with an uncle, Grant attended Brandon College, then a Baptist school. But he left after grade ten, his last formal year of schooling, when he discovered that his mother was using her limited resources to pay his tuition. Besides, "he hated it," his daughter, Susan, told me in a 2015 interview. In May 1912 Dafoe hired him as an office boy and messenger for himself and the paper's legendary agricultural editor, Cora Hind.

Within days of arriving in Ottawa for duty in January 1924, Dexter was papering page 1 with his reports and pinching himself. As he wrote to his sweetheart Alice Hunter, whom he would marry later that year: "What a sensation to feel that the ambition of one's life has at last come to pass! … I walked up to the main entrance, slowly to be sure and with the thought that even if no one else cared, I was making history in my own life.… Many score of newspapermen would have sold their souls to be in my shoes, and I knew it."

By today's standards, Dexter and his friends in the gallery did sell their souls — to the Liberal Party of Canada. Historian Allan Levine observes: "The line between being a good journalist and being a party hack was often blurred." Conservative leader Arthur Meighen dismissed Dexter's reports as "violently Grit" and "very often glaringly dishonest." At a press briefing held in conjunction with the 1933 Washington disarmament conference, Tory prime minister R.B. Bennett spotted Dexter across the room. "Ladies and gentleman," he intoned, "there will be no press conference. I refuse to say anything in the presence of Mr. Dexter, the emissary of John W. Dafoe of the *Winnipeg Free Press,* whose only purpose here is to distort and misrepresent Canada's position." Fake news?

Dexter's fellow reporters, not the least his friend Grattan O'Leary and Bennett adviser Bill Herridge, were shocked. O'Leary recalled that Herridge, who also happened to be Bennett's brother-in-law, "told R.B. that Dexter was one of the most honest journalists in Canada and that R.B. was just hurting himself. R.B. just stared stonily at the wall until we left."

There is no question about Dexter's political loyalties. Like Dafoe, in his Ottawa years Dexter cheerfully performed extracurricular services for the Liberals. As documented by Allan Levine, he attended Liberal strategy sessions, helped draft memos for the Cabinet, and wrote election propaganda. "The brotherhood was close," notes his daughter Susan Dexter, a senior journalist in her own right before she turned to teaching and community activism in Toronto. "He did everything. If they asked him to do a speech, he'd do a speech because he knew the argument. It's regarded today as unethical. But that was the system."

Dexter was not alone. His friend O'Leary was an unabashed Tory who worked on the side for the Conservative cause. (Despite that, the two men partnered on a political comment show aired by the CNR radio network in the early 1920s.) Several of Dexter's press gallery colleagues, notably Wilfrid Eggleston of Joe Atkinson's *Toronto Star*, Ken Wilson of Floyd Chalmers's *Financial Post,* and Arthur Irwin of *Maclean's,* were cozy with the Liberal establishment. During the Second World War, Eggleston and Fulgence Charpentier of *Le Droit* were among the reporters who joined the Canadian Censorship Board. (Jean Charpentier, Fulgence's son, also became a member of the press gallery with Radio-Canada and later was press secretary to Pierre Trudeau.) Farther afield, celebrated CBC war correspondent Matthew Halton made periodic return visits home to engage in patriotic rallies aimed at selling Victory Bonds and supporting the army position on partial conscription.

With his direct pipelines into key Liberal power brokers, Dexter broke major stories throughout his career. He relished doing that as much as anything. Within two weeks of arriving in Ottawa he revealed that King's efforts to lure two leading members of the Progressive Party into the Liberal fold had failed, thereby jeopardizing the prime minister's shaky hold on Parliament.

It was an era when co-operation among reporters in the press gallery, then numbering a mere thirty, and their colleagues around the country was common. Early in 1933, reporter Cora Hind in Winnipeg got a tip that a local cattle dealer was promoting a barter deal with the Soviet Union, exchanging Canadian cattle for Soviet oil. She passed the word along to Dexter, who in turn told Eggleston of the *Toronto Star*. "The story could not be broken first in Winnipeg without embarrassing Cora Hind," Eggleston recalled in his memoir, "so Grant and I made a deal whereby it would appear first in the *Toronto Star*." In Toronto, *Star* editors were delighted to flog a story that embarrassed the Tory government: Prime Minister R.B. Bennett had adamantly opposed trading with the dreaded Communists, while his agricultural minister favoured the deal because markets for western cattle farmers were under siege. But Eggleston rued the day. Managing editor Harry C. Hindmarsh was disappointed that the bureau did not dig up more dirt, and he forced Eggleston to resign from the *Star*. Eggleston recovered, however, and had a distinguished career as a public servant and founding director of Carleton University's School of Journalism.

Private life in official Ottawa was simple but elegant, built around a fraternity of journalists, politicians, and civil servants who socialized on a regular basis. At first the Dexters took an apartment, and then they moved to a four-bedroom house on Acacia Avenue in posh Rockcliffe with an expansive yard for Susan and her older brother and sister. Their neighbours on the street included the families of Grattan O'Leary and Blair Fraser. A nearby streetcar ran downtown.

For diversion the Dexters joined an informal Shakespeare Club, with the Egglestons, economist John Deutsch and his wife, and others. They met Sunday nights to discuss the play of the week. Sometimes out-of-towners like Bruce Hutchison or journalist Max Freedman would join the regulars. As the text required, Alice Dexter, a concert-level soprano, would perform Shakespearean-era songs. She also was an active promoter of the symphony and of emerging artists, her friend the painter Joe Plaskett being a favourite. Grant Dexter was no sportsman, but he did play the occasional golf game with Eggleston and other Hill reporters at the Chaudière Club. In the summer, to escape the heat, the Dexters would move *en famille* to their cottage on Whitefish Lake in the Gatineau north of Ottawa. Susan Dexter still remembers the night that Eggleston visited and recited "The Highwayman" who came "riding, riding, riding" her into such a state of terror "that I couldn't sleep for days." She also recalled the many sober discussions about world events and the mountain of reading her father did to compensate for his lack of schooling. "It was," said Susan, "a very rich household."

Dexter enjoyed the gossip that swirled through his world. He once incurred the wrath of King for violating, in the prime minister's view, the existing convention that a politician's private life was out of bounds for reporters. Dexter's offence? He had reported that the prime minister had taken a bath after delivery of the budget in 1930. We can only imagine what King would have done had reporters written about his curious relationship with long-time family friend Joan Patterson, who participated in his "table-rapping" spiritualism exercises.

It was also customary for reporters of the day to protect their sources from themselves. On one occasion in 1944 King's minister of defence for air, Charles "Chubby" Power, gave a briefing to reporters while he was intoxicated — "in his cups — deep in," as Dexter wrote in a private memo. He went on: "His deputy and officers could not hold him back. He insisted upon meeting the boys and made a scrambled, garbled kind of job of it. Half the material was off the record and half on, etc. The boys held a meeting afterward and sent somebody back to find out what they should print."

If Dexter did occasionally mention the personal side of political life, he mostly concerned himself with the big issues of the day: free trade, the looming signs of war, conscription, national unity, and anything related to advancement of the Canadian West. Dafoe's right hand in Winnipeg, executive editor George Ferguson, once explained the power of Dexter in a private memo: "Dafoe's paramount passion lay in federal politics. This made his Ottawa correspondent a figure of major importance, not only

Left–right: Victor Sifton, Grant Dexter, John W. Dafoe, and George Ferguson: the Liberal Party came first.

to the staff, but to the active politicians. The politicians both respected and feared Dafoe, and this feeling extended to his representative in the press gallery, Grant Dexter."

While Dexter kept members of the government informed of Dafoe's thinking on issues, the politicians were eager to explain their plans to Dexter in hopes of maintaining support of the respected "voice of the West" in Winnipeg. Dexter dutifully conveyed their supplications to the Chief and Dafoe's guidance to the government. The locales for his intel gathering were private offices, a quiet table at the Château Laurier dining room, or the Rideau Club. It would not be unusual for Dexter to visit five or six ministers in a day for an update.

The medium for the channelling was a Vesuvian outpouring of mailed memos and cables that flew between Winnipeg and Ottawa on an almost daily basis. They were never intended for publication. "Such information," Dexter wrote in a letter to Ferguson in 1942, "was always his [Dafoe's] information, given to me for him and not information which I could have obtained in the ordinary way. The secret memos really developed as a means of communication between various people here and the Chief."* They armed Dafoe with advance knowledge of government plans that he could support or, in the case of war policy, seek to change in his thundering editorials.

Dexter's discretion and easy manner in conversation flowed from his innate respect for politicians and his recognition of the heavy responsibilities they carried. "After all," he wrote in a letter to Alice in 1924, "it is not right to destroy public respect for a legislature or a commons. The people who are responsible for our laws deserve respectful attention, and a spirit of levity and disrespect will not improve our government."

Susan Dexter recalled that while her father could be playful, "he worked all the time. The dinner table talk was always about what he was doing and processing stuff." In addition to running the household and being a leading supporter of arts and culture in Ottawa, Alice was part of the Dexter machine, typing his memos, helping him to organize the scrapbook binders he kept as a vast personal filing system on events and policies, and driving him downtown. He was a serious man who worried about the big issues — and there were big ones in his time: two wars, conscription, French-English tensions, and the Great Depression. "There was always financial anxiety and concern over how the country was going to work," said Susan Dexter. "For my father, dread was not very far away. It didn't mean that he couldn't have fun. But life was very earnest and serious. There were grave things to be done. It was important stuff."

At the top of the list of worries was the rise to power in Germany of Adolf Hitler and his Nazi Party, and the seeming unconcern of the Canadian populace and the King government. In 1936 Dafoe dispatched Dexter to London with the thought, as historians Frederick W. Gibson and Barbara Robertson put it, "that informed press reports from London might help alert Canadians to their peril." The timing proved prescient. Dexter found himself in the middle of the action — and lending an ear to a disaffected Canadian diplomat, Lester Pearson, then second-in-command to High Commissioner Vincent Massey.

---

* The quoted memos were published in 1994 in an ambitious book edited by Frederick W. Gibson and Barbara Robertson, *Ottawa at War: The Grant Dexter Memoranda, 1939–1945* (Winnipeg: Manitoba Record Society, 1994).

At the time, King agreed with the British that appeasement of German grievances might temper Hitler's aggressiveness, while "Mike" Pearson wanted a more independent Canadian policy. He began sharing his secret intelligence from both Ottawa and the British Foreign Office with Dexter, who relayed it to Winnipeg, taking care to disguise it with a crude code (Hitler, ironically, was known as "Cohen"). Thanks to Pearson, Dexter was the first North American reporter to learn of British prime minister Neville Chamberlain's flight to Munich in 1938 for his infamous sit-down with Hitler about demands for control of the Sudetenland in Czechoslovakia.

Just days before the Munich agreement, Dexter and Alice celebrated their wedding anniversary by attending a performance of Wagner's epic *Ring Cycle*. In his diary that night, his jottings betray a sense of foreboding about the imminent signs of war:

> Alice looked down on all the young men on the promenade floor wondering what would happen to them. Driving home through Hyde Park — gangs of men swinging picks and shovels, digging air raid shelters and gun emplacements. Searchlights set about 3' above the ground — shadows thrown grotesquely on grass beyond — low hanging branches edging out the light — russet leaves — dying and glistening with dew. Fearsome scene. Al cried. So we drove along — sandbagging operations underway — trenches being dug in every park — guns with their snouts pointing skywards — RAF machines circling about above London.

After two years in London Dexter returned to Ottawa, his reputation soaring as a result of his reporting from Europe. In Winnipeg the circulation of the *Free Press* had bounced back after being pummelled by readers angry with Dafoe's denunciation of Munich and his hawkishness. Now, with the Nazis on the march through Poland, everyone was on the same page. Dexter's role was to supply the Chief and Ferguson with inside information that would allow the paper to defend Canada's war policy intelligently.

Dexter occasionally did use his channel to blow the whistle on policies he thought were wrong. One case was the government's decision in 1940 to brand 135,000 Italians as "enemy aliens" and to revoke citizenship of those naturalized after 1942. When disgruntled bureaucrats drew Dexter's attention to the xenophobic regulation, he wrote two damning comments about it in the *Free Press* and prompted Ferguson to write an editorial. Dexter's emotive opinion piece, "The Results of Panic," documented "the injustice which has been done to Canadian citizens of Italian origin." It went on to describe the craven collapse of the King government in the face of allegations about "fifth column" threats and the demand by the Canadian Legion that naturalized Canadians be classified as "enemy aliens." Two months later the government reversed course and restored citizenship to thousands of Italian and German immigrants. The internment of Japanese Canadians continued, though, without similar notice or outrage. Indeed, in January 1943 the King government authorized the liquidation of their confiscated property without a peep in Parliament — or from Dexter.

Astoundingly, Dexter also provided vivid detail of the deep Cabinet split over conscription that bedevilled King as war raged in Europe. But Dafoe and Ferguson kept it to themselves. Warring factions battled over the issue within King's Cabinet at the height of hostilities in 1942 and 1944. On one side was King and those loyal to the party's pledge, including many Quebec ministers, that they would impose mandatory service only for domestic, not overseas duty. The leader of the hawks was Colonel James Ralston, the minister of defence, who, with powerful allies that included Finance Minister James Ilsley, took their stand despite bitter memories of how conscription had torn the country apart in 1917. Dexter was plugged into both sides, from the prime minister on down, and his copious memos were startling in their detail and informality.

On March 4, 1942, he notes a private dinner staged by Horace Hunter of the Maclean-Hunter Publishing Company for General A.G.L. "Andy" McNaughton, the commanding officer of the First Canadian Corps in Britain, who was in Canada on home leave. Kenneth Wilson, parliamentary correspondent for the company's *Financial Post*, attended, took voluminous notes, and briefed Dexter, who sent the following to Winnipeg: "McNaughton's chief point was that Ralston was proving himself to be completely unfitted for his job and that unless he (McN) could obtain satisfactory action on a number of points, he would resign or ask to be relieved of his command and not return to England."

Journalists today would call that a "Holy shit!" moment. But there was more. Two days later Dexter, Bruce Hutchison of the *Free Press*, and Wilson sat down with the general. He elaborated on the fact that, actually, he had more than enough troops and that, instead, the money should be poured into equipment and armament. As Dexter wrote: "Brucie and I and Ken Wilson had a talk with McNaughton in the Woods building yesterday afternoon.... He emphasized the folly of the conscription issue.... It was tragic that the country should be thinking about conscription or military manpower when we should be thinking only of expanding war industry. Conscription would not be needed for at least a year."

By March 9, Dexter was reporting the blow-by-blow to Winnipeg in private memos to George Ferguson, but the paper was silent on the crisis. Ralston was threatening to resign because King, leery of reaction in Quebec, was unwilling to send conscripts abroad. On May 7, Dexter wrote: "What King really intends is never to impose conscription unless he can carry Quebec with him, that is, the bulk of the Quebec Liberals." Dafoe, who favoured maximum force against Hitler, nonetheless cautioned the government — via a memo to Dexter — to avoid "precipitate action" that could cause a national unity crisis. Dexter relayed that to the government. King heeded the advice. "Not necessarily conscription, but conscription if necessary" became his famous formula. Publicly, he put his faith in appeals to soldiers signed up for home duty to voluntarily go abroad. Dexter marvelled at King's ability to hold his government together. He noted that "casualties have been fantastically light and the army is embarrassed with an oversupply of men."

But by 1944 — after the D-Day invasion and intense fighting in France — the hawks began beating the conscription drum again. King fired the recalcitrant Ralston in front of his colleagues at a Cabinet meeting and brought in General McNaughton, of all people, as his successor. Without King's knowledge, on November 23, 1944, half his Cabinet was meeting and, reports Dexter, "they decided to act as a body and either force conscription or resign." This, mind you, was on the very day that the Allies had captured Strasbourg and the Americans were bombing Tokyo. Meanwhile, back in Ottawa, King responded with an amendment that would limit the overseas dispatch of home-based volunteer troops to sixteen thousand — in effect, limited conscription — but only after a Commons vote of confidence. That bought Cabinet peace. Two weeks later King survived the vote in the Commons, 143–73, with nineteen Quebec francophones in favour. In the end, only about twenty-four hundred men of the sixteen thousand actually arrived at the front line.

By the time the war was over, Ferguson, Dexter, and Hutchison were part of a divide-and-conquer troika established by publisher Victor Sifton to run the *Free Press*, Ferguson as editor, and Dexter and Hutchison as associate editors. Dafoe had died in January 1944, hoping that the hard-working Ferguson would replace him, knowing that neither Dexter in Ottawa nor Hutchison in Victoria had any interest in moving to Winnipeg and taking over the paper. But Sifton wanted it his way — having the final say. Still, Dafoe would have been proud of the way his boys hewed to his line on the volatile conscription issue of 1944.

Dafoe's death and the coming of peace signalled a shift in focus. At Ferguson's request, Dexter spent more time in Winnipeg and began writing editorials, a task he disliked. Ferguson worried that Dexter had trouble distinguishing the national interest from that of the Liberal Party. Ferguson reminded him sternly that his job, as historian Patrick Brennan put it, "was to help the *Free Press* provide its readers with the truth, and if that meant exposing a Liberal government's failings from time to time, so be it." By today's standards, the readers of the *Free Press* were denied relevant information with which to assess the performance of their government — one that in late 1944 had seemed to be careering out of control. In contrast to other papers, the *Free Press* sat on the wartime Cabinet crisis story until only a few days before Ralston's resignation. "The *Free Press*," Brennan wrote in *Reporting the Nation's Business*, "expressed mock surprise at these developments even though Dexter and Hutchison, both of whom fortuitously happened to be in Ottawa as the crisis broke, had known what was brewing for several days."

Such was the fate of the insider in those days. But Dexter could also keep his distance, as he did in analyzing an interview King granted him after his return from the Paris Peace Conference in 1946. Ever the internationalist, Dexter recoiled at King's dismissive attitude toward the United Nations and called for more public support. The next year King, preparing his succession, appointed Louis St. Laurent, a favourite of the press gallery even among Tory reporters, as minister of external affairs. In Winnipeg Ferguson failed to resolve control issues with Sifton and left to become editor of the *Montreal Star*. Dexter moved up to the top job at the *Free Press*, while St. Laurent replaced King as Liberal leader and prime minister. Dexter continued cheering the Liberals on from his post at the *Free Press*, as did Hutchison. The Liberals won re-election in 1949 and 1953.

By the time Dexter was back in Ottawa, St. Laurent was in failing health. When John Diefenbaker's Progressive Conservatives ousted the Liberals in 1957, the Liberal establishment press knew it was time for a change — of Liberal leaders. Dexter and Hutchison were there again to lend a helping hand to Lester Pearson. As Dexter put it, their work was "to help Mike shine."

Part III

THE PEARSON ERA

.

Chapter 6

BLAIR FRASER: THE DON

If the press gallery alumni had a Joe DiMaggio division, Blair Fraser would have been a unanimous inductee. Tall, graceful, and ruggedly handsome, with a silken style and analytical *gravitas*, Fraser became an influential don of the gallery. His writings served as a beacon of hope and a warning of potential shoals. He arrived in Ottawa in 1943 at the age of thirty-four as Ottawa editor of *Maclean's*. By 1945 his easy facility with radio made him a polished regular hosting CBC Radio coverage of the federal election, a role he played on radio and later TV until 1963. His *Backstage at Ottawa* column was fuelled by his insider connections with the new breed of senior officials, including Lester Pearson, Mitchell Sharp, and Jack Pickersgill, all destined to leave the bureaucracy and become Liberal Cabinet ministers on his watch. A friend and admirer of Lester Pearson, Fraser was part of an influential group of gallery correspondents who encouraged the diplomat to seek the Liberal leadership in 1958 following the retirement of Louis St. Laurent. And once the former diplomat was in office, they looked after "Mike," their friend and source.

In a friendly profile, "Meet Mike Pearson," that ran in the April 15, 1951, *Maclean's*, Fraser was unabashed in his affection for the external affairs minister. Noting how reporters would "pester" Pearson, Fraser wrote:

> It's the price of his unique popularity with the Press that
> we all feel entitled to ring him up at any hour of day or

Blair Fraser: a polished host on CBC Radio.

night.... Quite often he puts his official life in reporters'
hands with a clarifying, but grossly indiscreet, interpreta-
tion of the known facts. So far, he says, nobody has let him
down. Maybe that's one reason we all like him — he trusts
us. But a more important reason is simply his astonishing

gift for making friends. You meet Mike Pearson two or
three times and you begin to think of him as an old pal.

The friendly relations with senior reporters certainly helped Pearson at
key moments. In a January 1954 *Backstage* column, Fraser denounced a
"carefully phrased smear against Pearson" when his name got dragged into
the so-called un-American activities hearings during the McCarthy era in
the United States.

Many Ottawa observers came to regard Fraser as an apologist for the
Liberal government. Certainly he had no fond feelings for John Diefenbaker.
But in an introduction to a book of his father's pieces, *Blair Fraser Reports*,
his son Graham wrote: "The accusation that he was a Liberal bothered him
considerably because he worked at being non-partisan and felt no loyalty
to the Liberal Party as such." Blair once told Graham, "I've been identified
as a Liberal. The reason is that I am an old friend and tremendous admirer
of Mike Pearson. But I'm not a Liberal."

Added Graham, "I think this impression sprang at first from his feelings
about the need for a federal government that would be much stronger than
the provincial governments, and his feelings about French Canada. He had
no use for the view that the federal government should be kept weak."

It was a wonderful time on the banks of the Rideau. Fraser, his wife, Jean,
and the family lived in tony Rockcliffe, in a leafy neighbourhood they shared
with the likes of journalist Grant Dexter, Liberal MP Donald Macdonald,
Tory senator Grattan O'Leary, and diplomat Saul Rae and his wife, Lois,
parents of Bob, John, and Jennifer. He moved in elite circles and travelled
the world on assignment.

It was a long way from Sydney, Nova Scotia, where Blair had grown up.
His father, a farmer, had moved from rural Hopewell to work for DOSCO
steel and coal, eventually rising from steelworker to plant superintendent.
According to Graham's account, Blair was a frail kid who suffered from
asthma attacks. He regularly spent several months with two unmarried sis-
ters, friends of his mother, in Saint John to get away from the foul Sydney
air. Yet he worked summers at the steel plant to save money for tuition and

attended Acadia University, where he graduated with an English degree in 1928. For a year he taught at Stanstead College in Quebec's Eastern Townships; then he moved to Montreal where he worked for the *Herald* and the *Montreal Star*. He lived in an east end boarding house. That and covering the courts made him fluent in French. But he became dispirited, musing about getting an M.A. in English. His father, according to a letter Graham has preserved, was not amused. "I think you can write well enough now," he told his son bluntly, "and the next step should be to go out and find something to write about."

To save enough money to get married, like so many journalists in the day, he walked across the street to the dark side to work for the house organ of the Montreal Light, Heat and Power Company. He lost that job during the Depression. Coincidentally, his father had just been to Ottawa vainly attempting to get federal assistance to reopen his plant. A federal official told his father the government could not help DOSCO at a time when the whole country was in peril. The experience shaped Blair Fraser's belief in the importance of a strong central government with powers to control incomes, corporate taxes, and employment policies. Years later, recalling the grim times, he wrote: "Canada can't afford to have that sort of thing happen again."

In November 1933 Fraser got a job as a proofreader at the Montreal *Gazette*. The next year he became a reporter and, during the next seven years of six-day weeks, he rose to assistant city editor, city editor, news editor, and editorial writer. Graham wrote that his father was a voracious reader: all of Toynbee, Gibbon, Hemingway, and the poets. He was left of centre in his politics, an outspoken supporter of the Republican cause in Spain in the thirties. And while he remained skeptical about the Moscow purge trials, he wrote, "We still regarded Communists with something like the mixture of awe, admiration, and mistrust that Roman Catholics seem to feel for the Jesuits." As associate editor at the *Gazette*, Fraser got closer to politics — and further away from the paper's editorial line on national affairs. In 1943, when he moved to *Maclean's* in Ottawa, he was ready for the break.

Thanks to his sons, his journalistic legacy lives on in the pages of *Blair Fraser Reports*, published in 1969. He had many facets:

- A biting wit: Exploring whether there was "any alternative to the Mackenzie King government," he observed of Conservative leader John Bracken's team in the 1945 election that "some of its good men had been defeated; practically all of its most lamentable dolts had been elected."

- An eye for telling detail: He revealed that although William Lyon Mackenzie King disdained most reporters, he had collected four hundred thousand news clippings from 1921 to 1946, when his *Maclean's* story appeared.

- An instinct for the gobsmacking scoop: King consulted spiritualists in visits to London, a fact unknown until Fraser interviewed several mediums after King's death in 1950 for "The Secret Life of Mackenzie King, Spiritualist" in the December 1951 issue of *Maclean's*.

- An ear for anecdote: As a lecturer in history at the University of Toronto, Lester Pearson was responsible for assigning senior students to his seminars and those of his colleagues, all bachelors. Everyone noted that "all the prettiest girls happened to be assigned to Mr. Pearson. Within two years he was married to one of them — Maryon Elspeth Moody of Winnipeg."

On the big issues, Fraser understood Quebec and supported the sense of grievance that powered the Quiet Revolution. He believed in a strong presence for French Canadians in the national government and an independent foreign policy for Canada. He saw the battles over Quebec as the fundamental test of whether Canada would survive. After talks on a national pension plan broke down in 1964, he told René Lévesque, then a nationalist Liberal minister under Jean Lesage, "Lévesque, this may be the end of Confederation." Four years later Lévesque was leading a putative independence movement and Pierre Trudeau had been elected Liberal leader. Lévesque told Fraser, "If Pierre wins the next federal election — not this one [1968], the next one — that will probably mean it's all up with our movement."

Fraser had a deep attachment to Canada and its political affairs, but he also travelled widely and wrote about India, Indochina, and the Middle

East with flair and insight. For two brief and trying years he also served as editor of *Maclean's* in Toronto after the resignation of the legendary Ralph Allen in 1960. As Graham Fraser observed: "He was a reporter, and the editor's chair did not appeal to him." By prior arrangement he left after two years for fourteen months in London as roving *Maclean's* correspondent. When he returned to Ottawa, separatist flames were burning in Quebec and the acrimonious flag debate signalled the bitter political war on the Rideau between Lester Pearson and John Diefenbaker that would endure five more years.

I met Fraser during that period and was always impressed by the way he worked his sources in the bureaucracy, no doubt in the conviction that they would all be around long after the political cheering stopped. It proved to be a valuable personal lesson. He also was a collegial colleague. In an unpublished memoir, the CBC's great TV reporter Norman DePoe describes his experience as a newbie assigned to cover the 1952 Democratic and Republican conventions, both in Chicago's Amphitheatre:

> Blair quietly and unostentatiously — not being a visible instructor in any way — steered me to the right source, hinted that certain statements or developments were political gamesmanship, and [should] be regarded as such, introduced me to Governors and Senators and backroom power types; and also managed to get us tickets to "Guys and Dolls" and "Porgy and Bess." ... I don't know if Blair was consciously teaching me. I do know that if I became one-fifteenth as good a reporter and human being, my life may not have been totally useless.*

Another revealing example of Blair's quiet way of helping colleagues was the day that the Liberal justice minister, Lucien Cardin, was under attack from Conservative leader John Diefenbaker in the Commons and blurted out a line that would haunt the Commons for months: "I want the Right Honourable Gentleman to tell the House about his participation in the Monseignor case when he was prime minister of this country."

---

* Norman DePoe papers, Library and Archives Canada.

The Commons erupted. To my left, Martin Goodman of the *Toronto Star* led the charge out of the House back to the press gallery. Fraser Kelly, a new reporter for the *Toronto Telegram*, was in hot pursuit. He had no idea what the story was about, but he picked up a phone in the "hot room" and told his desk that he had a story about a scandal involving a monseignor — who knew? — perhaps from Toronto.

Blair Fraser overheard the conversation and, recalled Kelly, said softly into his ear: "'Fraser, the name is Munsinger.' And that's how I at least got the name right in the paper. I was saved by Blair Fraser that time."

The anecdote is doubly revealing: that Blair Fraser would save a young colleague from embarrassment and that he presumably knew all about the scandal involving two former Conservative Cabinet ministers and a mysterious East German woman, Gerda Munsinger. Pearson had learned of the scandal when he asked the commissioner of the RCMP for details of any security cases going back over the previous fifteen years. It was a fishing expedition that ended in a public inquiry damaging to the Conservatives.

The scandals and recrimination in the Commons in those years depressed Blair Fraser. He was encouraged by the arrival of moderate Robert Stanfield as leader of the Progressive Conservatives in 1967 and the election of Pierre Trudeau at the head of the Liberal Party a year later. At last the end of the corrosive Diefenbaker-Pearson feud was in sight. He had agreed to write a book on the election campaign then underway. Still, there were clouds on the horizon. "He rarely spoke of his fears or doubts; we could only sense some of them," Graham Fraser wrote. "He was also, particularly in his later years, subject to periods of acute depression."

Alas, Fraser did not get to observe the dénouement of the election or the national drama that had preoccupied him for two decades. As a warm-up to his annual multi-week canoe trip with a group of power brokers known as the Voyageurs, on May 12, 1968, Fraser took to the waters with friends for a weekend of paddling on the Petawawa River in Algonquin Park. As Fraser's canoe neared the takeout point just before the raging Rollway Rapids, things went terribly wrong. Paddling stern, Fraser missed the takeout, and the roiling waters pitched him onto the rocks and down the swirling chute that ended in a deep pool. He drowned, while his canoe-mate survived.

"He said once that if he could choose his own death," Graham wrote in *Blair Fraser Reports*, "he would choose to drop dead at the bottom of the Flying Mile at Mont Tremblant on the last good day of spring skiing. Certainly, drowning in the spring current at Rollway rapids, on that bright, sunny May Sunday morning, had a dignity and suddenness about it that would have appealed to him."

At the spot above the rapids sits a small memorial cross with the inscription: "In memory of Blair Fraser, 1909–1968. Erected by his Fellow Voyageurs." The monument also serves as an early warning sign of the shoals ahead.

Chapter 7

BRUCE HUTCHISON: THE DEAN

Bruce Hutchison met Lester Pearson at the Surrey home of Grant and Alice Dexter during an overseas assignment to cover the Imperial Conference of 1937 in London. At the time Pearson was undersecretary to Canadian high commissioner Vincent Massey, "in whose presence the ordinary man always felt like a naked savage," Hutchison recalled in his engaging 1976 memoir, *The Far Side of the Street*. As for the high commissioner's "pink and youthful factotum," Hutchison "liked his breezy manner, his lack of official gloss or diplomatic pose and I recognized even then that he had much greater qualities than his secondary job required." That was the start of a lifelong friendship that was an important part of Pearson's climb to the Liberal leadership and the prime minister's office. But first, there was William Lyon Mackenzie King to divine.

King sat down with Hutchison in his first few weeks on the Hill. Hutchison had a natural instinct for meeting and cultivating people in power, mainly because of his disarming, aw-shucks manner and his discretion. He admitted to being "charmed" when the prime minister, "a supreme artist of flattery," took "an hour to beguile an unknown young reporter, only because the remote *Victoria Daily Times* might come in useful someday." He did not stay in Ottawa long, but he quickly established himself.

His base for most of his career was on Vancouver Island, which granted him a tad more independence than his friends in the Liberal-leaning rat pack in hermetically sealed Ottawa. His flying visits to Ottawa and Washington were legendary exercises in harvesting sources for inside information and insight. He was on a first-name basis with twelve prime ministers, from R.B. Bennett and William Lyon Mackenzie King through Pierre Trudeau to Brian Mulroney. In Ottawa, his sources ranged over a host of Cabinet members, senators, journalists, and, above all, the mandarins of the Canadian civil service with whom he was closest in league. From his forays to Washington he was a friend of the powerful players in the New Deal and the New Frontier, including journalists Walter Lippmann, James Reston, and Walter Cronkite; senior policy advisers George Ball and Dean Acheson; and Harvard's John K. Galbraith. But it was Dexter who showed him the ropes and became his partner in exploring the subjects he loved most deeply, Ottawa politics and the future of Canada. Dexter would dig; Hutchison would pronounce.

In a career spanning seventy years he wrote an estimated twenty million words in thousands of articles and columns for the *Vancouver Sun*, *Winnipeg Free Press*, and *Victoria Daily Times*; and for the magazines *Maclean's*, *Saturday Evening Post*, *Fortune*, and *Collier's*. After his reporting days, he was editorial writer and columnist for the *Sun* (1938–44), assistant editor of the *Free Press* (1944–50), editor of the *Times* (1950–63), and editorial director of the *Sun* (1963–79).

Despite his management roles at three major dailies, he achieved the remarkable status of rarely having to go into the office. Instead he spent his days at home near Victoria in Saanich, at his woodland retreat on Shawnigan Lake, or on the road.

Hutchison wrote his last column only weeks before his death in 1992 at age ninety-one.

Three of his fourteen books won the Governor General's Award for non-fiction, notably *The Unknown Country*, his haunting 1942 portrait of Canada on the cusp of greatness. A piece he did for *Saturday Night* about a millionaire who sent his son to the bush to work with his hands became a Hollywood movie, *Park Avenue Logger* — "Really dreadful," Hutchison declared.

For all his *pensées* on politics, the piece that generated the most buzz was one he did for *Maclean's* on Zsa Zsa Gabor — "that inane dialogue in Hollywood," he sniffed.

Bruce Hutchison had a full life and lived with his beloved Dorothy, whom he called Dot, until her tragic death in an Ottawa traffic accident in 1969. After that, his loving daughter, Joan, and his son, Robert, looked after the old boy.

Hutchison and Dexter met in January 1925 when the *Daily Times* posted him to the Parliamentary Press Gallery in Ottawa. Hutchison was twenty-four, the youngest member of that small tribe of scribes. Dexter, "a tall, rosy-faced and outgoing youth of demonic energy," was twenty-nine — a gallery veteran of fully a year. After Hutchison married Dorothy Kidd McDiarmid later that year, they and the Dexters became fast friends. Bruce and Grant shared similar backgrounds. Like Dexter, Hutchison was born in a small Ontario town, and his father struggled in various enterprises, from farming to real estate. The family moved to Victoria where Bruce started writing and cartooning for the high-school paper and joined the debating club. The coach was one Benjamin Charles Nicholas who, impressed by young Hutchison, offered him a job on his *Daily Times*. At sixteen he started as a sportswriter at fourteen dollars a week in 1918.

On promotion to the police beat he observed a tableau of the local demimonde: "Each morning, drunks, bootleggers, brothel keepers, prostitutes, pimps, Chinese opium smokers, drug peddlers, burglars, and occasionally a genuine murderer, paraded through the smelly little police court." Within three years he was covering the provincial legislature. Ever the dutiful colleague, Hutchison — who remained a non-drinker into his forties — once did an all-nighter writing reports for five separate papers, covering for reporters who had passed out after a Conservative Party banquet, complete with "the partisan slant required by each in his impartial news columns." Hutchison also declined the cash bribes lobbyists routinely doled out to reporters.

In Ottawa his contemporaries included Grattan O'Leary of the *Ottawa Journal*, who later described Hutchison as "a poet who wandered into journalism." The cast also featured the peripatetic Charlie Bishop, who freelanced for a dozen papers before appointment to the Senate by William Lyon Mackenzie King; Toronto *Globe* correspondent Arthur Irwin, who ultimately became the outstanding editor of the era at *Maclean's*; and Ken Wilson, the pioneering business writer of the *Financial Post*. Hutchison recalled that when they met, Irwin "was seated at a piano in the secret hide-out of the Ottawa press gallery ... one hand on the keys of the instrument, the other clutching a bootlegged glass of neat whiskey, while he smoked a villainous-looking pipe and played Kipling's old song, 'On the Road to Mandalay,' the assembled company feeling no pain whatever and shouting out the chorus, plainly audible in the House of Commons."

That's about as raucous as these serious young men got in their day. Dressed in three-piece suits and clean-shaven, all of them brought an earnest zeal for politics, but also a respect for the heavy burdens carried by the political leaders of the day. The reporters worked long hours for low wages. Journalism was a calling. Their task was to inform a growing audience of newspapers about domestic affairs and, importantly, Canada's place in the world — not to bring down governments. The politicians were better at that, anyway.

Bruce Hutchison at the Liberal convention, 1958: on a first name basis with twelve prime ministers.

At the time of Hutchison's arrival in Ottawa, the focus was on the political war being waged between William Lyon Mackenzie King and Arthur Meighen. That led to the election in fall 1925 of Meighen's minority government and the subsequent King-Byng ("I'm not leaving") constitutional crisis of 1926 and King's return to power. Hutchison formed his impression of the two men early on. He respected Meighen's intelligence and oratorical skills, but came to believe that he was overrated. King, he pronounced, was "a great prime minister."

Shortly after arriving in Ottawa Hutchison became fast friends with Jack Pickersgill, an influential adviser in King's office. In 1937, encouraged by Pickersgill, King invited Hutchison for a private dinner at his residence, Laurier House. "We sat alone in a murky dining room lighted only by candles and decorated by shadowy portraits of eminent Liberals now departed," Hutchison wrote. "A ghostly setting, I thought, out of some inferior movie." For six hours, King talked without interruption, tackling his meal with gusto and, Hutchison reported, downing six glasses of white wine. His monologue ranged over attacks on the opposition, derision about some of his colleagues, and assurances that Hitler, to whom he had talked a few days earlier, would be fully satisfied with taking the Sudetenland from Czechoslovakia. At midnight he saw Hutchison off in the prime ministerial limousine, the scribe no more enlightened on the true motivation of this "secretive little man."

In 1952 Hutchison attempted a definitive assessment in a biography, *The Incredible Canadian*. It was critically acclaimed and a bestseller. But it shocked Liberal insiders because of its stinging assessment of King as a man driven more by ambition than principles. Still, his ambivalence surfaced in videos for the Canadian History Project ("Bruce Hutchison Interview") months before his death when he credited King with keeping the country together, creating "the welfare state of social services," and, during the war, leading "the greatest government" Canada ever had. "Now," he added, "let me be clear about this: I didn't think he was a very nice man. But can you afford to be nice if you can't govern the country properly?"

While the kind of access Hutchison enjoyed was remarkable, there were plenty of quid pro quos. In 1940 he was called away from Shawnigan Lake to join Dexter in Barrie, Ontario, where the King government was wining and dining a trainload of distinguished American reporters bound for Quebec and the Maritimes. His mission was to celebrate Canada's war effort and encourage Americans to join the fight "for the survival of North America." Hutchison called it "the propaganda train" and described himself with irony as "the clumsy, unpaid chore boy of the Canadian government."

The next year, "instead of a respectable war job," he accepted banker Donald Gordon's offer to become press officer for King's anti-inflation body, the Wartime Prices and Trade Board. Dexter was outraged. He telephoned King's office and demanded a meeting. Hutchison and Dexter were ushered in ten minutes later. In his memoir Hutchison noted wryly: "With an air of patriotic indignation Dexter told King that in the national interest, at a moment of deepening crisis, I could not be spared from my duty of reporting the work of government to the people of British Columbia." King agreed that as a representative of the *Sun*, the most important Liberal newspaper on the Coast, of course Hutchison should remain on the national news beat — as he did.

By 1943 *Free Press* editor John Dafoe was in failing health. He encouraged publisher Victor Sifton to woo Hutchison away from the *Sun* as assistant editor. Hutchison became the third member of the awkward governing troika: Hutchison in Victoria and Dexter in Ottawa — both refused to move to Winnipeg — and the brilliant Dafoe loyalist and workhorse, George Ferguson, handling the top editing chores in Winnipeg. They continued Dafoe's fine tradition of serious journalism and a daily editorial page whose long, grey columns overflowed with well-researched commentary and insights, despite its Liberal tinge.

Hutchison also embraced Dafoe's vision of the paper as free from direction by, but supportive of, the party: a place where a respectful relationship with the government would maintain access and influence. As he put it in his memoirs: "To us in the *Free Press* the Liberal Party, though flawed and often infuriating, was the natural party of government, the alternative much worse."

The troika honoured the wishes of their "chief" in supporting King during the crisis over conscription in 1944 — notably by holding back the story about the Cabinet crisis on the issue. In his 1952 King biography, Hutchison did recreate details of the Cabinet row, based in part on a secret diary that Senator Charles "Chubby" Power had kept while a minister in King's government.

Hutchison became an important vehicle for conveying context about Canada's postwar foreign policy — as seen through the eyes of St. Laurent's leaky external affairs minister, Lester Pearson. Often after returning from trips to Washington or London, wrote Hutchison, Pearson "would tell Dexter and me the top secrets of the British and American governments, his conversations with a prime minister or a president, even military secrets which both of us promptly put out of our minds and wished we had not heard."

In 1949 during a delicate stage of the negotiations on the North Atlantic Treaty Organization, Pearson privately briefed Hutchison on Canada's unhappiness with the hawkish U.S. position. "Our boys are thinking," Hutchison wrote in a memo to Dexter, "it may be time for a calculated indiscretion by our government. This is pretty important stuff it seems to me and I am given the green light to write it as I please." He and Dexter agreed to help the cause.

Hutchison's fawning approach to the minister sometimes was the equivalent of a lob shot at Roger Federer. In 1953, with a contract to write for *Maclean's* and the *Financial Post*, he asked Pearson if he would grant an interview "to our mutual advantage." Noting that he wanted to write "with reasonable accuracy and with proper guidance," he told Pearson that "if you can spare time to give me off the record some of your views of events I think it will prevent me from going off the rails and creating wrong impressions."

Hutchison was stunned when John Diefenbaker's Conservatives won the election of 1957, although they elected only a minority. He recognized that the arrogance of the St. Laurent government during the pipeline debate — using closure to ram a financing bill through Parliament — had tarnished the Liberals, but he still thought of them as the governing party. With St. Laurent's resignation, the leadership contest was under way. Hutchison, Dexter, Ferguson, and Fraser concentrated on Pearson's prospects.

On the eve of the leadership vote slated for January 16, 1958, Pearson was the clear front-runner, his image buttressed by having won the Nobel Peace Prize for his work resolving the Suez Crisis. But Liberals were divided about whether to try to defeat the minority Conservatives when the House resumed after the weekend convention. Hutchison and Dexter, now assuming roles as political advisers, not journalists, went to see Pearson the day before the convention to try to persuade him to let the duly elected government govern.

"Pearson listened impatiently," Hutchison recalled in his memoir, "and cut the conversation short. 'It's no use, Grant. I've made up my mind. We're going to force an election. That's final.'" Without revealing his plan to delegates, Pearson handily defeated rival Paul Martin Sr. Dexter and Hutchison filed their reports on his victory speech.

Hutchison flew off to Washington. Having barely arrived, Hutchison got word that Pearson needed him back in Ottawa immediately. The Liberals would not force a non-confidence vote the next day, they would up the ante: they would demand that Diefenbaker simply hand over the government because of its inability to manage the Canadian economy. "Tory times are tough times," they proclaimed. Pearson then planned a triumphant national television interview appearance, and he wanted Hutchison to host it with a list of pre-arranged questions.

It did not go well for Pearson in the House. Pickersgill, now a Liberal MP, had devised a strategy that proved too clever by half: Pearson would not actually move a traditional vote of confidence that would attract support from the Co-operative Commonwealth Federation (the CCF, forerunner of today's NDP) and cause another election. That was exactly what Diefenbaker wanted. Instead, Pearson proposed a motion noting only "the desirability" of "a government pledged to implement Liberal policies" — phrasing that the CCF could not support — and called on the Conservatives "to submit their resignation forthwith."

It was a disaster. The minute Pearson sat down, Diefenbaker rose to his feet in all his jowl-trembling outrage, and for two hours and thirty-five minutes he excoriated the new Liberal leader with a withering attack. He said it was cowardly to present such a "sham" motion. And then he produced a "hidden document" the previous Liberal government had received from senior officials before the election warning of a recession — a report that they had kept secret from the Canadian people. The report carried the signature of the then–associate deputy minister of trade and commerce, Mitchell Sharp, and had been available to the entire St. Laurent Cabinet well before the 1957 election when they boasted that Canada had never had it so good.

Underlining once again the close co-operation between reporters and government, as historian Denis Smith revealed in *Rogue Tory*, Diefenbaker had obtained the document from his friend Patrick Nicholson, the veteran Thomson Press correspondent in the gallery.

When the House adjourned, Hutchison and Dexter rushed up to Pearson's office. There they found a leader resembling a glassy-eyed boxer on the ropes. Asked about a script for the TV interview Pearson proffered notes for questions that "the boys have prepared." Hutchison threw the paper aside and said, "Look, Mike, this stuff's no good. Let's get down to business. What are we going to talk about?" They agreed on a half-dozen simple queries. With Blair Fraser of *Maclean's* they piled into Pearson's car bound for the TV station, the leader at the wheel. Hutchison did not remember much about the TV show, except that when the lights came on Pearson was cheerfully gritty, "as if he had just enjoyed a holiday of boyish frolic."

In fact, it was the beginning of the end. With the Liberals on the ropes, Diefenbaker called an election for March 31. After a masterful campaign Diefenbaker won the largest majority in Canadian history, a record that still stands in 2018. (Diefenbaker took 208 seats compared to 49 for the Liberals — including Pearson's — and 8 for the CCF. In the 1984 election Brian Mulroney's Progressive Conservatives won the most seats, 211, but his margin was 11 seats short of Diefenbaker's 151.) The redoubtable Maryon Pearson summed up the debacle with her distinctive black humour: "We've lost everything. We even won our own seat."

Having attacked Diefenbaker so often in years past, Hutchison's only good source in the new government was External Affairs Minister Howard Green, a friend of more than twenty years. Green, he said, trusted him "well enough to speak with an indiscretion that would have horrified Diefenbaker." He once got Hutchison to deliver a proposal to U.S. Senate leader Mike Mansfield about a change in the draft of the Columbia River Treaty, which Mansfield accepted.

When the Liberals returned to power with his friend Pearson at the helm, Hutchison was enjoying his new role as editorial director of the *Vancouver Sun*, all the more pleasing since new owner Richard Malone volunteered that his employee could stay on his beloved Vancouver Island. From there Hutchison dispatched instructions, editorials, and columns, and made occasional trips to Ottawa, Washington, and London. He published six more books, including *The Far Side of the Street* and *A Life in the Country.* He also wrote his history of the country's leaders, *Mr. Prime Minister: 1867–1964*, and the text for the National Film Board's stunning Centennial Year book of photos, *Canada: A Year of the Land.* Shortly before Hutchison's death in 1992, Prime Minister Brian Mulroney named him to the Privy Council of Canada, the honorary body at the service of the monarch for state and constitutional issues. Hutchison was one of the few non-politicians serving there. One of the perquisites of the office: access to all the secrets of the state.

Part IV

COVERING
DIEF THE CHIEF

Chapter 8

CLARK DAVEY:
ON THE RAILS TO VICTORY

Clark Davey was one of only three reporters, all of them from Toronto newspapers, with John Diefenbaker ("Dief the Chief") the night he became prime minister–elect in 1957. He had to charter a private plane to fly to Regina from Prince Albert late that night to make a televised statement to the nation. Back in Prince Albert, as if to underline the difference between himself and the patrician prime minister Louis St. Laurent, Dief took the boys fishing on Lac La Ronge. For four days Dief savoured victory among his people over a party that had been in power for twenty-two remarkable years. Davey reported in the *Globe* that it pleased Dief no end that he had put the lie to a misguided editorial in that month's *Maclean's*, printed ten days before the vote — but appearing *after* the result was in — which congratulated the Liberals for an "almost unexampled vote of confidence."

The lack of a live national broadcast news feed on election night in Prince Albert was not the only striking feature of politics in the 1950s. In those days, the Tories treated the reporters like royalty. While Dief's quarters were in an older railway car, the reporters each had two double rooms for sleep and a workspace in a modern coach. Fred Jones, the Chief's official photographer, doubled as wagon master, with instructions to give the reporters whatever they needed, especially their "hymn books" — code for Scotch bottles. Recalled Davey in a 2014 interview: "Mrs. Diefenbaker, recognizing that we weren't maintaining as close contact with our families as we should, would phone our wives and talk to them and tell them we were OK. It was a different era."

And so it was that Dief bundled two aides and three reporters into a small float plane for the hundred-and-fifty-mile flight to Lac La Ronge where they got into canoes for the five-hour excursion. (The others with Davey were Peter Dempson of the *Telegram* and Mark Harrison of the *Toronto Star*. Alan Donnelly of CP had worked himself into a state of collapse and had to leave the campaign just before election day.) At one point, Davey told me, Diefenbaker raised the issue on all their minds. Davey recounted the exchange:

Prime Minister John Diefenbaker and reporters, April 17, 1961, after the clos-ing of Parliament. Left–right: Norm Campbell, Jim McCook, Privy Council Clerk Derek Bedson, Diefenbaker, Victor Mackie, Peter Stursberg, Clark Davey, Tim Creery, George Bain, and Eugene Griffin.

John Diefenbaker: "I suppose you fellows are making my Cabinet for me?"

Clark Davey: "Well, we have to put something in the paper. It can't be all fishing."

Dief was never shy about aiding and abetting unattributed speculation, the better to get risk-free reactions to his ideas. This time, according to Davey, he tested potential Cabinet names. "He said, 'Have you got Donnie Fleming straightened out?' Someone suggested Finance. He said, 'Well, Donnie can have whatever Donnie wants.'" Indeed, Donald Fleming, the MP from midtown Toronto, became minister of finance.

———————

For forty days and forty nights Davey had tracked Diefenbaker on the campaign trail as he attacked the Liberals and evoked a vision of a prouder, more independent nation. The Chief's fiery speeches reminded Queen's University political scientist John Meisel of a nineteenth-century "revivalist preacher." Davey sensed that the crowds were growing in enthusiasm for Diefenbaker as his train chugged across Ontario and he gave stemwinders from a platform on the last car. When the party reached the Muskoka rail depot town of MacTier, Davey called his desk. He recalled saying: "I think there is something happening with this guy and I'd like to stay with him." The response? "And they left me with him."

Then came the victory. And then the aftermath. The atmosphere took a downturn after the fishing trip and reporters got a glimpse of the dark side of John Diefenbaker — a side that would prove fatal in the years to come. "As everyone who dealt with him did," said Davey, "we had a huge rupture about two nights after the trip." When Diefenbaker arrived back in Prince Albert he discovered that Trans-Canada Airlines, the forerunner of Air Canada, did not have room for his staff to accompany him on the night flight to Ottawa aboard the Douglas DC-4 North Star. St. Laurent, ungraciously, had not offered a government plane. So Diefenbaker sent his staffers on ahead and, on the eve of becoming prime minister, he was left to answer his own phones and check his own luggage. When one of his bags went missing, Diefenbaker blew a fuse, stomping around the terminal and demanding, "Do you know who I am? Do you know who I am?" Recalling the temper tantrum, Davey said: "I'm dictating to rewrite at that point and I said, 'We are going to start over.'" The new lede read: "An angry John Diefenbaker flew out of his home town tonight to keep his appointment with responsibility in Ottawa tomorrow." When the Diefenbaker party landed in Toronto, Dief saw the story in the morning *Globe*, and he unloaded a tongue-lashing on Davey, declaring: "Young man, I'll be in Ottawa long after you are gone."

Like so many journalists, Davey got his inspiration as a young man from a teacher. He aspired to attend Royal Roads Military College, but having worn glasses as a boy, his eyesight proved to be a barrier to entry. He was very disheartened until Miss Norma Stevens, his English teacher, reassured him and urged him to enroll in journalism at the University of Western Ontario. Some seventy years later he still remembers her saying, "Clark, people will pay you to write."

He graduated in the first class at the school in 1948. At twenty he joined the *Chatham Daily News* under his boyhood friend Richard J. "Dic" Doyle, an association that would last a lifetime. Davey then worked briefly as managing editor of the *Kirkland Lake Daily News* and moved to the *Globe* in 1951, where he covered city hall and met some of the larger-than-life characters who built postwar Canada.

One of them was Toronto mayor Bob Saunders who, after launching plans for a subway and clearing "slums," moved on to chair Ontario Hydro. There, along with New York Power Commission head Robert Moses, he was a chief architect of the St. Lawrence Seaway, including the flooding of several communities. Davey made his name covering Saunders — and coining "Seaway Valley" — while the waterway was under construction.

By the time he got to Ottawa in 1956, Davey was an experienced reporter despite his twenty-eight years. One of his biggest scoops involved the Suez Crisis that throughout the summer and fall of 1956 threatened to disrupt the Western alliance. Britain and France invaded Egypt to oppose President Nasser's nationalization of the strategic waterway and the threat to their oil supplies. In a key move, backed by the United States, Canada's external affairs minister, Lester Pearson, persuaded the United Nations to mount a peacekeeping effort designed to get the French and British to withdraw their forces. Canada planned to contribute a force consisting of the historic 1st Battalion of the Queen's Own Rifles (QOR) and a transport ship.

Assigned to cover the United Nations in New York, Davey had just seen off his wife, Joyce, at LaGuardia Airport after a weekend visit when he bumped into Pearson, just arrived from Ottawa. Pearson offered Davey a lift back to Manhattan. Said Davey: "In the limo, he said, 'Ah, this whole Egypt thing is going to blow up in our face. Nasser doesn't want Canadian troops.' I said, 'What's he got against Canadian troops?' He said, 'We wear British uniforms.' I said, 'Can I write that?' He said, 'As long as you don't know where you got it.' It was a big story."

And how. "QOR WON'T GO TO SUEZ," blared the "war type" headline in the November 19 *Globe* above Davey's byline and a detailed story on Nasser's objections to having such a close ally of Britain engaged. U.N. Secretary General Dag Hammarskjöld persuaded Canada to play an air transport role acceptable to the Egyptians. It was an embarrassing moment for Canada. The St. Laurent government tried vainly to explain why the Canadians were changing their plans and *not* bowing to Nasser's wishes, as they were. Eventually twelve hundred Canadians went to Egypt, the Brits and French withdrew, and Pearson won the Nobel Prize for the peaceful resolution.*

After the St. Laurent government fell in 1957, Davey was a regular visitor to Dief's office and a recipient of the occasional telephone call of complaint. He remembers one in particular when Diefenbaker "chewed me out" for reporting budget speculation that was remarkably accurate.

In January 1960 Davey moved back to Toronto at the request of *Globe* managing editor Dic Doyle to run the national and city desks. The two had been friends since their days growing up in Chatham, Ontario, and working together on the *Daily News*. After Doyle took over as *Globe* editor from Oakley Dalgleish, Davey became his managing editor, with a special focus on investigative journalism. His illustrious career in journalism embraced roles as publisher of the *Vancouver Sun*, the *Gazette* in Montreal, and the *Ottawa Citizen*.

Retired in Ottawa, he was spry and lively at eighty-seven when we talked in 2015. He was still active in journalism as a member of the Michener Award board and a fixture among the power brokers at the Rideau Club. For Clark Davey, journalism was never just a job, it was a calling.

---

* For an excellent account, see Antony Anderson, *The Diplomat: Lester Pearson and the Suez Crisis* (Fredericton: Goose Lane Editions, 2015).

Chapter 9

PETER DEMPSON: A LAST HURRAH

A heavy fog had rolled off the Ottawa River, enveloping the city in a damp chill when the train from Regina pulled onto the station. It was 6:35 a.m., August 25, 1945. The young reporter lugged his two suitcases across the concourse and hailed a cab: "Château Laurier." The driver smiled and pointed to the hotel — directly across the street.

It was Peter Dempson's first trip to Ottawa. He was a rookie, fresh off the city hall beat in Regina, and now he was going to take up his duties covering Parliament for the *Regina Leader-Post.*

Dempson ultimately worked that beat for seventeen years, a period that embraced five elections, four prime ministers, travel to thirty countries, the infamous pipeline debate, the ascension of John Diefenbaker's majority government, Dief's decline, the rise and fall of Lester Pearson, and a scoop about the Cold War–era expulsion of an alleged Russian spy.

In his candid memoir of his days in the capital, *Assignment Ottawa,* Dempson recalled being "stunned" by the proposal by *Leader-Post* editor-in-chief Dave Rogers that he cover the Hill for the upcoming fall session. "I had been a newspaperman for only two years," he wrote, "joining the *Leader-Post* after writing tourist publicity for the Saskatchewan government for several years."

Dempson was struck by the shabby decor of the third-floor gallery and the contrasting grandeur of its famous lifetime members, among them Grattan O'Leary of the *Ottawa Journal* and Charles Bishop of the *Ottawa Citizen*, then both in the Senate, and John Bassett Sr. of the Montreal *Gazette* (and father of the flamboyant John Bassett Jr. of *Toronto Telegram* fame). He marvelled at the clutter; at the cigarette, soft drink, and beer machines; and at the cuckoo clock whose hourly greetings seemed entirely appropriate to the setting. Everyone made way for the booze. Dempson wrote: "Huge, rubber-tired supply trucks wheel the spirits, beer or soft drinks up the corridors to the gallery. Often MPs have to stand aside, sometimes even a Cabinet minister, to let them roll by. Seldom is there a complaint."

Truly, the print reporters of the day ruled. And few of them cultivated the access to power as well as Peter Dempson. One of his early duties was to cover the speeches and activities of all the Saskatchewan and Manitoba MPs for the Sifton chain of Prairie papers, the *Leader-Post* in Regina and the Saskatoon *StarPhoenix*, as well as the *Winnipeg Free Press*.

One of his earliest and best sources was lawyer John Diefenbaker, the MP from Prince Albert, whom he had admired since he had covered him during a case before the Saskatchewan Court of Appeal. The feelings of admiration were mutual. Having returned home to Regina after the session ended at Christmas, Dempson encountered Diefenbaker coming out of editor Rogers's office. As Dempson recounts in *Assignment*, Diefenbaker told him: "I stopped off in Regina so I could personally thank your boss for the coverage you and your paper gave me while you were in Ottawa. It was just wonderful. I told him that I hoped to see you back in the press gallery before too long."

Dempson did go back, first as a sessional reporter for the Sifton papers, then as a full-time correspondent, and finally as the Ottawa correspondent for the *Telegram*. Like most journalists who get assigned to Parliament Hill, Dempson had paid his dues. Even when he worked as a lowly writer in the Saskatchewan government's publications division after graduating from the University of Ottawa, he freelanced for publications around the country. He sold a piece to the popular American weekly magazine *Liberty* for five cents a word. His work also appeared in *Saturday Night*, the *Weekly Star*, and *Collier's*, among others. After joining the *Leader-Post* and being assigned to the police beat, he'd spend time at RCMP headquarters in Regina developing crime stories for the many thriving police detective magazines with inside dope on murder cases fed to him by members of the force.

His work in dozens of publications across North America led Dempson into broadcasting and to a role as a regular contributor to the CBC and to CKCK radio, the Sifton-owned Regina station. When he finally moved to Ottawa full-time in 1949, his presence on several CBC programs heightened his profile. "In fact," he wrote in his memoir, "I discovered that, since I represented a newspaper that supported Tories editorially, I was in demand oftener than I would have been, perhaps, had I worked for a Liberal paper."

For CBC's *News Roundup* he delivered the first Canadian interview with Igor Gouzenko, the cipher clerk who defected from the Russian embassy in 1945 with more than one hundred documents revealing the shape of a major spy ring in Canada. The Toronto editor of the show, Norman DePoe, gave it extended play of four minutes. Of some six hundred broadcasts Dempson did for the CBC, that one "brought me more mail than any broadcast I have ever done."

When he arrived in Ottawa the press gallery was still a very clubby place. It was also a very intimate place. With the exception of the prime minister and minister of external affairs, whose offices were housed in the East Block, all the other ministers, the leader of the opposition, and the MPs and senators were within hailing distance in their Centre Block offices. Often they would drop by the press gallery for a drink or a chat in the lounge, while ministers would receive reporters in their offices.

Dempson was a stalwart in the tight circle of the power elite. He cultivated top members of the government and relied on key ministers, including Nova Scotia's George Nowlan and Manitoba's Gordon Churchill, to feed him inside information. He served on the press gallery executive and played on the press gallery curling team — and he participated in the system that was prevalent then of sharing his articles with other reporters, a "syndicate," as he termed it. Dempson acknowledges that he often traded "blacks" — carbon copies of his stories — with fellow gallery members. "As a result," he wrote, "I occasionally was tipped off to important stories that I would have otherwise missed. But in turn I came up with my share of exceptionally good yarns which I passed on to others."

Sometimes competition fouled the co-operative spirit. Dempson's *Telegram* colleague Norman Campbell had developed a scoop about secret rocket tests being conducted by the RCAF near the Ottawa airport. As he dispatched his story by wire, he asked CP Telegraph for a paper copy for his files. The next day *Toronto Star* correspondent Harold Greer handed Dempson the envelope with the copy of his story and, with a smile, said it had been left in his mailbox by mistake. When the *Star* hit the streets that day, a rewritten version of Campbell's *Telegram* story was splashed all over its front page. But not the *Tely*'s: the editors there had decided to hold it for a day to give it special treatment with drawings and photographs.

––––––––––

Perhaps the most significant domestic story of the era was the great pipeline debate in the spring of 1956. The issue was the singular determination of the autocratic minister of trade and commerce C.D. Howe and the St. Laurent Liberal government to ram a bill through the House authorizing an eighty-million-dollar loan to a U.S. syndicate to build a pipeline that would bring Alberta gas to Toronto and Montreal. The government turned over control of the pipeline to a shell company temporarily to allow it to pay for the pipe in hopes of driving the line to Winnipeg by summer. The terms of the loan to the shell company, TransCanada, were reasonable, and there was no doubt about the need for gas. But when Howe introduced the bill in May he also announced he would impose closure — for the first time since 1932 — to cut off debate and expedite approval.

The House exploded. Conservatives and NDP members opposed the bill at every stage, some shouting, others breaking into satirical songs. They forced some seventy votes, more than half on the partisan rulings of the sycophantic Liberal speaker René Beaudoin and his deputies. Black Friday, June 1, the speaker reversed a ruling he had made the day before that would have stopped the closure vote and allowed debate to continue. NDP leader M.J. Coldwell stormed the speaker's chair, waving his fist. Bedlam ruled. "COMMONS IN STATE OF RIOT," blared the *Globe*'s front page headline. But the Liberals controlled the Commons with a majority, and at 3:21 a.m. on June 6 the notorious pipeline bill got final reading.

It was one of the most tumultuous events in Canadian parliamentary history. Historian John English wrote in *The Worldly Years: The Life of Lester*

Pearson: "Howe had given the opposition a bloated target — Texas oil millionaires controlling Canadian resources plus an arrogant ministry that listened to the Texans rather than Canadians."

The debacle shook the foundation of a natural governing party that had ruled for all but six of the previous twenty-seven years under William Lyon Mackenzie King. The fiasco was the major factor in the Liberal government's loss the next year. And it caused an awakening among members of the press gallery about the abuse of power, especially among younger members.

George Bain of the *Globe* said, "It was the start of adversarial journalism." According to historian Allan Levine, "The Pipeline Debate left this new generation of Ottawa journalists a more questioning group, which made life more difficult for St. Laurent's successors. The days of the old quiet ways in the relationship between the press and the politicians were over."*

Nevertheless, with Diefenbaker's election as prime minister in 1957, Dempson relied heavily on Dief for inside information. Indeed, with his colleague Dick Jackson of the *Ottawa Journal*, Dempson would meet Dief most Fridays for tea with the clear intention of getting a scoop for the Saturday paper. "Usually," Dempson wrote, "he provided me with a story." But sometimes they were unwilling victims of the wily Chief.

Once, in 1959, taking a hint from Diefenbaker, Dempson and Jackson dutifully reported that Finance Minister Donald Fleming would be named to the external affairs post. Wrote Dempson: "It also became apparent to Jackson and me that Diefenbaker had used us, and our papers, to test public reaction about Fleming. When our stories evoked a prompt and negative reaction, he dropped the idea." A week later Dempson was back in Dief's office, pleading for a tip about the new external affairs minister. "Oh, I can't do that," the prime minister told Dempson. "Everyone in the Press Gallery would be mad at me. Who do you think it is?" Dempson replied that by a process of elimination he thought it was Howard Green. At this point Dief got out of his chair and walked to the window overlooking the lush lawns of Parliament Hill. "Those lawns," he told Dempson, "they sure are nice and *green*, aren't they?" Dempson continues: "That was all he said. I knew then that it

---

* Allan Levine, *Scrum Wars: The Prime Ministers and the Media* (Toronto: Dundurn, 1993), 199.

was Howard Green. The *Telegram* carried the story on the front page of all its Saturday editions." Green did get the job.

But it was not always about exclusives. In those days it was standard practice for parliamentary correspondents to cover for each other, often to the extent of filing a story in a colleague's name if the other journalist was indisposed. One such case Dempson cited concerned an announcement about a planned extension to Malton (now Pearson International) Airport outside Toronto. Noticing that his friend, *Telegram* correspondent Laurie McKechnie, was fast asleep in the gallery lounge after a few drinks, columnist Harold Dingman decided to file the story in McKechnie's name. Sometime later, Alf Cole of the *Star* did the same. Later that evening, aroused from his stupor, McKechnie spotted the announcement in the Hansard proofs of the day's debates and filed his own version. The managing editor cabled back congratulations on a "first-rate story," adding: "But was it necessary to send us three different versions?"

———————

Dempson had cut his teeth covering the 1949 election, the first one waged by Liberal leader Louis St. Laurent. Opposing St. Laurent was George Drew, a great friend of *Telegram* publisher George McCullagh. The *Tely* gave lavish play to positive stories about Tory leader Drew, most written by the crusty Ottawa correspondent Norman Campbell. Assigned to cover St. Laurent, Dempson found his stories banished inside the paper or squeezed onto the bottom of page 1. Frustrated, he sought Campbell's advice. "Give them a gimmick — a little twist," Campbell advised. "If St. Laurent is speaking and one or two people boo, play up the interruption. Pay little attention to the applause."

Dempson took the advice to heart. "I realized that what my stories lacked was the pro-Conservative slant."

A few nights later when St. Laurent addressed about two thousand people in a packed Ottawa theatre, Dempson took his photographer to a small section of fifty empty seats while noting some interruptions during the speech. He wrote: "The *Telegram* splashed the picture of the empty seats across four columns the next day.... From then on, it was nearly always the same. If 4,000 people attended a meeting and applauded enthusiastically, I paid little attention. If someone in the audience happened to boo or interject, that was the story." Dempson had no complaints about the play of his stories thereafter.

Meanwhile, across town, the Liberal *Toronto Star* was torquing its front page in similar fashion. For every *Tely* story that described a St. Laurent meeting of three thousand, the *Star* would put the crowd at more than ten thousand, all of them smiling and applauding in the pictures. That shameful episode in political coverage had its consequences. After St. Laurent won a powerful mandate of 190 seats out of 262, publisher McCullagh summoned his Ottawa reporters and senior staff for a tongue-lashing, as recorded by Dempson in *Assignment*: "I want you to know, that at no time did I suggest that we should cover the campaign as we did. I never issued any instructions to conduct a pro-Drew or an anti-St. Laurent campaign." He said, "the prestige of the *Telegram* has been harmed," and that "in the eyes of many readers, we looked a little silly. Now that the campaign is over, we're going to dig in and make the *Telegram* the best and fairest newspaper in Toronto. I want all of you, when covering a political meeting or any such event, to be objective."

At the height of the Cold War in 1964, Dempson had closely followed any rumours about spies in the woodwork. From a chat with Paul Martin Sr., then external affairs minister, Dempson understood that an *Izvestia* correspondent, Vasily Tarasov, was leaving the country. Two TASS news agency staffers had already fled in the wake of the Gouzenko revelations, and a third man posing as a reporter had been sent home. Seeking confirmation about Tarasov's expulsion, Dempson put in a call to RCMP commissioner George McClellan, whom he knew from their Regina days. McClellan pleaded with Dempson to hold off. "We're setting a trap for Tarasov," he told Dempson. He would get the exclusive when it happened. The reporter sat on the story. A week later McClellan called Dempson: "Tarasov was arrested last night while attempting to buy classified information from a government employee. We caught him in the act of passing money in a downtown hotel. The Soviet ambassador is now at the External Affairs Department." Dempson's story was the top line in the *Telegram*'s noon edition. At 2:30 p.m. in the Commons Prime Minister Lester Pearson confirmed the details.

Peter Dempson, 1964: tracking rumours of spies in the woodwork.

Dempson was also present when the Diefenbaker bubble began to burst in the late 1950s. It had been a great ride for the Tories: first, the arrogance of the Liberals in the pipeline debate; then a Conservative government in 1957, the first since 1930; and finally Dief's stunning sweep of 208 seats in the 1958 election. But within a couple of years the dollar had fallen and Dief was facing a defence policy crisis and defections by his senior ministers.

He became more paranoid and withdrawn. He even lashed out at Dempson during their regular meetings. His first run-in with Dief was in 1961 over a feature article that Dempson had nothing to do with. His press gallery colleague George Brimmell had written about a secret multi-million-dollar underground complex that the army was building at Carp, Ontario, near Ottawa, to house the Canadian government in the event of a nuclear attack by the Russians. It was almost ninety feet underground, complete with bathrooms and sleeping quarters, kitchens and communications equipment. An aerial photo showing the fourteen-foot barbed wire fence surrounding the complex dominated page 1 in the *Tely* under the screaming headline, "This Is the Diefenbunker." The Tory leader summoned Dempson to his office the next day. "Diefenbaker was livid. His hands were shaking. 'This is a dreadful story,' he said angrily. 'This is exactly the kind of information the Russians want.... You'd almost think that this article was Communist-inspired.'"

On another occasion Dempson was stunned when Diefenbaker complained that *Maclean's* had used larger type for the word *Liberal* than *Conservative* in a pre-election cover story — seemingly oblivious to the fact that his party's name had five more letters. To Dempson, it seemed to be the beginning of the end for Diefenbaker. The piercing eyes and ears of the young TV broadcasting industry also amplified Diefenbaker's woes. The visible shaking of his body led one newspaper to report that he had Parkinson's. Diefenbaker went to a Toronto hospital and produced a certificate from two doctors that he had no chronic illness.

One of the blessings of being a journalist is that you meet them on the way up and see them on the way down. Dempson continued at his *Tely* post into the mid-1960s, still meeting most Fridays with the fallen Diefenbaker, still relishing the scandals on the Hill. It was, though, the end of an era, and the start of a new one that ushered broadcasters into the press gallery. With Pearson now as prime minister, the press could feast on the bumptious relationship between a wounded Tory lion in opposition and an accident-prone diplomat in the prime minister's office. Dempson left the press gallery in the twilight of the Pearson years and became an associate editor of the *Tely* in Toronto.

Dempson died on August 19, 1976, of complications related to leukemia, a disease he had fought valiantly since his diagnosis in 1971, even achieving a temporary remission. True to form, before he died he sold a moving feature article on his battle to *Weekend* magazine.

Chapter 10

CLEMENT BROWN: DIEF AND THE FRENCH FACT

C lement Brown was a notable press gallery intimate of John Diefenbaker's. In a forty-year career on the Hill, Brown worked for the Ottawa daily *Le Droit* and two Montreal dailies of vastly different natures: the sober *Le Devoir* and the tabloid *Montréal-Matin.*

Born on October 25, 1911, in Saint-Joachim-de-Montmorency on Quebec's north shore, one of thirteen children, he did his classical studies at the Petit Séminaire de Québec in Quebec City's Old Town and defied custom by going on to university at Laval. He started in Ottawa at *Le Droit* as parliamentary correspondent in 1952. Over time he became one of the press gallery's leading lights, a frequent guest on TV, and a host of election debates. In 1962 he participated with journalists Gérard Pelletier and Jean-V. Dufresne in the first televised political debate in Canada, held during the Quebec provincial election. The same year, his press gallery colleagues elected him as their president.

He also was a lifelong Conservative, starting with the provincial Union Nationale. Before beginning his career in real journalism, he was the editor of *Le Temps*, the Union Nationale's partisan weekly promoting the affairs of Quebec *bleus* and their leader, Maurice Duplessis. Brown even took a leave as president of the gallery in 1962 to run as a "prestige" candidate for the federal Conservatives in Montreal; he returned to his post by popular acclamation after losing the election to the incumbent Liberal.

In Ottawa, Brown was a central figure in the Conservative-friendly cohort in the press gallery. In his early days as prime minister, Diefenbaker courted members of the gallery, seeking their views in private and meeting them in the corridor off the East Block after Cabinet meetings. Brown was first among equals. He told author Peter Stursberg in a 1974 interview, part of the oral history collection at Library and Archives Canada, "Mr. Diefenbaker used to call me any time of the day and say: 'Clement, what do you think of this? Put your views on paper and send them.'"

What most concerned the Chief after his 1957 election victory was the fractious Quebec caucus and the backlash against the paucity of Quebecers in Cabinet. Dief had elected a small, weak group of MPs from Quebec, and he generally relegated his few Quebec ministers to the second tier. His Quebec backbenchers tended to be unilingual, and they struggled to view issues from a national perspective: many were old-line Union Nationale organizers, more interested in patronage — or "pork" — than policy. They were nationalists who chafed under Dief's "One Canada" vision and his meagre cadre of three ministers from Quebec. Brown observed: "At one stage he told me privately that the Quebec deputation was a very poor quality and that he couldn't find any Cabinet timber there — and he was largely right."

Diefenbaker, Brown said, "felt he had been elected prime minister one election too soon because in '57 he had only nine members from Quebec and his selections for Cabinet posts were rather restricted." At one point there was a move to let Brown attend meetings of the Conservatives' Quebec caucus as an adviser. "I constantly refused," said Brown. "I would have been hindered as a journalist being privy to the decisions of caucus or the discussions."

Then came the sweep in 1958. Duplessis put his Union Nationale machine behind the federal Conservatives and the party elected fifty Quebecers, the second-largest provincial bloc among Diefenbaker's 208 seats. Still, Brown said that Diefenbaker failed to use the power of patronage — to "roll the pork" — to clear out the old guard and promote some of the new blood on his backbench.

Dief did try, Brown said. Although his French was "one of the worst that I had ever heard," he would gamely wade into a rural town meeting and sprinkle his English speech with "one or two sentences in French so as not to put the pressure on him too long."

Brown helped to organize what he called Diefenbaker's "famous trip in 1962," as the fortunes of the minority Tory government were fading. Dief roused a cheering crowd in an Eastern Townships village with a speech that went on for some thirty minutes in surprisingly good French. That night went down in Tory lore as "le miracle de Sainte-Perpétue." There also are stories, perhaps exaggerated, about the night Dief attempted to open with the conventional greeting, "J'espère que mes voeux sont appréciés," but to the locals it sounded more like "I hope my calves have been pooping." One farmer is said to have shouted back, "Moi aussi!"

Diefenbaker consulted Brown on a variety of other subjects. One was about the merits of appointing Georges Vanier as governor general in 1959. Diefenbaker was worried about the age of the distinguished general, who was over seventy at that time. Brown told Diefenbaker, as he recalled, that Vanier "was the best candidate that I could think of because he had never been involved in politics." When Dief was looking for people to appoint to a blue-ribbon commission on government administration, he accepted Brown's recommendation and called to thank him. And after the crushing loss of his majority in 1962, Diefenbaker turned to Brown again for advice on reorganizing the party. Brown suggested the appointment of a French-speaking national party director and two Quebec Tory senators who could — as the Liberals had done for years — concentrate on party organization. But those appointments were never made amid the revolt in Diefenbaker's Cabinet over defence and economic policies that saw the resignations of several key ministers.

The death of the autocratic Maurice Duplessis in 1959 marked a turning point in Quebec — and in Diefenbaker's own fortunes. Paul Sauvé's elevation as Union Nationale leader and, subsequently, Quebec premier, gave Diefenbaker a potential ally who did not make war with Ottawa. "I think that he dreamed of making Paul Sauvé his successor," said Brown. Indeed, unlike Duplessis, Sauvé accepted federal financing of universities and agreed to participate in the building of the Trans-Canada Highway. "Sauvé solved the two thorny issues that were dividing Quebec and Ottawa," said Brown. But after just 114 days in office Sauvé collapsed and died suddenly on January 2, 1960.

Jean Lesage became the province's Liberal leader and ultimately the premier who presided during Quebec's Quiet Revolution. Journalist Peter

Newman wrote: "In retrospect it seems clear that had Sauvé lived, Jean Lesage and his Liberals could never have captured provincial office in June 1960. Without Lesage's victory, and the resultant collapse of the Union Nationale, enough of the French-Canadian contingent in the Conservative Party would almost certainly have survived the 1962 election to give Diefenbaker the majority that would have extended his mandate."

At Brown's suggestion, Diefenbaker also had tried to recruit Montreal mayor Jean Drapeau as a minister and possible successor. "But," said Brown, "he wrote back to me at that time and said: 'I made every possible effort to bring Drapeau to Ottawa. Drapeau wouldn't come, he was not the type.'"

Ultimately, Diefenbaker accepted advice from his western flank to ignore Quebec. Brown said he rejected appeals from Quebec ministers to support the call for a royal commission on official bilingualism. And anglophone members of his caucus openly opposed Quebec's aspirations. As Peter Newman wrote, the Chief's clarion call for "One Canada" and "unhyphenated Canadianism" played well across Ontario and the West. But in Quebec it evoked memories of assimilation, going back to the Durham Report and the 1840 Act of Union. "None of this seemed to bother Diefenbaker very much. His calculations were based on the politics of the situation and it was evident there were far more votes to be gained in the country as a whole by questioning French Canada's motives than by defending Quebec's aspirations."

Brown was on the scene for the defeat of the Conservatives in 1963 and the transition to Lester Pearson. In all, his career in Ottawa spanned four decades. He had covered Quebec politics, worked for the Union Nationale, and served a stint as an official in the Quebec labour department before coming to Ottawa as an editorial writer for *Le Droit*. He was on hand when Diefenbaker won the leadership in 1956 and he declined an offer to join Diefenbaker's senior staff after he became prime minister in 1957. Clement Brown believed that his professional home was the press gallery. When he died in Hull, Quebec, on January 5, 2007, at the age of ninety-five, he had seen it all.

Part V

THEIR TIMES

Chapter 11

AMÉDÉE GAUDREAULT: SCOOP ARTISTE

Amédée Gaudreault was a curious boy. When he was a secondary student at the Séminaire de Chicoutimi in the 1930s, he discovered that the good fathers had a richer library of books than the students. With special permission, he was able to obtain access to complete texts of major works and such elite intellectual journals as *La Revue des Deux Mondes*. That curiosity would serve Gaudreault well.

In a career spanning thirty years as a journalist he became one of Quebec's premier reporters and analysts on the provincial and national stage, and an award-winning confidant of government and business leaders who never lost a sense of his small-town roots and his commitment to accuracy. From Maurice Duplessis to Pierre Trudeau, he pursued events with old-fashioned values: a passion for "*la primeur*" — the scoop on page 1 — and what he called "*une solide documentation*" and "*des textes irréfutables.*"

Growing up in the Maskoutain region around Saint-Hyacinthe northeast of Montreal, young Amédée played hockey, baseball, and tennis. He was also something of a budding wonk, having read Dale Carnegie's 1936 bestseller, *How to Win Friends and Influence People*. From that, the teenager decided to start at the top: he typed out requests to leading political and literary figures asking for information on their careers. That provided his first journalistic lesson: people love being asked — and talking — about themselves. To his surprise he received replies from former Quebec premier Louis-Alexandre Taschereau, colourful Montreal mayor Camillien Houde, and T.-D. Bouchard, who had served as mayor, reform-minded Liberal member of the Legislative Assembly, and senator in Ottawa. Bouchard also owned the local paper, *Le Clairon*, and was so impressed with young Gaudreault that he hired him in 1942 as a junior reporter at twelve dollars a week. He was twenty years old. Gaudreault immersed himself in all facets of the operation: covering news, sports, the courts, and the police beat; doing social notes from burgs like Saint-Damase and Saint-Pie; and correcting proofs in the print shop.

After six years of grounding at *Le Clairon*, he moved to *La Tribune* in Sherbrooke where, in addition to covering the local scene, he became the paper's first sessional correspondent at the sixteen-member Quebec press

Amédée Gaudreault interviewing Prime Minister Louis St. Laurent.

gallery. There he rubbed shoulders with top journalists, including the legendary Edmond Chassé, a veteran of *L'Événement* and *Le Canada,* and the young Pierre Laporte, whose *Lettre de Québec* column in *Le Devoir* was must reading in the heyday of the Duplessis government. Back in Sherbrooke, Gaudreault covered the infamous Asbestos Strike where he worked alongside *Le Devoir* special correspondent Gérard Pelletier, later a federal Cabinet minister during the October Crisis when the FLQ murdered Laporte, who by then was Quebec labour minister.

In 1954 Gaudreault moved to *La Presse* in Montreal where he covered the opening of the St. Lawrence Seaway by Queen Elizabeth and managed to wangle a minor scoop out of Prince Philip during a reception for reporters. As recalled in his memoir, *Trente Ans de Journalisme,* in 1958 a friend helped him enter a closed federal Conservative meeting undetected. There he reported on a clash among delegates over a new Canadian flag and immigration policy. A relative unknown, Roland Michener, later to become governor general, urged fellow Conservatives to support a motion for a "distinctive Canadian flag," a policy rejected by the new leader, John Diefenbaker. Gaudreault also made front page headlines by revealing the response of Defence Minister George Pearkes who, asked why he opposed liberalized immigration politicies, said: "We don't want to be flooded by Japs."

All of that was before Gaudreault moved to Ottawa in 1959 as parliamentary reporter and as correspondent for his paper's radio station CKAC. At the time, the gallery had only ninety-five members, but they had just voted to allow broadcasters as members, a move that would greatly expand the ranks. He and I became neighbours and, in addition to much banter, we also shared information. Like mine, his desk also was off the main "hot room" in a corridor leading to the Commons and Senate galleries. It was the beginning of the end of an era when reporters waited their turn to get to Ottawa: Gaudreault was only the third *La Presse* correspondent sent to Ottawa since 1926, his two predecessors having served a total of thirty-three years. One of them, J.A. Fortier, used to write out his dispatches in lavish calligraphic style and arranged to pay for transmission by weight of the paper instead of words.

Gaudreault also was delighted to discover that, in contrast to Quebec City, there was an official daily record of parliamentary debates and access to the "blues," the first drafts by Commons stenographers that were available at thirty-minute intervals in the press gallery. (Quebec began transcribing its debates in 1964. Until that time, Gaudreault and other reporters in the Quebec gallery established pools to cover the debates and share their accounts. All of that was in the days when newspapers demanded almost verbatim coverage of legislative and Commons debates.)

By the time Gaudreault got to Ottawa times were changing on all fronts, not the least in the media world. *Le Nouveau Journal* launched and quickly became *the* French-language Montreal paper, with aspirations to emulate France's *Le Monde* and the *Herald Tribune* with sophisticated opinion and analysis. Gaudreault signed on after only two years with *La Presse,* joining a who's who of defectors from other Quebec outlets. Among them: Jean-V. Dufresne, Raymond Grenier, Jean Paré, Jean-Pierre Fournier, and the cartoonist Roland Berthiaume, known as Berthio.

Television was forcing new demands on reporters for more context and background, and *Le Nouveau Journal* delivered to a fault. Critics argued that the paper sometimes left out facts and news, however, and the publication folded after two years.

Shifting to Quebec City's *Le Soleil,* Gaudreault, like many senior gallery members, was fortunate to have excellent access to Prime Minister Lester Pearson. Those confidences often allowed him to anticipate government plans with several *primeurs.* His experience with the secretive Pierre Trudeau was something else again. He had known him since his days as an activist professor in Montreal. Whenever they got together, Gaudreault made a point of passing on the latest gossip to Trudeau. But all he got in return were questions. One day he complained to Trudeau that he had never given him one tidbit. That's okay, Trudeau replied with a smile, "Keep coming, what you have to tell me is interesting."

Trudeau's arrival marked a welcome confirmation of French power in Ottawa for Gaudreault. He was a staunch federalist — at times denounced by nationalist colleagues — but he had been horrified by the ignorant argument against the introduction of simultaneous translation shortly after he came to Ottawa: How, Anglo critics asked, could unilingual Quebec MPs be expected to function in English? Gaudreault, an old-fashioned reporter, also was shocked to see instances of yellow journalism perpetrated by certain of his colleagues. He once challenged Richard Jackson of the

Ottawa Journal, who filed copiously to the *Daily Express* in London, about legendary exaggerations in his articles on Quebec. Jackson's defence was that he had to "jazz my copy a little bit." Jackson also made light of his lurid Fleet Street accounts of the Trudeau marriage breakdown by insisting, "No one in Canada wanted to publish them."

Gaudreault left the press gallery in 1971 as Trudeau's tide was ebbing. He joined the civil service as a public relations specialist until his retirement in 1987 at sixty-five. In 1988 he became a member of the Order of Canada. He died at age ninety-two in April 2015. In his memoir, Gaudreault provided a fitting epitaph: "Throughout my journalistic career, I viewed my work as that of *un témoin*" — a witness. In the best tradition of witness, Amédée Gaudreault always knew his facts and spoke them with authority.

Chapter 12

THE GANG OF SIX

The Parliamentary Press Gallery has always played host to a cast of characters and larger-than-life figures, and this was certainly the case when I first went to Ottawa in 1965. The ones I met there had come of age during the Great Depression and the Second World War. Most were from small towns and started at the bottom in the newspaper business. In an age when print ruled, they became key opinion makers for English Canada, with strong connections to the ruling powers. They tended to be fans of Lester Pearson and critics of Pierre Trudeau. They were still tapping their typewriters during my second and third stints in 1969 and 1975, when they set the tone for the Parliamentary Press Gallery.

———

Charles Lynch challenged the new prime minister, Pierre Trudeau, to allow the media to cover his scuba-diving trip to Mexico in 1969. Trudeau agreed as long as Lynch, a burly bull of a man, accompanied him to a depth of a hundred and fifty feet. Later that day, when Lynch related that challenge in a conversation with Lester Pearson, the former PM responded: "Of course you must accept. It won't be the first time you've been out of your depth." In telling the anecdote in *The Lynch Mob,* Lynch embraced the fundamental dichotomy of his long career: critics accused him of being a lightweight, but he loved consorting on the national stage with the powerful.

And consort he did. On assignment for British United Press (BUP), he covered the D-Day landings with celebrated CBC correspondent Matthew Halton, became friends with Walter Cronkite at the Nuremberg trials, exchanged barbs with Ernest Hemingway in France, reported for BUP from Brazil and Vancouver after the war, and covered the United Nations for the CBC. For three decades he was an Ottawa columnist for the largest newspaper chain in the country. He gave a hundred and fifty speeches a year in his prime, performed in more than thirty press gallery dinner shows, and once stood "in the full and complete presence of the Prime Minister of Canada" when John Diefenbaker dropped his drawers to prove that he had not been disabled in a fall.

Lynch pioneered celebrity journalism in the national capital. He arrived in 1947 at age twenty-seven, just before King transferred the Liberal hegemony to St. Laurent. "There were no spin doctors," Lynch recalled in an interview before his death with journalist Tom Earle. Reporters could talk to the prime minister and senior officials. "But the main thing," he added, "was you covered Parliament. That was where the news was." In 1957 he reported the federal election for the CBC and hosted the network's election night coverage. Southam then recruited him, and in 1962 he became a national columnist reaching millions and, fuelled by his TV profile, he generated handsome speaker fees in his prime.

He grew up in Saint John, New Brunswick, where, after high school, he got a job at a new paper started by K.C. Irving. That led to an assignment with CP in Halifax. From there he moved to Vancouver where he married his Halifax sweetheart Mary-Elizabeth Merkel, daughter of the legendary journalist Andy Merkel, with whom he had five children. (In the early 1980s Lynch scandalized official Ottawa and friends by leaving her for Conservative Party official Claudy Mailly, later an MP from Gatineau. They were together until Lynch's death in 1994.) After he wrote colourful accounts of the historic Churchill-Roosevelt meeting in Quebec in 1943, Reuters offered Lynch a job as a war correspondent. He and Halton were in the second wave of landings at Juno Beach, Lynch wading ashore with his typewriter atop his helmet. The army public relations gurus supplied carrier pigeons to take the first reports back to England. But, one after another, Lynch's thirty-six birds turned inland toward Germany. As the last one disappeared, Lynch shouted: "Traitors! Damned traitors!"

Charles Lynch with Winston Churchill and Field Marshal Bernard Montgomery.

He was a stocky, barrel-chested extrovert with a lyrical voice. His prime tools were humour and song — and provocation. His specialty was composing irreverent ditties about parliamentarians and playing his harmonica for any crowd that would have him. He once staged a sit-in at René Lévesque's first federal-provincial meeting on the Constitution, arguing that if the first ministers were going to remake the Constitution with the first separatist premier, the people deserved to see it. When Trudeau tried to clear the media after the traditional photo op, Lynch refused to go, bellowing, "Let the people see." Trudeau then started to leave the room. As Lynch recalled in his memoir, *You Can't Print That!*, "I yelled that he had said he could live with an open meeting, and he snapped back, 'Yes, but I can't live with you, Charles.'" Lévesque had the same reaction. "He said, 'Good issue, Chuck'

— he always called me Chuck because he knew I hated it — 'but not big enough. I'll walk out tomorrow.'" And he did. In the end, Lynch tired of the wrangling among first ministers. For the first time, he swung hard to Trudeau's side and supported the unilateral patriation of the Constitution.

Lynch always coveted the limelight and went out of his way to claim centre stage. In 1965 he had filed special reports from mainland China as a guest of the Chinese government. As president of the gallery he supported demands by authorities in China to expel the Taiwan correspondent and accredit their man (a proposal the members rejected overwhelmingly). He once outraged official Ottawa when he questioned Governor General Georges Vanier's dedication to the monarchy — simply because the distinguished old soldier had cautioned Lynch about the newsman's militancy in the cause. And the press gallery suspended him for three weeks after he reported on a private speech John Diefenbaker gave at an off-the-record gallery tribute to the outgoing Conservative leader in 1967. The reports by Lynch and the CBC revealed that Diefenbaker had told his audience that he would not be running again for Parliament. Lynch was right, though: it was legitimate news.

Critics came and went, but Lynch roared on. He recalled in his memoir that historian Frank Underhill once told him, "The reason your work is mediocre, Mr. Lynch, is that your mind itself is mediocre. You are doing the very best you can with what you have."

Charlie always got the last laugh. True to form, he composed his own obituary and, two weeks before his death, submitted it to the *Ottawa Citizen* where he was a freelance columnist in his later years. He wrote: "In his various guises, Lynch was a pioneer of celebrity journalism in Canada, and admitted he may have corrupted the breed, since everybody wanted to be rich and famous." To his great delight, Lynch is even memorialized below the main stairway outside the Senate where a sculptor, bored by chiselling gargoyles, carved the columnist's likeness in marble after the war. He is wearing a toque and smoking his iconic pipe. But most of all, he cherished his Order of Canada citation, which, in addition to newspaperman, broadcaster, and writer, credits him as "musician."

W.A. Wilson, known to all of us as Bill, was very close to Charles Lynch. In fact, when he was a fourteen-dollar-a-week reporter for British United Press in Vancouver in 1940, the two were job-sharing pioneers of a sort. Lynch worked the day shift and Wilson worked at night. That was a necessity. Wilson told journalist Tom Earle they "were so poverty stricken" that they had to rent a room together — and, since it had only one bed, one slept while the other was at work. In later years in Montreal, Wilson was one of the few reporters who could validly claim to have ridden the rails in search of work during the Depression. In another era Bill might have become a successful newspaper proprietor: an uncle owned the *Moncton Transcript*. But his mother and her siblings, the heirs, sold the paper for a quarter of its value on the uncle's death.

Wilson was born in Lethbridge, Alberta, and grew up there and on the family farm near the village of Barons. After his uncle died in 1935 and left him some money, Wilson went back to school and got his B.A. Young Bill parlayed his summer experience on the *Transcript* into work with BUP that took him from Montreal to Vancouver to Ottawa — and then to war.

By the time he turned twenty-seven, he had already followed the 1st Canadian Division into Sicily, and then on to Italy where he became critically ill from exposure on the battlefield. He flew back from hospital in North Africa in time to cover the D-Day landings from the cockpit of an RAF bomber. He was the first reporter back in London to file news of the landing. That evening at an aerodrome he got first-hand reports from returning pilots that the Allied march inland was under way and filed in time to make page 1 in several papers. Back in Vancouver his fiancée, Marion, was relieved and "filled with pride to see the byline, 'W.A. Wilson.'" Years later, recalling the vision of "the entire invasion fleet laid out before you" through drifting clouds, Wilson said, "You remember there'd been doubt about the whole thing, you knew that it was going to work."

After the war the Wilsons settled in London where he honed his economic skills working for *Newsweek* in Europe. In Montreal he was city editor of the *Herald* and, upon its demise, transferred to the *Star* as aviation correspondent and then Ottawa bureau chief in 1962.

In 1965 I had the good fortune of joining Bill's Ottawa bureau. At the peak of his career in Ottawa with the *Star*, and with the FP News Service (serving the former Free Press chain of papers across the country), Bill was must reading among the power elite, known for his serious analysis and knowledge of high finance and statecraft.

In Ottawa, W.A. Wilson conjured memories of times past with a neatly trimmed military moustache, his dark, three-piece bespoke suits, and his taste for fine whisky. In 1982 he was the only correspondent on the Hill who had parking stickers for both his Jaguar and a Land Rover (Fords and Pontiacs ruled). He took a similarly exotic view of the affairs of state; his nuanced prose reflected the seriousness of his subject matter. He was highly critical of Pierre Trudeau's handling of the economy, arguing that the government "virtually abdicated all responsibility for the soaring problem of inflation." He also faulted Trudeau for eroding the concept of ministerial responsibility "to the point that it became almost impossible … to pin responsibility for any government action on anybody." While he defended Trudeau's use of the War Measures Act in 1970, he was irate when he discovered the state intervening in his own personal life: he returned from covering Trudeau's Arctic trip in 1970 to learn that the Mounties had visited his home and questioned two of his five children about the shelter he and his wife, Marion, had apparently given to American draft dodgers. Wilson took his protest to the prime minister's office and got an apology from the solicitor general.

In 1969 Wilson, along with Anthony Westell of the *Globe and Mail*, obtained private correspondence from former prime minister Pearson about his handling of a series of scandals that had tainted his government. Publication of the documents in a national series of articles lent credence to Pearson's claim that he had not thrown his French-Canadian Cabinet ministers under the bus during a series of ministerial scandals. Wilson also went to the defence of Liberal minister Maurice Lamontagne when he was under attack for buying furniture on generous credit from a Montreal store. Wilson continued writing freelance opinion pieces and doing TV commentaries until shortly before his death at seventy-seven in 1994 following heart surgery. He made no apologies for his seriousness of purpose. "I've always had a preference," he said, "for knowing what I was talking about."

Lubor J. Zink became something of a parody of the red-baiting anti-Communist in the twilight of a thirty-year career in Ottawa as columnist for the *Toronto Telegram* and, after it folded, the *Toronto Sun*. Ronald Reagan read his portrayal of Pierre Trudeau as a crypto-Communist in the right-wing *National Review*; it contributed to the frosty reception the White House extended to the Canadian prime minister in the early 1980s. Zink was influential in the Czech government-in-exile during the war and was decorated for service in Sicily and France as part of a Czech unit in Montgomery's 8th Army. Less known was the indirect role he played in Lester Pearson's election as prime minister in 1963.

Zink was a nineteen-year-old student activist in Prague who fled the day before the Nazis closed the universities and rounded up and executed his colleagues. He joined the provisional government forces in London and ended up working for Jan Masaryk, foreign minister in exile, organizing anti-Nazi student rallies around the world. After the war, he worked as an aide to Masaryk at the foreign affairs ministry in Prague. But when the Communists took over, he fled to London with his wife and young son, just a day after Masaryk, an anti-Communist, was mysteriously found dead, the victim of an apparent murder. After a stint in London for the BBC, Zink moved to Canada seeking a better life for his family. As he told journalist Peter Stursberg in a 1977 interview about his experience in Britain: "You are branded a foreigner unless you have a string of ancestors going back to Hastings."

His freelance work for the Toronto *Globe* landed him a job in Manitoba as editor of the *Brandon Sun*. His editorials won a National Newspaper Award and attracted the attention of publisher John Bassett who offered him a job in Ottawa as a columnist with the *Telegram*. Before Zink left Brandon, Liberal opposition leader Pearson, on a campaign visit, invited Zink for breakfast and discovered that they were both friends of Masaryk, Pearson from his days as foreign minister in the St. Laurent government. When Zink arrived in Ottawa in 1962, he and Pearson saw each other on a regular basis.

The columnist soon found himself embroiled in one of the big issues of the day — the Diefenbaker government's decision to renege on a commitment with the United States to arm Bomarc surface-to-air missiles at two Canadian bases with nuclear warheads. The Pearson Liberals also opposed

Lubor J. Zink, 1962: the hardline anti-Communist.

the nuclear option at the time; the hawkish Zink worked on Pearson, trying to change his stance. Diefenbaker's Cabinet meanwhile was split on the issue, since the Cuban Missile Crisis in October 1962 had put a new focus on North American defence. Retiring North Atlantic Treaty Organization (NATO) commander General Lauris Norstad said during an Ottawa press conference — in response to Zink's question — that Canada was not fulfilling its role in NORAD, the shared air defence system. "So that blew it wide open," Zink said years later.

Zink went to see Pearson and learned that the Liberal leader was ready to change his policy. "I think he started really listening after the Cuban crisis," he told Stursberg. MP Paul Hellyer also was working on his leader to change his mind. Pearson told Zink that he would gladly support the government if Diefenbaker was willing to change his nuclear policy. "It took me a few days to catch Diefenbaker alone," Zink revealed, "and I wasn't even able to finish outlining what Pearson was offering." Diefenbaker was not interested in what Pearson was going to do. He stuck to his guns, and three of his key ministers resigned in protest: Defence Minister Douglas Harkness, Associate Defence Minister Pierre Sévigny, and Trade Minister George Hees. The fractured Diefenbaker government fell in February. Pearson came out in support of nuclear warheads, and Canadians elected Pearson as prime minister in April.

Zink, a slim, bespectacled and unimposing man, was back at the centre of a major controversy during the 1963 campaign, again involving Pearson. He had gone to see the Liberal leader in his room at the Queen Elizabeth Hotel in Montreal with other senior reporters, including Victor Mackie of the FP News Service. Zink said Pearson was lying on his bed in "a very, very depressed mood and he also was exhausted and altogether downcast." Once again, it appeared that Diefenbaker had defied the odds and the country was headed for another minority government. In unusually frank language, Pearson told the reporters: "Unless we have a workable majority I'll resign and hope that Mr. Diefenbaker will do the same. There are no unbridgeable differences between the two parties and new younger men on both sides, and I mean new men, not the old guard, might be able to join forces and give the country the strong stable government it needs so badly."

The bombshell took a week to explode. The chat with Pearson took place on a Sunday but, incredibly, Zink did not use the quote until the following Friday, and then as more of a throwaway line in a piece about how the election seemed to be heading for another impasse. The article in the *Telegram* carried the bland heading:

ONLY TWO WEEKS LEFT AND STILL NO CLUES

The story created a feeding frenzy by other outlets. As for the quote, said Zink, "I only used it to illustrate that Pearson was a sensible man. I had no idea of upsetting anything or betraying any confidence." Mackie argued that the quote should not have been used. "This was an informal talk, you know, it was off the record." He explained that to his editors when the story broke and, he says, they replied, "Forget it. This was obviously background."

Zink retained a good relationship with Pearson until the allegations surfaced about the Rivard scandal in 1964. Zink wrote that Pearson had been less than truthful with the Commons in answering questions about when his justice minister Guy Favreau had first told him of attempts by the PM's parliamentary secretary to help the mobster Rivard get bail. Zink argued that Pearson had thrown Favreau to the wolves to save his own reputation. "That's where the relationship cooled off remarkably," Zink recalled, "and from then on we practically didn't see one another." Yet when Zink made a foray to Vietnam in 1966 to check out the war he carried an official Ottawa letter urging foreign governments to assist him. It was signed personally by Lester B. Pearson.

With Pearson's retirement, Zink set his sights on Pierre Trudeau, implying that he was a Communist and a security threat. Twice Zink ran as a Progressive Conservative candidate in Toronto and lost in 1972 and 1974. With the fall of the Soviet Union and in failing health, the old warrior signed off his *Toronto Sun* column in 1993. He died in 2004 at eighty-four.

Doug Fisher was a blunt-talking, two-hundred-forty-pound "boy from the bush" in northern Ontario (born in Sioux Lookout) who never pulled his punches. In 1964 he went on CBC television and attacked the network for "metropolitanism" and ignoring the small towns. "The CBC," he said, "isn't Canadian in the wide sense." The programs, he went on, were for "some

kind of elite," to the extent that "these ordinary folk out in the bush —
lumbermen, trappers — are given an opportunity for all kinds of opera and
academic disquisitions."

As an Ottawa columnist Fisher was no less bold in his assessments of
prime ministers and colleagues alike. For forty-five years he was a respected
Parliament Hill commentator, as well as a political sage sought out by
several prime ministers for his strategic advice — and by not a few of us
junior journalists for context and background. When he retired in 2006
at age eighty-five he was the dean of the Parliamentary Press Gallery. He
was such an institution that for years Ottawa political junkies stayed up to
watch his local interview show after the late news on Sunday night. Fisher,
a man of many parts, also was the mastermind of the Canada-Russia hockey
series of 1972.

The son of a railway engineer, Fisher left high school in Fort William, as
it was then known, when he was eighteen. He worked as a lowly mucker in
the gold mines, and then as a logger and a firefighter. In 1941, at twenty-one,
he joined the army and, refusing a commission, fought as a trooper in heavy
action from Juno Beach, through Falaise and into Germany with the 12th
Manitoba Dragoons, an armoured car regiment. After the war he attended
Victoria College at the University of Toronto on his veterans' benefits. There
he fell under the influence of legendary professors Northrop Frye, Frank
Underhill, and Donald Creighton — and sparred with student president
Keith Davey, later Pierre Trudeau's key campaign strategist. After graduating
with honours in history and library science, he studied in London and then
taught school back in Port Arthur.

On the side he helped local industries with grant applications and individuals confronting provincial and federal bureaucracies. That led to his
selection as the thirty-seven-year-old candidate for the social democrats, then
known as the Co-operative Commonwealth Federation, in the 1957 election.
Ahead of his time, Fisher bought time on local television and, using folksy
fireside chats, captured the rising anger with the arrogant Liberals in Ottawa.
With his victory over "Mr. Everything" in the St. Laurent Government,
Industry Minister C.D. Howe, the author of the 1956 pipeline debacle,
Fisher was an overnight sensation. His hard work in the riding allowed him
to survive the Diefenbaker sweep of 1957 as well as the elections of 1962
and 1963. He was one of the most active opposition MPs and an orator

who could hold his own with Diefenbaker. But increasingly he felt out of line with the ruling powers of the social democratic movement, including David Lewis and his son Stephen, and opposed the merger with big labour that led to the formation of the NDP.

He did not run in the 1965 election. In addition to fights with his party, the costs of raising a young family of five boys with his then-wife, Barbara, a librarian as well, propelled him into writing for money — a comment on the ten thousand dollars a year in pay then accorded MPs. Publisher John Bassett offered him a thrice-weekly column in the *Toronto Telegram*, later syndicated, as well as a show on his CFTO station in Toronto. When the *Telegram* folded in 1971 Fisher signed on with the *Toronto Sun*. He also became a regular on national shows such as *Question Period*. What Fisher brought to the public was a profound sense of the political game. His awareness of the influence of the press gallery was acute. He saw it as essential because, as he put it, "politics more and more *is* the media, and the media, politics."

He was a true iconoclast. He had the nerve to advocate for higher pay and better resources for MPs, yet he decried the high-spending ways of officials in the post–Expo 67 period — except when it came to sports. With Cabinet about to deny a twenty-five-million-dollar increase in the federal budget for sports, which he helped draft, Fisher contacted Trudeau's principal secretary, Jim Coutts and, with Keith Davey's support, got the money approved.

Readers of his column were often unaware of Fisher's conflicts of interest. As a sometime adviser to Pierre Trudeau's Liberal government he wrote about the subjects in which he was involved. One example was the key role he played in negotiating the terms of the 1972 hockey series, including the television rights, and his subsequent government appointment as chair of Hockey Canada. Yet Fisher did not receive payment for most of his extracurricular work. He maintained the respect of his peers, especially the politicians, with whom he shared a bond.

Pierre Trudeau was something else again. Fisher was never intimidated by the prime minister and was fearless in his questioning. Trudeau once refused to go on a TV panel unless Fisher was disinvited — which he was. His main regret about losing an election bid for the NDP in 1968 was not being able to confront Trudeau in the House. "I knew I could take Trudeau on, head-on, and drive him up the wall," he told interviewer Tom Earle. "I would have had a field day with him."

Doug Fisher: "I knew I could take Trudeau head on."

Fisher was never a fan of official bilingualism or Trudeau's constitutional patriation. He twice went to London to argue against the measure and the Charter of Rights. "I still don't want judges being the final determinant of our legislation," he said in 1993. He once caused a row at a conference at Laval University when, in response to René Lévesque ("you need us more than we need you"), he said that his average constituent's perception of Quebec culture, apart from political corruption, was Maurice Richard and stripper Lili St. Cyr. Twenty-five years later Lévesque and Fisher had a happy reunion at an Ottawa book launch. Fisher's son, Luke, who arranged the encounter, told me: "Lévesque said that he and Doug became friends that night of the debate because they enjoyed listening to each other talk. He also said, 'Your dad and I have different priorities, but there is one thing that brought us closer together. We can't stand Pierre Trudeau!'"

Not only was Fisher insensitive to the aspirations of French Canada, but he also espoused a dismissive view of First Nations culture. "This is brutal," he said in 1993, "but I grew up with them, and I have lived with them, and I represented a lot of Indians. Their culture simply cannot stand up to modern technology and the forces of the modern world."

Fisher got along much better with Jean Chrétien and Brian Mulroney, like him both sons of the hinterland. He and his family were Mulroney's guests at the PM's Harrington Lake retreat. Chrétien said no one understood political parties better than Fisher. As he told researcher George Hoff, "There are no others who have done it like him."

He was a true original. In his final column for the *Toronto Sun* on July 30, 2006, Fisher provided a clue: "I carried the opposition MP mentality into journalism." Fisher died three years later on September 18, one day shy of his ninetieth birthday.

Victor Mackie was thirty-five when the *Winnipeg Free Press* sent him to Ottawa to cover Parliament full-time in 1951. He had already been a visiting correspondent for the session of 1942–43. That's when he first met Prime Minister Mackenzie King. Grant Dexter of the *Free Press* was going to see the prime minister for an evening chat and took the cub reporter along. Mackie parlayed the introduction into regular corridor chats with King that yielded news for his paper. Mackie continued the practice when he came back as a full-time correspondent.

This tradition continued after King retired. There were only about forty people in the press gallery, but Mackie was one of the few reporters who talked weekly to Prime Minister Louis St. Laurent. "I was getting stories that nobody else had," Mackie told journalist Tom Earle. "It got so I could phone St. Laurent and get him on the phone and talk to him." Gradually other reporters joined Mackie in the corridors. Little did they know the practice would forever alter how politicians went about official business. Today we know it as "the Ottawa scrum."

But it was a different era, when reporters were more chroniclers than antagonists. Even though he reported to a Liberal paper, Mackie made a point of having good sources on both sides of the political divide and attempting to report fairly. "I never, ever betrayed a confidence from Dief or a confidence from Mike," he told interviewer Peter Stursberg in 1977.

In return, the politicians treated reporters with respect. Typically, King would attend the reception in the lounge after the gallery's annual general meeting. "Both King and St. Laurent had a very high regard for the Parliamentary Press Gallery as an institution," said Mackie. "They thought of it as a part of Parliament and a very important part of the parliamentary system."

Mackie was typical of the breed of parliamentary reporters of the era. He had wide experience as a journalist and editor in Saskatchewan and Manitoba. He started as a cub reporter for his hometown *Moose Jaw Herald* after high school, covering funerals, the police beat, and city hall — and he played gin rummy with the Mounties in their barracks. Rejected for military service for health reasons, he landed a fifty-dollar-a-week job in Regina with the Sifton-owned *Leader-Post*. There he covered the riots and the beatings of the "On to Ottawa Trekkers," who were protesting against dismal conditions and pay in relief camps in the mid-1930s. To his surprise he spotted one of his gin rummy Mountie buddies embedded with the marchers. "He just looked at me and put his fingers up to his lips," Mackie recalled, "so I shut up and didn't say anything." His big break came when he returned from Ottawa and covered the 1944

Saskatchewan election victory of Tommy Douglas and his Co-operative Commonwealth Federation. The first social democratic government in North America was big news, and Mackie's freelance reports appeared in *Time*, the *Financial Post*, and *Maclean's*.

After Mackie moved to the *Free Press* in 1948, editor George Ferguson assigned him to cover the election campaign of Tory leader John Bracken with the admonition to "stay on the train and travel with him until he stops making news." The lacklustre Bracken had trouble making news, a point Mackie took up with Mel Jack, Bracken's chief adviser. "Is he as dumb as he seems to be?" Mackie inquired. "And [Mel] said, 'He's dumber. He can't put two words together.'" With that, Mackie suggested a couple of lines for the leader to use — which, in turn, generated front page stories. "Next morning at breakfast, Mel Jack said, 'Well, it went great. Have you got any ideas for today?'"

In all, Mackie covered fourteen federal elections and six prime ministers before his official retirement in 1981. He commiserated with Lester Pearson when his farewell speech remained in his pocket, undelivered, after Pierre Trudeau abruptly dissolved the House for an election in 1968, "a terrible slap." He was in the House the night the Joe Clark government fell by misadventure. He was president of the gallery during the historic year in which members voted to accept the first radio reporter, Sam Ross, as a member.

Looking back in a 1984 interview, Mackie said that the pipeline debate of 1956 was "the most lasting and vivid" he ever covered. The "bedlam" made his stomach churn. He recalled the pre-pipeline period as a golden age when there was a "clubby" atmosphere in the Commons and warring factions could still be friends away from the floor of the House. After the pipeline debacle, he added, "all that dissolved and you've got the bitterness, which is still here today."

The arrival of radio marked another turning point. "There was a more adversarial attitude," he said. "The politician began to realize that he was being pinned down. When he saw that recording machine and the tape and the microphones in front of him, he was very cautious. He no longer treated the press, radio, and writers as great friendly fellows."

Mackie continued freelancing after his retirement and wrote a weekly insider's view of Ottawa for select clients, which he based on his discreet connections. He died in December 1992 at the age of seventy-six, leaving only a few secrets unreported.

———————

George Bain embodied many of the traits of the ancient Greeks. He was as prodigious in his writings as Sophocles and had the wit and verve of Aristophanes, but an instinct for the jugular — and the foibles — of Hercules. He dropped out of high school at sixteen, became a six-dollar-a-week copy boy at the *Toronto Star* and, despite a fear of flying that lasted all his life, flew as a pilot in Bomber Command during the Second World War. Later he covered provincial politics for the *Globe* and, at thirty-four, joined the Ottawa bureau. Bain said his new environs resembled "some odd sort of sweatshop," but the elegance of his prose soon elevated Bain from the reportorial ranks to the lofty pedestal as first regular parliamentary columnist for the *Globe and Mail* — and the writer who set the gold standard for all the Ottawa columnists who followed. The post came with, in the words of Dic Doyle, the *Globe* editor who appointed him, "the most valuable piece of real estate in Canadian journalism": a broad plot on page 6.

His musings beneath the editorials on page 6 were a must read. His thrusts were always delivered deftly. In an early column he described Conservative operative Dalton Camp as "sort of the keeper of the Conservative principles, the first of which is that the party ought to get elected in the next election." He often reserved his most acerbic barbs for his own kind, once accusing Hill reporters of "willful ignorance and an indecent lusting after page 1, where it is known that conflict and confusion play better than concord."

His main target over the years was Pierre Trudeau. Whether it was a result of the war veteran's dislike for a man who had irreverently avoided the conflict, or the product of a simple personality clash, his dislike of Trudeau was so great that he resented even being in the same room with him. The morning after Trudeau proclaimed the War Measures Act against the Front de Libération du Québec (FLQ), Bain denounced the move in his column. "What is going on here?" he began. "Up to the moment there have been too many drastic actions taken and too few explanations." Either the government

George Bain, July 1964: the most valuable real estate in Canadian journalism.

"grossly underestimated the potential of the FLQ," he added, or "its recent extreme actions are the result of panic."

Bain also blew the whistle on Trudeau when, during an exchange over rising unemployment, the prime minister mouthed an expletive at Tory MP John Lundrigan but then denied saying anything more racy than "fuddle duddle." The next day in his column Bain wrote that Trudeau had

"mouthed at him the words which Mr. Lundrigan read to be: 'Fuck off.'"
And so the phrase entered the good grey columns of the *Globe* for the first
time. The incident, Bain concluded, "reflects again the snotty rich kid from
Outremont syndrome." It also revealed Bain's habit of pounding the beat
in search of facts and quotes.

Trudeau never granted him an interview.

Although shunned by Trudeau, Bain was the toast of the town. Urbane,
neatly coiffed, and nattily dressed, he had the air of a corporate director, not
a muckraker. He was in demand as an after-dinner speaker and TV panellist.
He won a Leacock Award for humour, and received honorary degrees from
Carleton and King's College universities and the Order of Canada.

He was a journalistic pioneer. After his initial stint in Ottawa, in 1957
the *Globe* assigned Bain to open the paper's first London bureau, from
where he covered Europe, the Middle East, and Africa for three years.
Next he became the paper's first Washington bureau chief and covered the
civil rights movement, the Cuban Missile Crisis, and the assassination of
John F. Kennedy.

In 1964 he returned from Washington to Ottawa and started his beloved
column. Saturdays were special: the mythical "Clem" would convey his
(Bain's) thoughts about national events in the homey *Letter from Lilac*, the
Saskatchewan town born of Bain's prolific imagination. In 1973, feeling
the strain of writing five times weekly, Bain moved to the *Star* in Toronto
as head of the editorial page. Bain was angered that *Globe* editor Dic Doyle
refused to allow him to write a farewell column. Noting Bain's sudden dis-
appearance from the *Globe,* Pierre Trudeau sent a one-sentence letter about
his old nemesis: "Where in the hell is Bain?"

At the *Star*, Bain chafed under the second-guessing and editing from
the corner office. After only a year the *Star* honoured the promise of moving Bain to London if his new job was not working out. Characteristically,
Bain left his successor a typed quote from veteran American newsman
William Ringle: "Writing editorials is like wetting your pants while wearing a blue serge suit. Nobody notices and it leaves you with a warm
feeling." After three years in London and two more in Toronto, Bain
took his leave. He and his wife, Marion, moved to Mahone Bay on Nova
Scotia's South Shore where his custom-built home housed his extensive
wine collection. He became director of journalism at King's College, and

wrote a wine column and features for *Saturday Night,* and a regular weekly column once again in the *Globe.*

To the end, Bain had a habit of rubbing his superiors the wrong way. In his memoir, *Hurly-Burly, Globe* editor Doyle cited a note he wrote to Bain after yet another clash over one of his decisions: "I'd like to know what compels you to think the worst and expect the worst of whatever might be done or not done in Toronto." A bitter disagreement led to Bain's second departure from the *Globe.* In 1987, editor Norman Webster decided not to continue his column. When the paper refused once again to run his farewell column, Bain took it to his friend Doug Fisher — who ran it in his regular space in the *Toronto Sun.* Bain's friend Clark Davey, a colleague in the gallery back in the 1950s, observed upon his death in 2006 from Alzheimer's, "George had his view, and the rest of the world could go to hell, which is a great thing in a columnist and a helluva problem in an employee."

I stayed in touch with George after he moved to Nova Scotia. After the Liberal leadership convention in Ottawa that elected John Turner in June 1984, we went for a nosh on *Maclean's* dime — "a decidedly vinous dinner," he recalled. "The next morning I found in my jacket pocket a note that said, 'Call Bob Lewis about column.'" That led to his *Media Watch* in *Maclean's,* at the time the only regular accounting of the fourth estate in Canada and the fodder for Bain's 1994 book, *Gotcha! How the Media Distort the News.*

The book summed up some of Bain's popular themes over the years: how the national press had been unfair to Conservative leaders Joe Clark and Brian Mulroney; how pack journalism in the gallery had unfairly ruined the careers of some Liberal ministers in the 1960s; how a 1992 CBC documentary had dishonoured the role of Bomber Command in the Second World War. Above all, he lamented the loss of civility in parliamentary reporting. "What we have had instead," he wrote, "is a predisposition to suppose persons in public life, and particularly those in positions of power, to be villains — and to insist at the same time that they maintain higher standards than the average citizen (such as, for example, a journalist). In other words, the pendulum has swung too far in the other direction." That was not a popular sentiment among the post-Watergate generation of reporters. But Bain was not troubled. He was used to speaking truth to power, whoever held it.

Part VI

ENTER THE
BROADCASTERS

Chapter 13

TOM EARLE: GENTLEMAN PIONEER

Tom Earle was an unlikely trailblazer. He was a shy, soft-spoken Montrealer who had no great ambition other than to be a good radio broadcaster. Unwittingly, he became a revolutionary figure — the first TV reporter sent to Parliament Hill with camera and tape recorder.

Until the CBC assigned Earle to cover Ottawa in 1955, the press gallery had refused membership to anyone who did not report for a newspaper or magazine. And the gallery traditionalists — he called them "Neanderthals" — were intent on maintaining that stance.

"The thought of the Gallery breaking tradition and admitting broadcasters was anathema to me," wrote *Toronto Telegram* reporter Peter Dempson. "It was motivated, in part, by selfishness. I realized, as did many newspapermen, that as soon as CBC representatives were granted membership some of our freelance earnings would disappear. However, I never said anything publicly about this."

Arthur Blakely of the Montreal *Gazette* was not so reticent: "Why in hell should we admit the CBC? And besides," he added with a grin, "I'll lose more than a thousand dollars a year if the CBC comes into the gallery and starts its own broadcasting."

The CBC mounted an effective lobby campaign on Earle's behalf. While the gallery hid behind its musty constitution, Speaker Roland Michener allowed Earle and Sam Ross, head of the private Ottawa Radio News Bureau, to sit and take notes in a gallery adjacent to the press gallery overlooking the Commons. By this point CBC TV had been on the air three years and Earle had scored several key interviews on the Hill. But still the ink-stained wretches fought to keep him and Ross out. Fortunately, both men were exceptionally able — Earle an urbane Montrealer with blueblood roots and solid reporting skills, Ross a distinguished war correspondent and veteran of several western newspapers and CP. They were well liked and more talented than many members then in the gallery who looked down on them.

Still, without membership, they could only attend press conferences; they could not ask questions or record them. Earle would have to do his interviews in the hallway, "re-asking" the questions. Earle faced "a lot of hostility," including attempts to sabotage CBC tape recorders and incidents where fellow reporters shouted crude remarks as his camera was rolling. The *Montreal Star*'s James Oastler, who later became a good friend, once hung his hat over the lens of a CBC camera during an arrival speech at the airport by the U.S. secretary of defense.

But the lure of TV was irresistible. By this time, television in the United States was drawing massive audiences for coverage of political conventions. In Canada some ten million Canadians tuned in to the CBC on June 10, 1959, to watch anchor Charles Lynch and commentator Blair Fraser — two print guys — cover election night with a cast including a young Montreal lawyer, Pierre Trudeau. The show's producer was the CBC's Morley Safer, who would go on to fame as a foreign correspondent for the network and later as a host on CBS's *60 Minutes*. The hidebound members of the press gallery *were* starting to look like Neanderthals. Finally, the gallery admitted Earle and Ross as full-fledged members in 1959. Still, it hurt to be left out. "I was always on the outside looking in until membership was fully granted," Earle recalled in a melancholic interview with fellow journalist Doug Small recorded for the national archives.

Tom Earle grew up in Westmount, Quebec, the son of a grain broker who had separated from Tom's mother. Life in Westmount and in the west end of Montreal was insular and anglophone, with a focus on U.S. entertainment and news from stations in nearby Plattsburgh, New York. After finishing Westmount High School he went to work at a series of jobs, first as an editor on a shipping magazine, briefly in a misadventure as a young reporter for the Montreal *Gazette*, and then as a publicist for the so-called

CPR News Bureau. His main job with the rail and steamship company was meeting the Empress Cruise Line ships near Quebec City, interviewing passengers of note, and sending photos and stories to the newspapers before the vessels docked in Montreal. In those days, working for the CPR was a leg-up to a "reputable job," as opposed to newspaper work. Not only was the CPR work considered a better job, at the time it seemed one more in keeping with his abilities than reporting on "real" news. As Earle admitted, when *Gazette* managing editor William Weintraub fired him, he did so because "I just wasn't very good." Weintraub, incidentally, later went on to write the hilarious *Why Rock the Boat*, a novel about a corrupt managing editor.

As an only child, Earle loved listening to the radio and playing announcer by imitating broadcasts on imaginary microphones in the family basement. "The radio," he said, "was companionship": listening to Rudy Vallee, *Amos 'n' Andy* (played by two white actors on radio), Foster Hewitt doing the NHL broadcasts, and baseball announcers Red Barber and Mel Allen. Later as a teen he was riveted by the wartime broadcasts of the CBC's Matthew Halton and Peter Stursberg. Early radio was "where I got my interest in being a broadcaster."

In 1953, at age twenty-six, Earle left the CPR and joined CBC in Montreal as a writer at a then-handsome seventy-five dollars per week. Two years later the CBC posted him to Ottawa as a TV editor. It was the autumn of the St. Laurent Liberal government and the rise of John Diefenbaker. "That's when I became conscious of being a Canadian," said Earle. "Until then I was an Americanized Montrealer without realizing it."

At first his main duty was to line up print reporters to do on-air coverage of Parliament, including the likes of Blair Fraser, Charles Lynch, and Arthur Blakely, and to film interviews with politicians. Said Earle: "Some of the top members of the gallery became very adept at doing reports, standing with a microphone in front of the Peace Tower and doing their minute-and-a-half report, or doing it out at the studio at CBOT." Graham Fraser recalls that his father, Blair, routinely did TV interviews outside the Commons after question period, much like the present-day scrums of politicians.

Why print reporters on TV? There were no broadcasters in the gallery and, besides, the CBC brass was leery of having its staff cause offence with the government. Earle's other job was to ship clips for TV news to Toronto.

It was a great time in the old town. For hours on end Earle would stand in the lobby under the Peace Tower interviewing MPs on the big stories of the day: Lester Pearson on the Suez Crisis, Trade Minister C.D. Howe on the pipeline debate, Diefenbaker on Diefenbaker.

On one celebrated occasion in 1961, Earl told visiting U.K. prime minister Harold Macmillan he had a question about a free trade agreement proposed by Britain — a question he had already answered at a press conference. Prime Minister Diefenbaker, who opposed the deal, cut Earle off abruptly and said: "No, you're not going to ask that question."

"I was flummoxed. I didn't know what to do," Earle said.

The other reporters certainly did; they reported that the prime minister had tried to censor the CBC. The Liberal opposition took up the cry in the House of Commons. Said Earle: "Paul Martin described me as a young man being corrupted by Dief in the pursuit of honest journalism. It was a very embarrassing period for me. I had a call in the morning from Davidson Denton, the last great head of the CBC. He cut right through all the bureaucracy and asked me what had happened, and I told him. I never heard another word about it, but it was a very uncomfortable period."

Earle did not fault Diefenbaker for shutting him off: "He did it because he felt it might be embarrassing to the Canadian government. It was a perfectly natural reaction. He told me later he wasn't mad at me personally. Dief had a great ego. I adored him. There was nothing personal in this. There really wasn't. It was Dief reacting like Dief." In fact, Earle became very close to Diefenbaker, who fully understood the power of television — and Tom Earle — and used both well.

Tory George Hees, with leadership aspirations burning in his breast, was another master of TV. He went to unusual lengths to ensure a presence on the French-language CBC. Earle would rehearse questions with Hees and his staff, and someone would write the answers on a laundry shirt cardboard in French and tape them to Earle's chest. Noted Earle:

You'd ask him a question in French and he would reply, looking at you. He'd be reading the answer, in French, off your chest. It was in the early pioneer days, before moral ethics played a big role. You didn't question this. This was

John Diefenbaker at head table, gallery dinner. From his right: Tom Earle, Victor Mackie, Jean-Marc Poliquin, and Bob McKeon.

his way of getting to a French-network audience. It was a very smart move on his part. There was no attempt to change my questions.

It was a different era. And change was in the air. In the early days of the Liberal reign, Earle used to join a squad of other gallery reporters in the East Block to interview the prime minister after Cabinet meetings. On one occasion Pearson stumbled on the TV cables and almost toppled over in the scrum. "I never saw him mad in his life," said Earle, "but he was really upset by all of this and he successfully banished the press gallery from the East Block, with no argument. That was the end of the press gallery going to post-Cabinet meetings in the East Block. It had been a great tradition, particularly in the off-session, to go to talk to the prime minister."

Still, gallery reporters had solid relationships with the young ministerial aides on the Hill and pretty well got to go where they wanted. When Earle went to Europe on assignment for CBC, he hitched a ride on a defence department plane at the invitation of Bill Lee, the powerful executive assistant to the minister of defence. Upon Earle's return to Lahr, Germany, to catch his ride back to Ottawa, the base commander informed Earle curtly that he didn't fly civilians around. Earle responded, "Bill Lee told me it would be okay." *Globe* reporter Geoffrey Stevens recalled Earle's account of what happened next: "He said he could hear the guy's knees hit the desk as he snapped to attention. 'Are you ready to go now, sir?'"

It was also a time when reporters and politicians worked in close quarters, unlike the fenced off pens of today. Said Earle: "You could sit on a crate at an airport talking to C.D. Howe while you were waiting for some VIP to arrive. You had a much better relationship. I don't mean you were suppressing news, being suborned, or anything like that, but you had much easier access to politicians in those days." Earle lamented the tone of so much post-Watergate reporting in an 1994 interview. In his day, he said, things were different:

> You would not argue and fight with people on camera. I am thinking of Nixon when he bowed out as president of the United States. Some of those Washington press conferences became a fright. That is not the purpose of journalism. The purpose is to elicit information. You don't have to scream and shout and inject yourself, as so many people do today. That's not the job of the reporter. The person tells the story. If the person lies, he will be found out.

A soft-spoken gentleman of the old school, the bespectacled Earle eventually concentrated on reporting for radio, his true love, and broadcast almost daily on such CBC standbys as *The World at Eight* and *The World at Six*. Official Ottawa respected his calm manner and courtly ways. The government even tapped him to join the official party that would descend into the Diefenbunker to be the reportorial voice of the government in the event of a nuclear attack. Happily, the Cold War never came to that.

In 1967 Earle was honoured to serve as the president of the Parliamentary Press Gallery during Centennial Year. Looking around at the very first coed crowd, he declared: "I am the first president of the gallery in its 100 year history who has ever been able to say, welcome ladies and gentlemen."

It was a celebratory year with special events and attractions — including an all-expenses-paid junket for gallery members and their spouses to Montreal for a preview of Expo 67 sponsored by Seagram's distillers and

Player's cigarettes. The next year, Sam Ross, the first radio reporter granted membership, followed Earle as president.

Earle left Ottawa in 1971 for a rewarding seven years in the CBC's London bureau. Upon his return he spent seven mostly unhappy professional years as a manager of radio operations in Ottawa, a period he described as "the nadir, my darkest moment." The CBC bureaucracy and infighting among staff finally drove Earle to a long sick leave and, ultimately, retirement.

He ended his days on the Hill as a freelance correspondent for the BBC and doing interviews for the oral history project of the Library of Parliament. He died at seventy-seven in Ottawa on October 19, 2004, having blazed a trail to the top for broadcast journalists on Parliament Hill.

Chapter 14

NORMAN DEPOE:
THE GOLD STANDARD

A nother reason for the early acceptance of broadcasters in the press gallery was the arrival of Norman DePoe of the CBC in 1959, four years after Earle. At that time DePoe had just over a decade of broadcasting experience on major shows produced in Toronto. He was a war veteran and, at forty-two, a contemporary of the existing stars of the press gallery. He was well read in history and politics, with a passion for news. He had a crisp, no-nonsense style of storytelling that captivated as it enlightened. His grilling of politicos was so commanding that other broadcast reporters customarily stood back recording while Norman elicited answers; then they inserted their own version of his questions in their taped reports. His reporting on national affairs set the bar for all broadcasters. The voice, seemingly tuned to the sound of rattling gravel, coursed from beneath a neatly trimmed moustache, in a distinctive staccato cadence that ranged from accusation to sympathy. Trussed in three-piece Brooks Brothers suits, with his wavy hair combed tightly, he evoked images of Humphrey Bogart at midnight.

DePoe's performances at live events were spectacular. His idol and model was Edward R. Murrow of CBS News. "A news broadcast," he once told *Maclean's*, "should be a clear, concise, frankly conversational account of what's going on. You shouldn't be pompous about it. There is no need to be a stuffed shirt." That technique was in full evidence in 1962 when the CBC assigned him as the first staff member to anchor election night live. His co-host Blair Fraser, the legendary *Maclean's* columnist, said: "Norman put on a fantastic performance of ad-lib commentary. About all I did was hand him new material from the Teletype. It was a real *tour de force* and it established Norman as someone who could do something no one else could."*

He got rave reviews as well from his later contemporaries. "He was the best newsman-broadcaster Canada has ever seen. He had no equal," observed the late Bruce Phillips. That was no small praise from a journalistic icon in his own right who led CTV coverage in Ottawa during the 1980s before becoming director of communications for Brian Mulroney.

In his interview with Doug Small for the Parliamentary Library's oral history project, Earle elaborated: "Norman very quickly became the equivalent of Blair Fraser, the best of print journalists. As Dief used to say, if when you came into a crowd you saw Norman DePoe, you would know it was important. He was not being facetious."

Veteran CP reporter Dave McIntosh observed: "Television's greatest asset was Norm DePoe of the CBC who, day after day, summed up the affairs of Parliament and government clearly, crisply, briefly, and fairly. And he did it live on camera without notes and, what the rest of us envied most, he could do it half-bombed."

David DePoe, the eldest of Norman's seven children, has fond memories of his father, despite his battle with alcohol and some tempestuous times. In a 2015 interview he recalled meeting his father in the press gallery and strolling with him over to the CBC studio in the Château Laurier to do a live report:

> He'd make a few notes and compose his report in his head during the walk. He had a Bulova watch with a stopwatch and would run through his report and time it. He'd usually argue with Toronto about the time. He'd get on the phone and say he needed two minutes because

---

* DePoe papers, LAC. Like many clippings, this one is unsourced and undated. The author was George Brimmell, a colleague of DePoe's in the press gallery.

the story was so complicated. They would say, "a minute." He'd say, "I can't possibly tell this story in a minute." He would get a minute-thirty. Sometimes he had to turn the camera on in the studio. No matter how much he had to drink, he would snap to in his reporterly mode. But we always could tell watching at home: he would slightly slur his *s*'s.

His CBC colleague Tom Leach marvelled at his "ability to improvise a report and make it sound as though he was reading a script." Gail Scott, then a junior reporter at CBOT-TV in Ottawa destined for a national role as a parliamentary correspondent and co-host of CTV's *Canada AM*, described the DePoe technique in a 1988 interview with the *Ryerson Review of Journalism*: "He knew what film he wanted for a story and knew when words weren't necessary to tell a story. He would phone the newsroom, saying, 'I want 10 seconds of film of the Parliament Buildings, 12 seconds of film of this' and so on. We would get the shots, and without having seen the footage, he would go on the air and get it bang-on every time."

In the course of his three decades with CBC, he did some five thousand reports; covered thirty-one elections; the leadership victories of Diefenbaker, Pearson, and Trudeau; U.S. elections; and Winston Churchill's funeral. He said the Freedom March in Washington in 1963, culminating in Martin Luther King Jr.'s famous "I Have a Dream" speech, was the most thrilling story he ever covered. His instinctive Canadian nationalism bubbled over in 1967 when French president Charles de Gaulle endorsed Quebec separatism with his "*Vive le Québec libre*" call from the balcony of Montreal's city hall. That night in a report that stepped into personal comment, he said, "We neither need the Queen of England nor the president of France to tell us how to be Canadians." DePoe's reportorial reach extended across the country on a variety of subjects. In 1969 *TV Guide* heralded his special, "Northwest Passage," as "the season's finest documentary."

Norman Reade DePoe was born in Portland, Oregon, on May 4, 1917. A neatly typed — and unpublished — manuscript on faded pink sheets of CBC paper in the DePoe fonds of the national archives in

Ottawa betrays the pain of his early childhood and the Depression in suburban Seattle. "I remember clearly the empty house in Multnomah," he wrote, "and my mother piling suitcases into our 1921 Oakland touring car after seeing the furniture off. I suppose my sister and I eventually got in for the resolute drive north that was to make me a Canadian, and it was apparent that we wouldn't be living with my father anymore." Norman was six.

Growing up on Howe Street in Vancouver, Norman delivered newspapers during the Depression while his mother converted their modest house to take in a motley crew of boarders. A series of men came and went. But hard times forced them to abandon the home. In the 1930s young Norman joined the Single Unemployed Protective Association, whose goals were to rally and get relief for the unemployed. "The outfit was Communist-inspired and Communist led: we all knew it and supported it anyway," he wrote. After the RCMP busted heads and broke up a demonstration, "we used to call the Mounties and the city mounted cops 'Cossacks,' with some justification." Norman started attending meetings of the Young Communist League in hopes of joining the volunteer International Brigades heading for Spain to fight against the Franco regime.

Instead, he used his savings to enroll at the University of British Columbia where, over three years, he studied chemistry, history, and English. Before finishing his studies, he signed up for the Royal Canadian Corps of Signals in 1938. During training in Brockville he met Madeline Mihalko, a teacher, at a base dance. They married in 1942. Norman left for Europe as a wireless officer, eventually rising to captain. Madeline quit her job, because in those days the rules barred married teachers. Norman was overseas when David was born in 1944.

Service in Europe was a turning point. The action in Italy and Holland brought him face to face with death. In one incident a comrade managed to get off a deadly shot at a sniper who had drawn a bead on both men. DePoe was on leave in Nijmegen when the Germans surrendered northwest Germany, Holland, and Denmark to Field Marshal Bernard Montgomery. It was May 4, 1945 — Norman's birthday. "Our part of the war was over," he wrote in his memoir. Four days later, VE day marked total victory in Europe. DePoe rejoiced: "There was a magic feeling about that day. We were suddenly eternal: nobody would ever shoot at us again, and nobody could kill us now."

Back from the war, DePoe studied arts and modern languages at the University of Toronto and served as the managing editor of the *Varsity* newspaper, in those years a daily. He was a top student, but the scholarships and veterans' benefits were not enough for a growing family. On September 5, 1948, he joined the CBC as a news writer, while he continued to take classes at the university and write freelance articles for magazines. His big break came when the CBC assigned him to fill in for a colleague who was ill and cover the 1952 Republican convention in Chicago. A star was born. By 1958 he had become editor and on-air host of the newsmagazine *Assignment*; the next year he was named host of CBC's weekly *Newsmagazine* show. The subsequent posting to Ottawa would redraw the road map for television reporting on the affairs of the nation.

David DePoe remembers a busy household in Ottawa where Cabinet ministers, MPs, and senior officials were frequent guests. Davie Fulton, the Tory justice minister, was a regular who loved to come by for buckets of Scotch and to play the piano while Norman belted out Irish laments. Another regular was columnist Charles Lynch who teamed with Norman to write many of the irreverent ditties they would perform at the annual press gallery dinner, one of their very favourite nights.

Based in Ottawa, DePoe ranged widely throughout the world. One of his most celebrated hits was the first TV interview in 1966 with Gerda Munsinger, the German prostitute who had been at the centre of a sex and security case involving members of Diefenbaker's Cabinet. Millions sat rapt as DePoe first brought viewers behind the scenes of the "get." His breathless description of how he got the interview was pure Norman, a mixture of tabloid hype and self-deprecation. For three days in Munich, he reported, he and producer Donald Cameron haggled with Munsinger's agent — and then scored the big scoop.

Then they immediately flew to Montreal for a CBC *Newsmagazine* special hosted by Knowlton Nash. DePoe, now live on air wearing his usual three-piece suit, noted that he had been up for twenty hours and "just for once I don't think I have to apologize for a haggard appearance and a hoarse voice." He then noted pointedly that the interview had been done under "a world copyright agreement." He went on: "We sneaked out of our hotel in Munich in a wet snowfall in separate taxis and ducked the trailing reporters and landed, with a few glances in the rear-view mirror and checking our shoulder-holstered automatics [thin smile], at an apartment house in suburban Munich. It was the sort of pad that Hugh Hefner writes about in *Playboy:* a spiral staircase, a balcony, one or two carefully chosen antique pieces of furniture."

And then, before Munsinger's appearance on camera, a stern warning: "Any of you red hot newsmen who are getting ready to take a snap off the TV screen when you see Gerda Munsinger will be sued right down to your socks, because she's got the sharpest agent I've ever encountered in a long time." Pure *Front Page*.

With former associate defence minister Pierre Sévigny at his side in the studio, DePoe then rolled the interview. Throughout, Gerda insisted that she and the minister had just been "sociable" friends who had met for cocktails and dancing. She saw him "off and on, and we were very good friends." She also allowed that she had seen former trade minister George Hees "a few times" for cocktails. She denied being a former East German spy or a CIA double agent. With a commission of inquiry into the affair getting under way back home, the CBC had scored a major coup.

Norman DePoe (left) with Lester Pearson, August 14, 1963.

At his peak in 1962 DePoe was making a handsome sum from his salary and freelance income.* But by 1968 he had had enough of Ottawa. He was drinking heavily, and his marriage had ended in bitterness five years earlier, in part because of his romantic interest in Susan Dexter, an Ottawa journalist who was twenty years his junior. Dexter cited his drinking — dating from the Second World War — and his newfound celebrity in Ottawa for his downfall, along with boredom in a job that had ceased to be challenging. In an interview over lunch in October 2015 she said:

> Because he was very quick and a very good synthesizer, it was almost too easy for him. He was also capable of doing that while leading quite a social life and a domestic life.… For Norman it would have been easier if there had been more structure, or it had been more difficult to do what he was doing. It might have kept him going for longer. He might not have been so self-destructive. He was very definitely driven by the booze. It was basically he got to be this big star and he just couldn't reconcile the two parts of himself. Celebrity played into it. It is very hard to keep your head if you are mobbed at every airport. It wasn't vanity. It was more inadequacy. If he had been of my father's generation, he would have been busy working on a book, or doing something like that. As things stood, he was not a dilettante, but it was a dilettante's lifestyle.

Dexter knew something about the Hill. In addition to personal experience as a reporter for the *Ottawa Journal*, she was the daughter of Grant Dexter, the legendary journalist who dominated the press gallery in the 1940s and 1950s.

Back in Toronto, DePoe co-hosted the current affairs show *The Public Eye* and was a regular on specials and the news. In 1970 he remarried, to

---

* His earnings that year were the 2018 equivalent of about $150,000. His tax return in the archives also indicates that his speaking fee was $150, or about $1,200 in 2018 dollars.

Mary Blackwood. She and CBC friends tried to get help for Norman and his drinking, but the cause was a lost one. He became a newsroom fixture with few assignments and, eventually, only occasional radio reports. Still, he correctly predicted the looming victory of René Lévesque's Parti Québécois in 1976, largely on the basis of sitting in Montreal taverns and conversing in colloquial French with the regulars.

He was a student of language who learned the craft of writing at the hands of Ralph Allen at *Maclean's* in the fifties. In his unpublished memoir, DePoe wrote that of all of Allen's editing notations in "his small precise handwriting … the one I treasure most was at the left of a sloppily written paragraph. He did not tell me how to recast it, or what words he might have used. He merely wrote: 'Come on DePoe, you can write better than this.'"

In retirement, DePoe wrote a critically acclaimed column on the uses of language in the *Ottawa Citizen* called *Speaking of Words*, where he weighed in on such topics as the best desk dictionaries and the proper use of the word *media* as the plural of *medium*. The DePoe archives in Ottawa also contain his wartime sketch pads and watercolours of the English countryside and, intriguingly, a petal from a dried pink rose.

His son David remembered that his father was a stickler for proper English and grammar. He had a huge library and was well read in such diverse fields as constitutional law, history, and literature. "In his political views," said David, "he was a left-leaning liberal. He was a very strong nationalist. He loved Mike Pearson. He liked Red Tories too."

David and Norman became estranged in the mid-1960s, largely over the son's radical politics. But during the second night of a mass hippie demonstration in Toronto's Yorkville district, as police moved in to break up a sit-in, Norman waded into the crowd, inebriated, shouting at the cops: "Cossacks, Cossacks, arrest me!" On orders from the officer in charge, the police *did not* arrest the CBC icon. In an interview in early 2015, David, a seventy-one-year-old grandfather and still a social activist, said: "That was our reconciliation. I've taken a lot of my values from him. He had a strong belief in fairness and justice."

Norman DePoe died on March 13, 1980, three weeks short of his sixty-third birthday. Five hundred people attended his funeral; his will stipu-lated that the drinks at the wake were on him. He is buried in Toronto's

Mount Pleasant Cemetery, facing Yonge Street in midtown Toronto — not far from Knowlton Nash and Larry Zolf, two other CBC legends. As he wanted, the inscription on the footstone beneath a towering copper beech reads: "He was a good reporter."

Part VII

TRIPLE PLAY

Chapter 15

PETER C. NEWMAN: COURT JESTER TO POWER

Peter Charles Newman was on the run again. At eleven he and his sister escaped from the Nazis in Czechoslovakia with their parents, landing at Pier 21 in Halifax in September 1940. As a Jewish schoolboy at stuffy Upper Canada College, Peta was an outsider, struggling to speak English and to gain acceptance.

In the winter of 1957 he arrived in Ottawa, fleeing a failed marriage and leaving a baby daughter behind in Toronto, to prove himself once more in another hostile environment, the Parliamentary Press Gallery. He was twenty-eight and underwhelmed. "The Crown Jewel of Canadian Political Journalism was a dump," he wrote in his autobiography, *Here Be Dragons*. As for his new colleagues, "They had become stenographers instead of investigators, agreeing on the story 'line,' operating as a captive Rat Pack."

When Peter left the gallery eleven years later he had moved over to *Maclean's*. He and his talented new wife, Christina, had revolutionized the coverage of politics in Canada and launched a multi-million-dollar industry based on his books, TV shows, and public speaking. Restless as ever and lured by the cash, he took a new job as editor-in-chief of the *Toronto Star*. However, troubled by the lack of independence he experienced there, he went back to run *Maclean's* and turned the struggling monthly into a successful weekly newsmagazine. In 2018, amid plummeting advertising sales, it reverted to a monthly publication with a weekly online edition.

As the author of a series of books on the Canadian business elite, Newman became the most celebrated — at times, the most reviled — journalist in the country. In his own words, "I donated myself to various causes, the main one being to gain recognition for myself as the authoritative Boswell of Canada's various establishments." Or, as he also put it, "a court jester to the Establishment."

Before the war, the Neumanns (as they were known before Pier 21) had it all. His father was the sugar beet king of Břeclav, *his* Czech company town an hour north of Vienna, where Peter was born on May 10, 1929. Young Peter had a pet deer in his private zoo on the grounds of the family estate. There was a pool and toys were everywhere. He was chauffeured to school and entertained by doting nannies, and he enjoyed everything in life except "a feeling of acceptance" by austere but loving parents. As Hitler's storm troopers marched closer to Břeclav, Oscar Neumann decided it was time to flee. With one bag each, and Wanda Neumann's valuable jewellery as a cash generator, the family set off on a harrowing eighteen-month exodus, first to Prague, then Venice, and then Paris, Bordeaux, and Biarritz, where they survived German machine-gun strafing on the beach and boarded a battered freighter for England and safety.

These lessons in human survival helped Newman to navigate the strange world of Upper Canada College — with its canings, sexual tensions, and bullying — and to speak fluent English, if only to avoid the mockery of his classmates. He joined the navy reserve, mainly because the "CANADA" flash on the uniform signalled that "you are a Canadian." Later he also became editor of *Crowsnest,* the navy magazine. During an interview in 2015, he told me: "It wasn't much of a job, but I loved it. Instead of parading around, I was writing."

After leaving the navy he attended the University of Toronto where he discovered a world of Canadian writers, from historian Donald Creighton to political columnist Bruce Hutchison to novelist Hugh MacLennan — all must reading to this day — as well as international stars Norman Mailer, Ernest Hemingway, and Aldous Huxley. He also published his first poem in a literary journal and won a prize.

He left school in search of a paycheque after his father's death in 1950 and his marriage to Patricia McKee the next year — he was a self-styled twenty-one-year-old virgin. He landed a lowly job at Ron McEachern's *Financial Post*, summarizing corporate reports. But he had flair. In an article on a baldness treatment, he wrote, "the only thing that stops hair from falling is the floor." His natural ability led to a posting in the Montreal bureau where his fluent French — he also spoke German and Czech — proved an asset. After a brief stint back in Toronto, *Maclean's* recruited him as Ottawa columnist while incumbent Blair Fraser was on an extended European assignment.

Then John Diefenbaker entered his life — and the rest is history.

In the 1957 election campaign, when Diefenbaker toppled the St. Laurent government and ended twenty-two straight years of Liberal rule, the Tory leader managed to brand the Liberals as an arrogant party that abused the rights of Parliament. But there was more. He evoked a vision of a proud and united nation, with a northern vision for resource development, increased Canadian ownership, and reduced taxes. When new Liberal leader Lester Pearson maladroitly demanded that the Tories hand back power to the Grits in his first session, Diefenbaker seized on the debacle in the House and called a snap election for March 1958. Newman described the prime minister in full campaign mode as "a personification of the national will for whom all things were possible." He added: "When he stood bareheaded in the rain addressing a small outdoor crowd at Penticton, B.C., I watched some of his listeners deliberately closing their umbrellas. In Fredericton, a crush of swooning women held their children up to touch him."

Actually, Diefenbaker's massive majority victory served only as a prelude to a decade of rancour and bitterness on the national stage, leading to new elections in 1962, 1963, 1965, and 1968. It was a period when separatism was on the rise in Quebec and other demands reverberated from the rest of the provinces. The backdrop on the global stage was the Vietnam War and women's liberation, but Ottawa got Diefenbaker vs. Pearson. At the beginning Diefenbaker launched several positive initiatives: a nationwide highway, a new bill of rights, tax cuts, assistance to Prairie farmers, and a Commonwealth leadership role on world issues.

But even in the early months there were rumblings about dissent in Cabinet. Despite the greatest majority in Canadian history, Diefenbaker proved to be indecisive. Cabinet spent months toing and froing about the cost of building a supersonic interceptor before finally killing the CF-100, known as the Avro Arrow, along with numerous jobs and the pride of Canadian aviation. While Diefenbaker atoned for Riel and reclaimed Quebec for the Tories with fifty seats in 1958, he ignored the province by failing to appoint any francophones to senior Cabinet posts. That neglect haunted the party for a generation. He bowed to Washington and approved the installation of Bomarc missile bases for northern defence, but refused to arm them with nuclear warheads despite his NATO commitment. He picked a public fight with the Bank of Canada governor over interest rates that ended badly: James Coyne left after making his case before the Liberal-dominated Senate. Diefenbaker was unable to forge a solid relationship with U.S. president John F. Kennedy. Along the way to defeat, Diefenbaker devalued the dollar and saw seventeen of his ministers quit his Cabinet or retire. He lived for campaigning, but he failed at governing. As Newman observed: "His government never demonstrated any clear purpose except to retain power."

Still, the gritty campaigner managed to hold the Liberals to a minority in the 1963 and 1965 elections. Then he forced his party into a messy and protracted leadership confrontation that culminated in the election of Robert Stanfield in 1967. But Diefenbaker and his rump of westerners remained in the Commons, upholding their angry vision of "One Canada."

The gory details of Diefenbaker's Cabinet revolt and his demise formed the heart of Newman's 1963 book, *Renegade in Power: The Diefenbaker Years*. It was a sensation. Newman employed the creative devices of the novel, where the story had a beginning, a middle, and an end. There were good guys and bad girls, racy dialogue, and anecdotes from behind the curtain. And telling detail — in one illustration of the disorder that characterized the prime minister's office, Newman wrote: "In the fall of 1957 Diefenbaker lost a personal letter from President Dwight Eisenhower, although it contained some points that required reply. After weeks of searching by his staff, Diefenbaker found the letter himself — under his bed at 24 Sussex Drive. Some eighteen months later, when Eisenhower asked Diefenbaker to Washington, his invitation went unacknowledged for three weeks."

Newman's accounts of the Coyne crisis and the Cabinet revolt over defence policy were riveting. The detail revealed a reporter with a firm grip on the nation's finances and public policy. At the heart of his disclosures were diaries that a dozen insiders agreed to keep, on condition that their contents would be revealed only after Diefenbaker was no longer prime minister. "Most of the book came from those notes," Newman told me. One of the key government insiders was Roy Faibish. Officially he was executive assistant to the agricultural minister but, Newman wrote, in actual fact he was "the government's only intellectual" — and Newman's greatest source for the book. When I noted with surprise that Newman could get people to be so free with state secrets, he replied: "Well, so was I, frankly. It was because people who worked for Dief found him very ungrateful."

That certainly was the word for Dief's reaction to *Renegade*. He considered suing for libel, but abandoned the idea. In a note in his own hand, preserved at the Diefenbaker Canada Centre of the University of Saskatchewan, the Chief wrote:

> Then there is Newman. Here is the literary scavenger of the trash baskets on parliament hill. He is in close contact with the Liberal hierarchy and gets his briefings from them as that what [*sic*] he should publish.... He is an innately evil person who seems intent on tearing other people to pieces. Seems honourable people have no protection from his mind and pen. He makes his fortune in doing so. NOTE: He is an import from VIENNA!

In the beginning, Newman admired Diefenbaker. Their relations were friendly — as were the Chief's dealings with other key members of the press gallery. "He liked that I was from Czechoslovakia — Hitler and all that stuff — and that I survived," Newman said. "For a while we had a really good relationship. Then I could see he was a really great orator and a great presence, but he wasn't a great prime minister. He had never administered anything more complicated than a two-man, walk-up law office. He had a country to run, and he couldn't."

But the runaway success of *Renegade* had a profound impact on Newman as well. As Conservative political guru Dalton Camp astutely observed, "Newman's fame soon became his notoriety: the true victim of *Renegade in Power* was not Diefenbaker, but Newman." Newman admitted in his autobiography: "Truer words were never writ. The success of the book was the beginning of the end for Peter Newman and the end of the beginning for Peter C. Newman."

Years later, after their marriage had ended, Christina wrote to Peter about the changes she saw in him after *Renegade*: "From that time on, the tendency already in you to make a fiction out of yourself began to distance you from reality.… The intense fame became too much for you and gradually took more and more of your real self, until you were left as nothing much but a terrified ambition."

That strikingly brutal passage appeared in Newman's own autobiography. When I asked him to elaborate, he was visibly uncomfortable. "All of this was mixed in with Christina and I drifting apart. That really was the end of me. It was a very happy marriage for seventeen years." What did she mean? "Well," he replied, "I guess what she meant was that I had illusions of grandeur. It was probably true. I don't deny anything she wrote because I really admired her. She was incredibly intelligent."

Bathing in his newfound celebrity after *Renegade*, Newman turned his sights on Lester Pearson and the Liberals after their minority government victory in 1963. And he jumped at the chance to become Ottawa columnist for the *Toronto Star*, following his mentor Ralph Allen who had moved from *Maclean's* to be the paper's managing editor. With that, Newman acquired a syndicated column in thirty Canadian dailies with a combined circulation of two and a half million readers, the largest of any columnist in the country. Diefenbaker and Pearson provided the grist. "During the curious decade when this odd couple ran our affairs," Newman wrote, "the two men expected the worst of each other and were seldom disappointed." As for his new role, "I became chief chronicler of the carnage, secure in the knowledge that the worse the government, the better the copy."

Under Lester Pearson, things tended to go from bad to worse. His initial "sixty days of decision" featured enough indecision to give Diefenbaker, intent on toppling the minority government, one opening after another. Finance Minister Walter Gordon produced an ill-advised budget that slapped a 30 percent tax on foreign purchases of Canadian stocks and then had to admit under Commons questioning that it had been prepared with the help of three outsiders from Bay Street. Newman was getting all of the background detail down for his *Star* readers from the likes of Keith Davey, then national Liberal Party director, and Mike McCabe, executive assistant to Finance Minister Mitchell Sharp. He got so many scoops on Cabinet secrets that Pearson once threatened to fire any minister who leaked to Newman — a fact Newman duly reported in his column two days later.

"The sixty days of decision had unaccountably turned into ninety days of disaster and the character of the man who was to be Prime Minister of Canada for the next five years was thrown into cruel relief." So wrote Newman in his next mega-seller, *The Distemper of Our Times*. Like *Renegade*, the book was in the style of *The Making of the President*, the groundbreaking 1960 work by U.S. political journalist Theodore H. White. Christina was his able editor and muse. The couple became the toast of official Ottawa. They partied with Pearson and with renowned photographer Yousuf Karsh, and entertained Pierre Trudeau, the dashing minister of justice, and his date, Madeleine Gobeil, a noted journalist and professor of French literature. Newman had known Trudeau as a professor in Montreal and was among the first to promote him in print as the next Liberal leader. When Trudeau won the prize in 1968, Newman congratulated him. "Now," he told the prime minister, "I'll be able to obtain leaks from all the departments, not only Justice." Trudeau retorted: "Listen, the first Cabinet leak you get, I'll have the RCMP tap your telephone."

Newman abandoned Ottawa in early 1969 to become the *Star*'s editor-in-chief. There was little love lost with his old Ottawa colleagues. "You didn't much like the press gallery," I recalled. "They didn't much like me," Newman responded. Indeed, Newman was bitter that the gallery's pooh-bahs denied him the traditional leave-taking gift — an engraved pewter mug. Years later he reminded me that I had arranged for his very own gallery mug. He seemed pleased.

In Toronto, Newman quickly found out that his direct responsibilities embraced only the editorial and opinion pages. That, in addition to having the "second to last word" on editorial direction under publisher Beland Honderich, made his *Star* stint a short one. In 1971 he went back to *Maclean's* as editor. Wily Lloyd Hodgkinson, the head of the parent company's magazine division, had told Newman that if he did not accept the job he was going to close the money-losing magazine. That tugged on the Canadian nationalist in Newman, who plunged onto creating a rival to *Time Canada* — and used his Ottawa connections to secure federal support for Canadian magazines.

It is a testament to Newman's work ethic — and able senior staff — that he not only edited a magazine and published major books on the Canadian establishment through the decade, but also continued mining his Ottawa sources for political insights and news. Just like his idol Bruce Hutchison in years past, Newman would swoop into town from Toronto, make a call on his magazine's Ottawa bureau, and then head off into the night, vacuuming the town for tips and tidbits.

Newman made one of his most dramatic finds while still at the *Star*. He uncovered a rumour about the real reason for the Trudeau government's imposition of the War Measures Act in 1970: to abort a plan by influential Quebecers to replace the floundering regime of Premier Robert Bourassa with a provisional government. The *Star* was jittery. Publisher Honderich and a libel lawyer reviewed the text word by word. It was a secondary story placed on page 1 of the October 26 edition — its provenance disguised by a "From our Ottawa bureau" byline — and it mentioned no names of alleged plotters:

BEHIND WAR MEASURES ACT
PLAN TO SUPPLANT
QUEBEC GOVERNMENT
CAUSED OTTAWA TO ACT

Citing unnamed "top-level sources," Newman wrote: "The Trudeau administration believed that a group of influential Quebecers had set out to see whether they might supplant the legitimately elected provincial government with what they conceived of as an interim administration having enough moral authority to restore public order." According to the story, the feds believed that "could have ended in the destruction of democracy in Quebec."

Peter and Christina picked up the rumour while making the rounds in Ottawa. According to Newman's memoir, Marc Lalonde, Trudeau's chief aide, summoned them to his East Block office. After warning that he would deny talking to them if his name became attached to the report, he said a group of prominent Quebecers, including separatist leaders René Lévesque and Jacques Parizeau, militant union boss Marcel Pepin, and *Le Devoir* editor Claude Ryan, were plotting to replace the Bourassa government. With disbelief, the journalists said they would not publish the report unless Trudeau confirmed it directly. Back in their hotel room they received a call from Trudeau. In *Dragons* Newman quotes the prime minister saying, "I can confirm it.... This move toward a parallel power must be stopped."

The next evening Peter and Christina attended *the* social event of the season, the annual party thrown by the town's reigning power couple, Bernie and Sylvia Ostry, at their Five Oaks mansion across the Ottawa River in Quebec. Amid the tinkle of glasses, talk of the conspiracy was rife. Back in Toronto, Newman was astounded when Mayor Jean Drapeau, in his re-election victory speech on October 25, thanked supporters for resisting revolutionary attacks "but also attempts to set up a provisional government." That was the confirmation Newman needed, although he insisted he was only "reporting what I had been told, without subscribing to the notion myself."

But it was not a double-sourced story in the standard journalistic sense, as history would reveal. Ryan, as well as Lévesque, roundly denounced the report, several news organizations discredited the tale, and credible historians said it never happened.

Ryan, as it turned out, was the indirect source of the rumour. After the FLQ kidnapping of Quebec justice minister Pierre Laporte, Ryan called an emergency Sunday editorial board meeting at *Le Devoir* to discuss ways of strengthening the hand of Premier Robert Bourassa. One of the options mooted, but rejected by staff members in attendance, was enlisting community leaders to restore Bourassa's slipping grip in a provisional government. That night Ryan discussed the proposition with Lucien Saulnier, chairman of Montreal's executive committee. Appalled by the notion, Saulnier in turn reported it to Drapeau and Lalonde. By the time it got to Trudeau, Ryan's trial balloon was a full-blown *coup d'état*.

Ryan and Lévesque initially denied they plotted to form an alternative government. But both later conceded that discussions had taken place, according to an excellent summary of events by former Bourassa minister William Tetley in *The October Crisis, 1970*. Despite the denials of any conspiracy by Ryan, Lévesque, and others, forty-five years later Newman said bluntly: "Whether they were actually going to do it or whether they were just talking about it, I don't know. Certainly there was a conspiracy." It was, as Peter prophetically told Christina at the time, "the story of the decade."

For the next eleven years, in addition to saving *Maclean's,* Newman produced his towering series of books on the Canadian business establishment. His 1979 marriage to Camilla Turner, his third, ended in 1990. Six years later he settled down with psychologist Alvy Bjorklund, whom he playfully called "my last damn wife." Newman also continued inventing new national leaders. Trudeau, in the end, was a big disappointment. "We took him on faith and he broke it," he concluded. He actively promoted the Liberal leadership ambitions of "the Honorable Member from Bay Street," John Turner; he was dismayed when the hero of corporate Canada could not seem to shake off the must accumulated in his burgundy-toned banquette at Winston's, then the financial district's lunchtime haunt. Joe

Peter Newman interviewing Brian Mulroney at Harrington Lake.

Clark he dismissed, in one of his many crazy metaphors, as resembling "a wild fawn caught eating broccoli." He then ushered Brian Mulroney onto the national stage, but eventually fell out with him in a dispute over rights to a book based on taped interviews with the Tory prime minister. "To give him his due," Newman told me, "he never complained about what was in the book. He complained that there *was* a book." Next, Newman put down Jean Chrétien's longevity in office not to bold policies but to the unpopularity of his rivals. His next white knight was Michael Ignatieff, made Liberal leader in 2005 — someone, said Newman, who "could be just the man for our time."

We now know how that ended. Newman ran with his "man for our time" idea for a while and started writing an upbeat book on Ignatieff. The project ended as the sad story of the leader's demise in Newman's 2012 book, *When the Gods Changed: The Death of Liberal Canada*.

The critics accused Newman of constantly chasing stardust. In a 1989 *Books in Canada* review of Newman's *Sometimes a Great Nation*, writer Norman Snider argued: "Newman has indefatigably mythologized a rogue's gallery of swarthy pols and carpetbagging CEOs with the 'glowing light' of his undiminished enthusiasm. In sensibility, if not taste, he is Canada's Andy Warhol, displaying a promiscuous adoration of wealth, power, and celebrity, in whatever form they may take."

Newman tended to apply the *coup de grâce* after the battle was over. True, he did curry favour with the elite, and he protected his friendly sources from scrutiny. But in the end he also ushered his main characters to their inevitable demise, usually gleefully. His usual reaction to the downfall of the people he venerated was one of lamentation — for the lost hope of the leader who might have been, for the country he genuinely loved. In truth, Newman said it best in *Here Be Dragons*: "I was in search of a hero, all right. But the hero, I blush to admit, was me." In the winter of 2016 the quest went on. Peter C. Newman, stooped and shuffling at eighty-six, his memory fading, was putting the finishing touches on a book about the United Empire Loyalists of Upper Canada — another tribe that went out across the wilderness in search of acceptance and respectability.

Chapter 16

ANTHONY WESTELL: THE CONTRARIAN

Tony Westell was a studious schoolboy during the blitz in England when German incendiary bombs rained down on Exeter, the cathedral city in southwest England. He became a "firewatcher," one of the countless volunteers who donned a steel helmet to fight the flames with buckets of water. Little did young Anthony know, but his alertness to bombshells would prove useful in a journalistic career that took him from the banks of the River Exe to the halls of Westminster and the press gallery in Ottawa — with not a few explosions that his own work ignited along the way.

A contrarian who opposed the conventional wisdom of politics and journalism — and even the rules of his own trade — Westell became a role model as a reporter, columnist, and journalism professor. He was a mature thirty-eight, well schooled in the ways of politicians, when he arrived on Parliament Hill in the fall of 1964. Those years were the nadir of parliamentary politics, with poisoned battles between Prime Minister Lester Pearson and Conservative leader John Diefenbaker. Mercifully, that gave way to Pierre Trudeau and Robert Stanfield, and changing times. Westell was a chief witness. But he was also a player who made a difference with his journalism.

He landed the first blows during the 1965 campaign, his first, by calling John Diefenbaker to account in unique fashion. Through the election, Pearson struggled to obtain an elusive majority government against a backdrop of ministerial scandals and the renewed fire of the old Tory leader, a man who lived to campaign. Whistle-stopping by train across the land, his jowls shaking, his arms waving, Diefenbaker enthralled audiences with tales of Liberal skullduggery. But he also dispensed "fake news." He would read from "secret" documents that were not secret, or cite imaginary quotes from Hansard. Diefenbaker, Westell concluded, was "careless with the truth." The reporter found himself constantly inserting brackets in his copy, correcting the-record-according-to-Diefenbaker. "I was determined to be fair, but it seemed to me that simply to report what he said lent credibility to what was untrue as a matter of established fact," he wrote in his autobiography, *The Inside Story: A Life in Journalism.*

It also bothered Westell that constantly inserting notes in his copy seemed to betray bias and feed the notion that press gallery reporters were out to get Diefenbaker. So Westell, with the *Globe*'s agreement, dropped off the campaign and went to the library for several days of research. In a resulting op-ed analysis, he cited chapter and verse of Diefenbaker's untruths, mainly linking Liberals to mobsters — one of whom had actually entered Canada when the Conservatives were in power. Westell dismissed the idea that reporters should simply be "stenographers," and wrote in the *Globe*: "At the back of many reporters' minds there was a memory of the McCarthy years in the United States. The press helped boost McCarthy to power by reporting factually and uncritically his allegations which were known to be untrue…. Diefenbaker in this campaign is conducting a witch hunt not for Communists but for criminals in the government."

In an interview in his condo overlooking downtown Toronto in August 2014, Westell, then eighty-eight, told me: "I filed the story with great trepidation. I felt this is breaking all sorts of rules. Actually, the *Globe* loved it. The piece caused a stir in the press gallery because it was a different sort of reporting — and it was different for me, too. I hadn't tried that before."

Diefenbaker eventually paid Westell the ultimate compliment when, challenging one of his articles in the Commons, he referred to "Mr. Weasel — I beg his pardon, Mr. Westell."

The 1965 election gave rise to another mini-drama over reportorial accuracy, one that is instructive in this age of instant digital communications. This time Westell did not prevail. During a visit to a Liberal committee room in Toronto late in the campaign, Pearson gave his troops an impromptu pep talk: "Now, it's very important to get the Liberals elected because we're the only party that has a chance of forming a majority government. If we don't get a majority government, we're going to get another election in a year or a year and a half — and who wants that?"

CP reporter Dave McIntosh rushed a bulletin to newsrooms across the country: "Prime Minister Pearson said today there will be another election in a year or 18 months if the Liberals don't win a majority on Nov. 8." In the meantime Pearson and his entourage had climbed on an airplane to attend a rally in Vancouver. Not until he arrived was he made aware of the controversy that was brewing. Both of his chief opponents, Diefenbaker and the NDP's Tommy Douglas, had denounced him for arrogance. People phoning in to the hotline shows were raging about the implied threat of another election. Livid, Pearson denied making the statement. "When did I say that?" he demanded. "I said no such thing."

The trouble was, Toronto radio station CFRB had a tape of the Pearson quote. Ted Rogers, the Conservatives' radio strategist, put the Pearson statement and his denial together and distributed the package to some eighty stations, including his own CHFI, ensuring that the contradictory Pearson quotes would play every hour for days.

Globe correspondent Geoffrey Stevens, travelling with the Liberals, argued that the Pearson quote was a rhetorical statement of the obvious and urged the paper not to go with the CP angle. Westell also weighed in, supporting Stevens. But the paper, whose editor was no friend of Pearson, went with the McIntosh version and the headline: "PM's Hint of New Vote Called Arrogance." Pearson won the election but not his coveted majority.

———————

As a boy, Westell had faced adversities with stoicism. When he was six his mother died from complications from a gallstone operation. "The death of my mother," he wrote, "must of course have been a defining moment in my life, but I have few memories of her." Although he passed the Oxford entrance exams at fifteen, he left school in 1941 because his father did not have enough money to send him on. He took an apprentice job at the local newspaper, the *Express & Echo*, where he was required to learn typing and shorthand — the latter an essential tool in assuring factual accuracy. His first assignments were writing notes about local films from theatre publicity handouts and covering funerals; a mention of the funeral home garnered a few shillings from the undertaker. He also covered the police courts and, under threat of dismissal, learned the correct usage of *affect* and *effect*.

After twenty months, at seventeen he signed up for the Royal Navy and saw uneventful service in Hong Kong and the Pacific. Back from the war, he moved upcountry to bombed-out Bristol in 1948, where he became a reporter for the *Evening World* and, more importantly, met a fellow reporter, the tall, attractive Jeannie Collings. Although her rooming house had no running water, Westell recalls, she came to work "every day like a butterfly, with clean gloves and starched blouse, having done her laundry in a bowl on the gas ring."

They married on January 10, 1950, spending only a few shillings for a licence and two doormen at St. Pancras Town Hall — "a cost we have amortized at four cents a year, which seems a reasonable bargain, at least for me." Sixty-five years later they were still a strong, supportive unit when I visited with them in Toronto, proud of their two children and their partners, and two grandchildren. Westell's dedication in his 2002 biography was telling: "For Jeannie, who made my career possible at the cost of her own."

From Bristol he made it to London in 1949 as a "lobby correspondent" (political reporter) for the ten-paper Northcliffe chain, covering Conservative opposition leader Winston Churchill's attempts to unseat the minority Labour government. On the side, he stepped into "the real Fleet Street" as a freelance contributor to the *Sunday Express*, eventually writing editorials and the *Crossbencher* column. That piece parroted the thinking of Canadian-born owner Lord Beaverbrook, who called in his *pensées* by telephone. In 1954 he moved to the *Evening Standard* as diplomatic correspondent and deputy editor under patron Charles Wintour.

Events conspired to give Westell a run of international travel and front page news, including the death of Stalin, Khrushchev's debut as Communism's salesman on the world scene, Churchill's retirement, and the emergence of Anthony Eden as foreign minister. On Fleet Street Westell learned two valuable techniques that served him well throughout his career: an ease with formulating an analysis of the facts and a comfort with dictating a story live on a deadline. After meeting the *Globe's* managing editor on a visit to London, Westell parlayed his record into a job and a new life for

his young family in Toronto. He started on general assignment in 1954 at
$111 a week, one dollar above union scale (about $1,000 in 2018 dollars),
but was soon covering local politics.

From the city hall beat he moved to editorial writing under editor
Oakley Dalgleish and, after his death, under Dic Doyle. After less than eight
years in Canada Westell took over the *Globe*'s bureau in Ottawa. Because of
the paper's agenda-setting role in the capital, Westell admits, "I had standing
and access long before I had earned it." But like the new breed on the Hill,
he kept a distance between himself and the people he covered. Westell also
rattled the conventions of the boys' club in the press gallery during the
gender wars of the late sixties. A rump group forced a surprise vote that
changed the policy preventing female members from attending the annual
off-the-record black-tie gallery dinner. To prevent a scheme to reverse the
decision, Westell got a colleague to invite Secretary of State Judy LaMarsh as
his guest, and Westell escorted the popular Conservative Flora MacDonald.
Westell also picketed the annual Press Club ball after members voted to ban
women as members.

The year 1967 was a special time in the affairs of the country. The
highlight of year-long Centennial celebrations was the magical Expo 67
World's Fair in Montreal on islands created in the St. Lawrence from earth
dug from tunnels for the new subway system. In politics, there was a major
tilling of ground as well, as both Conservatives and Liberals staged leadership
conventions. The major question in the Liberal Party was whether Pearson
would hang on for a major upcoming constitutional conference or make
way for a new leader. Westell, along with several of his senior colleagues,
liked Pearson. They embraced his social policies, his internationalism, his
commitment to accommodate Quebec's aspirations, and his recent proposals
for official bilingualism. His summary was succinct: "I always got on well
with Pearson. I admired him. He did eventually achieve a great deal as prime
minister. He was not an inspiring leader."

In November 1967 Westell took the mood of the Liberal caucus and
wrote a devastating piece about Pearson's government on the second anniversary of its 1965 re-election. The decay, he wrote, was in part because
of uncertainty about Pearson's own leadership. Under the headline, "A
not-so-happy Liberal anniversary," it read in part: "With three years of
its mandate still to run, the Pearson Cabinet today is showing symptoms

of disintegration that may be the prelude to its collapse.… The Liberals are now in danger of following the Conservative course over the edge of the precipice."

Later that day Pearson's minister of finance, Walter Gordon, had what he called "a straight talk" with the PM in his office after question period. In a private memo, he later wrote: "I said the Westell article in the *G&M* this morning is a fair reflection of the situation in my opinion — and the views expressed by members. Mike agreed." Six days later Pearson announced his intention to retire, insisting later that he had long intended to resign at that time. "So," Westell concluded, "I cannot claim to have persuaded him out of office, but I may have nudged him."

In retirement, Pearson was stung by assertions from within his party and the press that in 1965 he had sacrificed French-Canadian Cabinet ministers — Justice Minister Guy Favreau and his successor, Lucien Cardin — to save his own skin when the government was under assault over its handling of influence peddling and espionage cases. The issue came up at a lunch Westell arranged for Pearson, then in retirement, in 1969. Joined by gallery friend W.A. "Bill" Wilson at the Rideau Club, Westell listened as Pearson told the two journalists he had been "wounded" by accusations in books from his former minister Judy LaMarsh and journalist Peter Newman. Wilson and Westell were among the gallery thought leaders at the time and had a shared vision of journalism based on analysis and context, not flash headlines. They offered to write Pearson's side of the story, provided he turned over his personal papers and diaries.

Pearson was an inveterate note-taker and pack rat. While he did not keep a regular diary, his custom was to dictate memos to himself after key events. In the trove, Westell and Wilson found letters from Favreau and Cardin thanking Pearson for honouring them with Cabinet posts and apologizing that they both had let him down.

Westell and Wilson produced a lengthy series that ran in papers across the country, including the *Toronto Star* and the *Winnipeg Free Press*, reviving memories of the two scandals that dominated the politics of 1965. In the most vivid affair, a member of Favreau's staff and other Liberal aides had attempted to secure bail for mobster Lucien Rivard, but Pearson said he did not remember Favreau briefing him on the case. Cardin, meanwhile, had rejected demands that charges be filed against a Vancouver postal clerk for selling information to the Russians but, in the heat of the battle, Pearson authorized a public inquiry. One royal commission criticized Favreau's handling of the Rivard affair, and he resigned to take a lesser Cabinet post and eventually left government and died at age fifty, they say, of a broken heart. The second inquiry into allegations about the alleged post office spy exonerated Cardin, who went on as justice minister to launch accusations about the famous Munsinger case, in which a third inquiry determined that Diefenbaker had mishandled a security case.

In 1969, when Peter Newman left the gallery to take up the post as editor-in-chief of the *Toronto Star*, he recruited Westell to take over his Ottawa column, which came with a then-considerable $20,000 salary (about $140,000 today) and 50 percent of the syndication revenues. But after two years — and having won his third National Newspaper Award — Westell decided to give up the three-column per week grind for academia. More interested in analysis than reporting, Westell also was concerned that journalism was fast becoming "adversarial and destructive rather than supportive of democratic institutions. We seemed to be exercising power without responsibility."

As a visiting professor at Carleton University, Westell continued writing a weekly column for the *Star* and started research on what became an important book: *Paradox: Trudeau as Prime Minister*. He also began picking away at a paper on the future of journalism that he had promised to do for publisher Beland Honderich before leaving the staff. It was an eye-opener in 1973 and is remarkable today for its extraordinary prescience. The day of the mass circulation, something-for-everyone newspaper, Westell proclaimed, was dead. "The first generation of the post-industrial society is now emerging from the universities to become citizen-consumers," he wrote. "The price of survival will be to meet the needs of this market of specialists." He added:

> What is the role of the newspaper when the city worker hears three radio newscasts as he drives home from his office, turns on the 6 p.m. TV news as he has a drink before dinner — and then picks up his afternoon paper? … Further, there will be more and more news on TV as channels multiply and satellites relay the world to the

world. The TV mass market is already fragmenting and as
it divides into smaller sections broadcasters will become
increasingly specialized. Movies on one channel. News
on another channel, 24 hours a day. And already much
of the commentary and analysis on TV is equal to that
in newspapers.*

The *Star* confronted the reach of TV by switching publication to a
morning paper, but declined to enter the brave new world of specializa-
tion. Publisher Honderich and editor Martin Goodman had encouraged
Westell to pursue his ideas, though, by approving a new "super bureau" in
Ottawa, headed by Westell. The idea was that an expanded bureau of ten
would specialize in key policy areas. Westell recruited veteran journalist
Carl Mollins from CP as bureau chief, hired Richard Gwyn to replace
Global TV–bound Peter Desbarats as columnist, and assembled a crack
team that included reporters Eric Malling, Ian Urquhart, John Gray, and
David Crane. The daily file was to be edited in Ottawa with minimal
involvement of the desk in Toronto.

The experiment lasted two years and blew up during the 1974 election.
It became clear to Westell, as he put it, that "news editors in Toronto
were not prepared to surrender to us their authority to decide what we
should be reporting and how we should write it. They were happy with
any exclusives we could provide, but their first priority was to match
whatever was on the CP news wire, on the CBC TV news, or in the early
editions of the *Globe*." The desk assigned former *Star* Ottawa bureau
chief Val Sears to the campaign, bumping one of Westell's crew. Mollins
posted his resignation on a bulletin board at the *Star*. Westell penned his
resignation letter to managing editor Ted Bolwell, blaming himself for
the debacle and describing the *Star* as "quite the most extraordinary and
infuriating place in which to work." Said Westell, "That was the end of
my career in journalism."

But it was not the end of his impact on journalism. He went back to
Carleton, first as a visiting fellow in Canadian studies. Even though he
had dropped out after high school, he became director of the school of

---

* Anthony Westell, *The Inside Story: A Life in Journalism* (Toronto: Dundurn, 2002), 186.

journalism and associate dean of arts. He continued writing a column for the *Star*. Along with colleague Alan Frizzell he turned what started as a class exercise into regular election polling for CBC and Southam News. And the old democratic socialist became a post-nationalist believer in free trade, a view he expanded in his 1977 book, *The New Society*, and

Anthony Westell, 1957: lamenting the intrusion of opinion in the news.

in a massive article for the policy magazine *International Perspective*, whose thesis Donald Macdonald embraced in his Royal Commission report on free trade.

Westell also had time to reflect on journalism — and he did not like what he saw. Canadian journalists, he asserted, "suffered an acute attack of Watergate-envy." His journalism students were "gung-ho to investigate and overthrow somebody, anybody, but preferably a politician." Journalism was becoming more personal, "with the journalist as actor packaging the news in dramatic and often judgmental mini-dramas." One of Westell's major complaints, shared by many consumers of media, was the intrusion of opinion in news stories. As Westell wrote: "Who takes the trouble, and the space, to tell us what a politician actually said in a public speech? Instead we get an opinion on whether or not the speech was a political success." It was a lament for the days when reporters specialized in shorthand notes and faithfully reporting who said what to whom, no exceptions.

Westell died in Toronto in April 2017 after complications from metastatic prostate cancer. He was ninety-one, and he went out agitating for reform — in this case, protesting against a doctor's refusal to approve his assisted death.

Chapter 17

RICHARD GWYN: THE REPORTER

When Richard Gwyn agreed to take over the Ottawa column for the *Toronto Star*, Martin Goodman, the managing editor, told him, "What we are looking for from you is a sense of the inside." Gwyn, by then a veteran journalist who had just spent five years as a senior adviser inside the Trudeau government, knew what was expected. "I said to myself," he recalled during a conversation in 2015, "I've got to have something in every column — it might be a small thing — but it had to be new."

It was a code Gwyn mostly honoured during more than a decade at the helm of what became one of the best-read political columns of the era. Every day Gwyn made the rounds of ministers, political aides, and MPs. At the many federal-provincial meetings he could be espied popping in and out of hotel suites after hours for briefings by premiers and officials, or hanging back from a scrum talking quietly to a senior bureaucrat. Typical of his handiwork was the column he produced for the *Star* on Thursday, November 2, 1978, reporting on private meetings between Prime Minister Trudeau and the premiers at a crucial point in the constitutional discussions. Gwyn described how they spent fifteen minutes over a seafood lunch wrangling about the wording of a press release: "During the rest of the time, they agreed to remove from the draft communiqué any reference to anything they had agreed on — except to set up a committee.... At the traditional private dinner at 24 Sussex Tuesday night, one premier told Trudeau to 'take your bill of rights and stuff it.'"

It was not a happy night, although, as Gwyn noted, it was Halloween. Secretly, Gwyn hoped for success in the talks. Although born an Englishman, with a British accent modulated only slightly after six decades in the country, he is a proud Canadian. He calls the constitutional saga "the greatest single event" he covered. "You really had a sense that, if we don't get this, we probably are going to break apart," he said in an interview. "There really was a sense of privilege, of having some kind of inside insight. It really was, 'Can Canada make it?'"

Canadian patriotism came early to Gwyn thanks to a charming Newfoundlander he met on the ferry from St. John's to Halifax shortly after he arrived in Canada at the age of twenty. Her name was Sandra Fraser, and she, too, was going to Halifax after a visit home. At the time he was struggling to make a go selling magazines in St. John's, so he decided to try Halifax and a starter job at a local radio station. Their friendship blossomed and in 1958 they married. He was twenty-three and she was twenty-two, three years out of Dalhousie. Until her death from breast cancer in 2000, they formed a deep bond as partners in love and writing, her touch evident as his prose blossomed through the years. (Gwyn later married another writer, dance historian Carol Bishop, who published an acclaimed biography of the National Ballet of Canada founder, Celia Franca.)

In their Ottawa period, largely bookending the Trudeau era, the Gwyns were one of the capital's power couples. She was Ottawa editor for *Saturday Night* magazine. Her majestic look at post-Confederation Ottawa, *The Private Capital: Ambition and Love in the Age of Macdonald and Laurier*, won the Governor General's Award for non-fiction in 1984. Every year the Gwyns returned to their Newfoundland summer retreat. In honour of Sandra Gwyn and her devotion to the island's arts and culture, Richard established the annual Winterset Award to recognize outstanding writers.

Both were recipients of the Order of Canada. Over the years, Gwyn's work was recognized in a National Magazine Award for investigative reporting and in four National Newspaper Awards. As the author of seven books, most notably on politicians Joey Smallwood, Pierre Trudeau, and John A. Macdonald, Gwyn carved a legacy of excellence that stands the test of time. In the early 1980s his colleagues voted him the leading journalist in the press gallery. Dalton Camp, the Tory insider who was one of the most engaging writers about the game, once described Gwyn as "perhaps our best political journalist." His last book, the second volume of his history of John A. Macdonald, was a finalist for the Governor General's Award in 2011 and winner of the Shaughnessy Cohen Prize for political writing in 2012.

Gwyn shrugs off the recognition with typical insouciance. Approaching his eighty-first birthday when we talked, he said with a chuckle: "The big thing in life is to time your birth. I was just ahead of the baby boomers. You didn't have to worry about getting jobs. Women weren't competing with us. Immigrants weren't competing with us. It was just a bunch of people like you and me. Today, you and I would be struggling."

Richard John Philip Jermy Gwyn was born on May 26, 1934, in Bury St. Edmunds, an East Anglian town one hundred and thirty kilometres northeast of London, the son of Brigadier Philip Jermy-Gwyn, an Indian army officer, and Elizabeth Edith Tilley. They sent him away to Stonyhurst College, a private coed Catholic boarding school run by the Jesuits. After that he briefly attended Royal Military Academy Sandhurst before landing in Newfoundland on a planned tour of the world.

From his radio station reporting job in Halifax, Richard moved to United Press International (UPI), where he became low man in the Ottawa bureau in 1957 under bureau chief Bill Neville, later one of the outstanding public policy advisers in the capital. While at UPI, Gwyn scored a world exclusive that Princess Margaret, then twenty-seven, had asked that John Turner, a twenty-nine-year-old Montreal bachelor, be added to the guest list for an official ball in Vancouver in the summer of 1958 where they danced the night away. After three years with UPI, Gwyn "crawled up the ladder" to Thomson Newspapers, "writing little squiggly reports" for the chain of small papers. Then he made "an advance" to Maclean-Hunter business publications, a stable of worthy but grey trade papers (distinguished authors Arthur Hailey and Roy MacGregor also were graduates).

By then Gwyn was starting to get radio and TV work on the side. "For some reason," he notes, "I was good on radio. I had one big disadvantage, which was my English accent. Most listeners hated me. But I was not bad. I started to become a 'small name,' someone who could talk on television and radio."

That major profile boost landed him a job in 1962 as Ottawa correspondent for the Canadian edition of *Time,* which then offered a weekly
section on domestic politics, business, and the arts. While there, Gwyn
took a leave to publish *The Shape of Scandal* in 1965, a penetrating look at
the Pearson government's many self-inflicted wounds. In 1968, during a
stint in Montreal as an associate editor in the magazine's Montreal-based
writing shop, he published *Smallwood: The Unlikely Revolutionary* in 1968.
Time "wanted to send me abroad," he recalled. India was a possibility. "I
realized if I went there, I was a *Time* person for life. I said no. I didn't want
to leave Canada." He knew then that he had to leave *Time.* "If you say no,
that's the end of you."

Next Gwyn signed on with the CBC co-hosting a local TV show, *Seven
on Six,* with journalist Peter Desbarats. "But there was a problem: Desbarats
was the lead, the important one," said Gwyn. "I was running behind him.
I couldn't see how that would change. He was very good looking. He was
very good on air and he was a good guy."

On the side, Gwyn had been working quietly writing speeches for his
friend Eric Kierans, the former head of the Montreal Stock Exchange who
was making a run for the Liberal leadership. Although he lost to Trudeau,
when Kierans got elected to Parliament and became minister of communications he recruited Gwyn as executive assistant. "That's going to be the
end of your career in journalism," Sandra told him. Two years later Gwyn
moved into the bureaucracy under deputy minister Allan Gotlieb, which
proved an invaluable study of government — and, as it turned out, a useful
connection to insiders.

He put all of that to good use when he came back to journalism in
1973 as the *Star*'s syndicated Ottawa columnist. He replaced Desbarats,
who moved to Global TV as a news anchor. Although policy was his beat,
Gwyn liked nothing better than chasing a news scoop. One of his biggest
was his front page exclusive on Sunday, July 1, 1984, revealing that Prime
Minister John Turner, the new Liberal leader, would be calling a summer election. "Circle the date of Sept. 4 on your calendars," Gwyn wrote.
Because the Queen expected to be in Canada later in the month, Gwyn
revealed, Turner "has made plans to fly to London late this week to call on
the Queen at Buckingham Palace to ask her to reschedule for the fall her
July visit to Canada."

Turner's office and the Palace promptly said they had no knowledge of any such plan. But by July 6 the confirmation was there for all to see in the *Star*'s main headline: "Liberals Increase Lead in Gallup as Turner Flies to See the Queen." The election took place, as Gwyn predicted, on September 4. Brian Mulroney defeated Turner.

Luck has always been a key factor in the careers of the best journalists, and Gwyn was no exception. In early 1979, at publisher Jack McClelland's behest, he began researching a book on Pierre Trudeau. Unexpectedly, Joe Clark's Tories won the election and Trudeau stepped down as Liberal leader on June 4. "What was good for me," Gwyn said with a twinkle, "was that he resigned. So suddenly an enormous number of Cabinet ministers, back room types, civil servants blabbed, and with extraordinary candor. They were angry with him, disappointed with him." But then, equally unexpectedly, Trudeau returned to fight the next election. "I thought," said Gwyn, "I am totally screwed. But then I realized I had heard a whole lot of things. I got really terrific insight and reportage on Trudeau. I was sitting on a gold mine."

The result was a 399-page blockbuster, *The Northern Magus*, its cover featuring Trudeau in black and white, garbed in a rakish, broad-brimmed hat and cloak, the only colour a red rose in his lapel. The portrait inside ranged over the petty and personal to the grand moments. There was Trudeau denouncing the press as "crummy" and apologizing to a departing press secretary: "I know I've given you a hard time, but I just can't stand those guys." Gwyn revealed that Trudeau was so infuriated with Margaret's tell-all 1979 autobiography, *Beyond Reason*, that he called the election that year "a couple of months earlier than his advisers had wanted, mostly, as one of them put it, 'to show Margaret.'" (The night he lost she was dancing at Studio 54 in New York.) There was the stunning detail of the backstage manoeuvring that brought Trudeau back from retirement to contest — and win — the election of 1980. And, in the end, there was an assessment of Trudeau's role in defeating the Quebec independence movement and ushering in official bilingualism and a bill of rights in the repatriated Constitution. For all of that, Gwyn placed Trudeau in a league with Sir John A. Macdonald. Alone among all the prime ministers, he wrote, these two "have reinvented history in their own image."

Richard Gwyn at Eden Mills Writers' Festival, 2012: a belief in Canada.

Gwyn, the perpetual optimist, believed that Canadian values were worth fighting for. When he left Britain in the mid-1950s the country was bankrupt. Meanwhile, Canada was booming and as a British immigrant he didn't need a passport. Postwar social programs were taking the sting out of the flinty-eyed meanness of the Depression years. The country flourished. Gwyn never looked back. As he argued in 1997, "the Canadian values of tolerance, civility, and decency are precious and are becoming more and more rare the world over." Returning to the theme of Canadian exceptionalism in his *Star* column in March 2016, Gwyn proclaimed: "A terrible truth can no longer be denied. Its starting point is that for some time now it's been obvious that Canada is one of the most successful countries in the world."

Part VIII

MY TIME

Chapter 18

THE TRUDEAU ENIGMA

Pierre Trudeau was many things to many people, but he was no morning person. Certainly not at eight o'clock. Certainly not in a stale conference room at an Ottawa hotel, the guest at a table of Ottawa journalists. The prime minister was there, at the invitation of our regular breakfast group, because his handlers had told him to make nice with the press.* Boy, was he grumpy.

"What do you want to talk about?" he inquired after some desultory small talk. The Montreal Canadiens had defeated the Philadelphia Flyers the night before in a Stanley Cup playoff game, but Trudeau had gone to bed after the first period and didn't know the score. What *he* wanted to talk about was "selective distortion" of the facts by the press — and this man, who said he never read the papers, had his list of errors: that his father-in-law paid Margaret's shopping bills (not so); that he doesn't have coffee during Cabinet meetings because of the cost (not true). There were some revelations as well. He allowed that he would be out of politics when his eldest son, five-year-old Justin, turned ten. (He missed by two years, but there were extenuating circumstances.)

---

* The group included organizers Peter Desbarats and Geoffrey Stevens, and Richard Gwyn, John Gray, Marjorie Nichols, and Bruce Phillips. Other guests over the years were Tory leader Joe Clark, Ontario premier Bill Davis, and Supreme Court Chief Justice Bora Laskin.

That breakfast, on May 14, 1976, was one of only four times I had the opportunity to engage on a personal level with Pierre Trudeau. The others: a 1978 interview for *Maclean's* at his official residence with bureau colleague Ian Urquhart, on the occasion of his tenth anniversary in power; a convivial dinner aboard his jet with three other gallery members on a return flight to Ottawa from meetings in Tokyo in 1976 (with customary wit, he corrected me when I suggested that he would have had the RCMP after us if we had criticized him the way he had gone after Maurice Duplessis: "Not the RCMP — the army"); and on a chance meeting before another trip abroad at CFB Uplands in Ottawa, when he bent down to shadow box playfully with my two young boys — and mercifully did not take a direct hit. For most of his years in office, I, like most members of the gallery, was a close observer, travelling the world on his plane, reading his speeches and writings, questioning him at press conferences and debriefing his friends, advisers, and opponents. Early on, a friend of mine on Trudeau's staff gave me an important clue to covering the man: read his lips — because he uses exactly the same language in public as he does in private.

Keeping a distance worked best. He had a job to do and so did we. He was a challenging subject to cover, a public man of indisputable intelligence and style who elevated our game. You needed to know your stuff when you confronted him. If you happened to land a telling blow he could be delightfully unpredictable. When my friend and colleague John Gray once demanded to know if he had actually dismissed the Quebec government of Robert Bourassa as "weak" — as he had — Trudeau shot back: "How's your grandmother?" She was dead, as it happened.

In October 1970, CBC reporter Tim Ralfe asked Trudeau how far he would go in dealing with terrorism and elicited the famous reply: "Just watch me." In April 1977 after Alberta Tory Jack Horner crossed the floor and joined the Liberals, Trudeau said at a press conference that the only incentive he had offered was "a chair" in the Commons. That didn't seem like much of an offer, I observed. "Well, he wasn't offering much either," Trudeau responded, as his aides flinched in the background.

He was equally irreverent with the public. In 1968, during his last swing through rural Quebec before the party leadership vote, he defended his bill legalizing homosexuality, explaining patiently that Canada was a pluralistic society.

"What about masturbation?" someone shouted, to audible gasps. With his patented shrug, Trudeau replied: "Well, I suppose everyone has his problems."

In office he told striking Montreal mail delivery workers, "*Mangez de la merde.*" He hoisted his index finger at protesters in Salmon Arm, B.C. He called MPs "nobodies," and he told one MP in the House of Commons to "fuck off."

He really didn't like the newshounds. He once broke off a discussion with a senior adviser because of a looming press conference. "I must go meet the vultures," he said. In 1977, at the height of his very public split with Margaret, he decided to skip the annual press gallery dinner because he was ill at home. "Dying with the sniffles," one aide told me.

Trudeau did not pretend to flatter reporters by asking them for their thoughts. In his breezy memoir, Patrick Gossage, his affable press adviser through the late 1970s, wrote that Mike Duffy, then a CBC reporter, once told him "how hurt he was that Trudeau never personally recognized him in the hundreds of scrums he had thrust his mike into." George Radwanski, a bilingual Montrealer, spent some eight hours interviewing the PM for his 1978 biography, *Trudeau*, yet in a private dinner with other reporters when he retired, Trudeau repeatedly called him Peter.

Despite the slights he inflicted and egos he bruised, he sure was great copy: his pirouette behind the Queen's back at Buckingham Palace in 1977, captured by CP photographer Doug Ball; his boast to reporters in London during a 1969 Commonwealth Conference about having lunch with an unnamed "blonde."

Most of us found his disdain for our ilk amusing. We actually admired his intelligence, his passion, his commitment. We followed him from his earliest days in public life — as the cool justice minister bringing in reforms of the criminal code — and then as the prime minister with a majority government, recognizing mainland China, lowering the voting age from twenty-one to eighteen. He brought to the office a style that Canadians had never seen before. He put us on the map and usually made us proud when he strode the international stage. In the words of former *Globe and Mail* bureau chief Anthony Westell, Trudeau was "the man we would all like to be." My colleague Marjorie Nichols observed astutely that Trudeau was "a phenomenon created by middle-aged men, not women … he was more of a role model, a post–John Kennedy figure, for every middle-aged man in Canada."

When I returned to Ottawa in 1975 for my third stint on the Hill, the bloom was coming off the Trudeau rose despite his majority win the year before. John Turner had resigned as finance minister to go into exile on Bay Street and the power lunch crowd at Winston's. Inflation was at 14 percent. Trudeau mused about a new order to replace the "market system." He brought in gun control and mused that maybe it was time to reconsider the Liberals' historic opposition to the death penalty. There was an overall sense that the government was tired and prone to scandals and cronyism. As I observed in a column in 1976: "After 13 uninterrupted years of Liberalism, Ottawa has become a candy store for party faithful. The distinction between civil service and party duty is now blurred."

Trudeau was ever an enigma. He went from his early days as the philosopher king to Mackenzie King, as Larry Zolf famously put it, falling into the hands of Liberal back-roomers and pollsters as the majority of 1974 evaporated in the defeat of 1979. I tried to sum it up in a profile in 1978:

> He has been purist and pragmatist, arrogant and humble, dashing and dull, a reformer of the head but a conservative of the heart, a self-described "solitary sort of fellow" who perfected the politics of the mob, a government leader who preached economic restraint even as, the *bon vivant,* he sailed the Adriatic with the Aga Khan, a man of fixed personal ways who has never lived in a house of his own — a paradox, in sum, who has provoked every emotion, except indifference.

He was indeed a "solitary sort of fellow." He once told Radwanski, "I know I can be as hurt as anyone and therefore I don't, I never did, just let anybody in." That reserve complicated his relationships with even his closest colleagues from the 1950s. He once said, "Management of men — or women, for that matter — was not my strong suit." Gérard Pelletier once told me that had Trudeau made clear he needed him, he would have stayed in Ottawa as a member of the Cabinet instead of taking the post as Canadian ambassador in Paris. When Jean Marchand resigned and arranged to say farewell to the prime minister over dinner, Trudeau told him he had to be out of the house by nine thirty. It is widely assumed that John Turner would not have left the Trudeau Cabinet if the PM had stroked his ego or given him another senior portfolio.

Perhaps his biggest human relations failure was with Margaret, the dope-smoking flower child he married in 1971. Tellingly, he hesitated at first because of the twenty-eight-year gap in their ages. By 1974, according to Margaret, their communication had broken down and she was starting to seek her independence. She felt isolated, stifled, and ignored. By 1977, when they announced their separation, coincidentally in the wake of the 1976 election of René Lévesque's Parti Québécois, it was as if he had chosen the country over his marriage. In an interview with *Maclean's*, Trudeau told us he would "be lying" if he said that the election of the PQ government "didn't motivate me to stay on for a little longer and make sure I didn't leave the field to separatists."

The first time reporters saw Margaret Trudeau's instability up close was during the prime minister's official Latin American trip in late January 1976 with their youngest son, Michel, then three months old. During a state dinner in Mexico she made impromptu remarks. Then, in Caracas, she turned diplomatic heads when she rose at dinner and sang a halting ode to Blanca Rodríguez de Pérez, wife of the Venezuelan president. Columnist Charles Lynch praised her derring-do ("Sing out, sweet Margaret!"). But mostly Margaret Trudeau faced reprobation. She did not help herself by coming to the back of the plane where she sang her "Ode to Mrs. Perez" into *Toronto Star* reporter Bruce Garvey's tape recorder and took a swig from photographer Rod MacIvor's bottle of rum. Still to come were her freedom rides to New York with the Rolling Stones and several extramarital affairs documented in painful detail in her 1979 book, *Beyond Reason*, published on the eve of her husband's epic confrontation with Lévesque on the future of Quebec in the 1980 referendum.

At one painful press conference in that period that he bore with stoicism, virtually all the questions to Trudeau were about his marriage. It was one of the few press conferences where I could not bring myself to ask a question. It might have been better if Peter Desbarats, a Don Draper figure in his own *Mad Men* day, also had refrained. Did the PM feel his official role was affected by his marriage difficulties? Trudeau: "What about you, Peter, do you think your marriage troubles affect your performance?"

Years later the full extent of Margaret Trudeau's battle with mental health issues shed new light on many of her activities — and the strain it placed on the prime minister at a crucial period in the affairs of the nation. By 1982 a contrite Margaret wrote: "I shall mind all my life that I robbed Pierre of his dignity at various stages of our life together by my unreasoned, hysterical outbursts…. What I did was unpardonable."

For all his woes, Trudeau was present at the big moments. He stood firm against bottle-throwing hoodlums at the final rally of the 1968 election on the night of the Saint-Jean-Baptiste celebrations in Montreal. As other officials, including Mayor Jean Drapeau, ran for cover, Trudeau brushed off his security detail and remained glaring from the stands. Across the street the travelling press corps from Ottawa stood and applauded.

Trudeau's major acts were polarizing. He stood against the FLQ in 1970, incurring the wrath of civil libertarians for the War Measures Act but knowing that the polls showed it was very popular. Arguably, Trudeau prevented the breakup of Canada in the referendum of 1980, but separatism then flourished on his watch. His Charter of Rights established the ground rules for historic decisions — but, critics said, diminished Parliament's sovereignty, resulting in judge-made law. His interventions were a major factor in the defeat of the decentralizing trend of the Meech Lake and Charlottetown accords, but they also killed the attempt to have Quebec sign the Constitution. His implementation of official bilingualism and his recruitment of top politicians and professionals from French Canada altered the face of the federal government, but they caused a backlash in English Canada.

It was difficult for many Anglos to fully appreciate the ardour behind Trudeau's campaign to seize the federal government. He, Jean Marchand, and Gérard Pelletier — the Three Wise Men, as they were dubbed in English, and *les trois colombes* in French — had been leaders in the reform movement during the dark days of the Duplessis regime and its alliance with the clergy in Quebec. They were on the front lines of the Asbestos Strike when provincial police crushed the workers. Later, they watched from the sidelines as Jean Lesage, René Lévesque, and the Liberal reformers swept to power in Quebec City. Meanwhile in Ottawa, a series of French-Canadian ministers in the Pearson Cabinet fell under a barrage of corruption accusations from Tories in western Canada — amplified by the national press corps. Even once he and his comrades had taken over, Marchand displayed his lingering animosity. In an interview in 1978, he told me: "I know damn well that the English press has been repeatedly looking for wrongdoing by French Canadians and has publicized the wrongdoings — or what may seem to be wrongdoings — on the part of French Canadians. It's partly a prejudice against French Canadians."

When *les trois colombes* arrived in Ottawa, the government members of the National Assembly in Quebec represented the centre of power for French Canada. People who wanted action turned to Quebec, not Ottawa. But under Trudeau's leadership French Canadians assumed important roles in government and the bureaucracy. As Trudeau put it famously in the 1968 election, "I am trying to put Quebec in its place — and the place of Quebec is in Canada." How then to explain the rise of separatism on his watch? Trudeau's response in the 1978 *Maclean's* interview: "Ask yourself if that movement would be stronger if we hadn't in the past 10 years done all we did in Ottawa to make French an official language and to show

Cabinet changes, April 4, 1967. Left–right: Pierre Trudeau, John Turner, Jean Chrétien, and Lester Pearson: "The place of Quebec is in Canada."

that French Canadians in Quebec and Ottawa could pull their weight and exercise sufficient power."

At the time, many of us in the gallery had come around to that view. We cut Trudeau some slack because of that. You had a sense not only of an epic story unfolding, but also a conviction that if the federal drive failed, the route led to the breakup of Canada. It was important stuff and you became steeped in the exotica of amending formulas, notwithstanding clauses, and the conflicting demands and personalities of the first ministers. Quebec, indeed, became Trudeau's obsession, often at the cost of issues of concern to other parts of the country, particularly western Canada, where the National Energy Program produced the grievance that fuelled the rise of Reform after Trudeau left office.

Quebec was our big story, too. For two decades Canada was a cauldron of uncertainty: the rise of René Lévesque's Parti Québécois, a series of federal-provincial negotiations on the Constitution, two Quebec referendums, two federal referendums, seven federal elections, five prime ministers, and the installation of Lucien Bouchard's Bloc Québécois as the official opposition. You got to know and deal with premiers and their advisers from coast to coast. Peter Lougheed was in regular contact, having accepted me as a reporter from the East he could trust (perhaps also knowing that I had parents and siblings in Calgary). The gallery teemed with outstanding reporters who competed for exclusives on the national story, including Jeffrey Simpson of the *Globe*, David Halton and Don Newman of CBC News, Daniel Lessard of Radio-Canada, Bill Fox of the *Star*, Lise Bissonnette of *Le Devoir*, and Ian Urquhart of *Maclean's*, among many others. Elly Alboim, the CBC's parliamentary bureau chief, recalled that in the heyday of constitutional talks, the network had fifteen TV reporters on the Hill and often would go live covering constitutional talks for a whole day. Said Alboim: "It was not unusual to have three or four items on the national news that night. We helped set the agenda for the next day."

The culmination of all the talk, including the fabled "Night of the Long Knives" (a secret meeting held without Lévesque to settle on a compromise constitutional formula), and the court battle over patriation, came at 11:35 a.m. on April 17, 1982. That morning Trudeau sat down with Queen Elizabeth at an outdoor table on Parliament Hill to sign the new Constitution — "a defiant challenge to history," in Trudeau's words. Yet, as if to mark the official dissent of the Quebec government, which refused to sign the deal, the first drops of an eventual downpour splattered the Queen's red-lettered introductory protocol greetings, and the proclamation was delayed on its way to the printer for drying out. "We are being royally screwed," Quebec's vice-premier Jacques-Yvan Morin declared. Clearly, the great fight about Canada's future was not over.

One of the dignitaries in morning coat and striped pants in the crowd that day was the new leader of the opposition, Conservative Joe Clark. Only two years before he had been the prime minister, his government emboldened by its defeat of the Liberals and by Trudeau's retirement. But hubris and a lack of basic arithmetic led to the defeat of the Clark government in under nine months. Miraculously, or so it appeared, Trudeau came back to power. Canadians had turned again to the strong man who had been their prime minister for most of the past twelve years. As Trudeau summed up his approach during our breakfast group meeting that May morning in 1976: "You asked for leadership and we've given it."

Chapter 19

THE CLARK INTERREGNUM

I felt for Joe Clark that day in 1982 as he sat with his wife, Maureen McTeer, among the dignitaries in the April sunshine watching Pierre Trudeau and the Queen signing the new Constitution. A thoroughly decent man, he deserved better. No question, if it came down to sharing a beer with Pierre Trudeau or Joe Clark, the more agreeable mate would be Clark. Many of us had known him as a good source when he was a young assistant to Conservative leader Robert Stanfield in the early seventies. He was the subject of an article I wrote for the *Montreal Star* in the fall of 1965 when he was president of the Young Conservatives and concerned that university students returning to school could not vote in the federal election on campus. He had briefly worked as a reporter himself. Although he was physically awkward and given to pompous phrasing in public, in person he was open, genuine, and candid, with a self-deprecatory sense of humour. When I once asked him about reports that he could not swim — a shortcoming I shared — he replied: "My head sinks."

As prime minister he believed in access. Compared to Trudeau, he was a breath of fresh air. Indeed, Clark was disarmingly open with reporters. The night he was elected Tory leader, he invited me to his hotel suite for a lengthy interview, knowing I was on deadline. At an early press conference he readily agreed to post his daily schedule when I asked.

Later, before he met Parliament, he gave me a forty-five-minute interview during a drive from Hinton, Alberta, to nearby Jasper, where he was in strategy meetings with key advisers. Fatefully, we touched on the sensitive issue of the looming Quebec referendum. In contrast to all-guns-blazing Pierre Trudeau, he said the Quebec vote was not "the only issue." Clark offered the promise of lower temperatures between Ottawa and the provinces after years of wrangling among Trudeau and the premiers. He also gave a voice to the West in Ottawa and, having learned passable French, he worked hard to build the party in Quebec.

But his openness never guaranteed Clark any breaks with the national press. Dalton Camp observed astutely and sardonically that reporters found it difficult to take Clark seriously because he was "of their own age and too much one of them: they shared with Clark a common history, a life's experience as brief and unremarkable as their own."

His government also suffered from a series of self-inflicted wounds. At his first press conference after being elected, he told columnist Allan Fotheringham that, yes, he still planned to break with historic Canadian policy and move the Canadian embassy in Tel Aviv to disputed Jerusalem — a policy he ditched later under a political storm.

Despite leading a minority government, Clark stubbornly decided that he would govern as if he had a majority. His pledge to fight the deficit with a four-cent hike in the tax on a litre of gas and his plan to sell off Petro-Canada in the midst of an energy crisis proved toxic. The most telling issue he faced, the price of oil and gas, was one that he could not resolve while two Conservative premiers, Peter Lougheed of Alberta and Bill Davis of Ontario, warred in the bosom of a single party. That and the looming referendum convinced Canadians to bring gunslinger Trudeau back to power in 1980. Clark lasted in office eight months and two days.

If only …

Clark had his chance to avoid the non-confidence vote on Finance Minister John Crosbie's budget that brought down his government on December 13, 1979. But he had allowed the opposition to pick the day of the budget vote — when three of his MPs were absent. He rejected advice that he make a deal to get the Créditiste rump in the Commons to vote with the government. Even the night before, you could tell the Grits were in a toppling mood, despite Trudeau's retirement as Liberal leader. As I wrote: "That evening at the annual [Liberal] caucus Christmas party, the booze flowed, the faces reddened and the laughter rolled. Montreal backbencher Thérèse Killens confided soberly: 'We're going to do it.'" After the vote, the Liberals set about the task of luring Trudeau out of retirement.

In defeat, bitterness overcame the Conservatives, already Canada's "natural opposition party" for most of the century. There were those who accused the media of slanting their stories against Clark. Even today there are critics who insist that unfair coverage of Clark's world trip as opposition leader in January 1979 was the root cause of his loss twelve months later. That madcap adventure around the globe was best remembered for TV camera gear and personal suitcases that ended up in Bangkok, not New Delhi.

A word or two about the lost luggage. There was none. The only lost luggage was one bag that went astray when we landed in Athens. It was mine. It went on to Rome. It was back in my hotel room later that day. "You're not going to write about that, are you?" Clark handler Ian Green pleaded. I didn't — until now.

When Clark, his official party of five, and fourteen journalists gathered on Sunday night in Tokyo for a reception on January 7, 1979, the Tory leader was ten points ahead in the Gallup poll, while Trudeau's Liberals were running out of time to call an election. This was the PM-in-waiting, and we were anxious to assess his readiness for power, none more so than columnist Allan Fotheringham, whom Clark later singled out as the leader of the rat pack. According to Andrew Szende, writing in the *Toronto Star*, Clark described Fotheringham at a Tory caucus meeting as the "leader of the pack of negative reporters" that included Doug Small of CP and Don Sellar of Southam. "He thought Bob Lewis of *Maclean's* was fair and he praised the *Globe's* Jeffrey Simpson and the *Star's* Stephen Handelman for giving the best coverage of his tour."

Clark's organizers actually invited coverage before the tour. They had stressed the importance of his high-level meetings with the leaders of Japan, India, Israel, and Jordan. Ahead lay a mind-numbing fourteen-day tour through twenty-four time zones embracing Tokyo, New Delhi, Tel Aviv, and Amman, with touchdowns in Manila, Bangkok, and Athens.

The Conservative's Ottawa travel agency had booked the entire voyage on various scheduled commercial airlines, including one fateful flight on EgyptAir 865. The Boeing 707 was to take us from Tokyo to Bangkok with a change of planes that allowed for a mere sixty-five-minute connection to the ongoing Lufthansa flight 661 to New Delhi. The EgyptAir flight was late taking off and arrived thirty minutes late in Bangkok after a scheduled stop in Manila. Canadian officials had managed to hold the Lufthansa flight, and Clark's executive assistant Green made the decision to have Clark board the flight, keep his scheduled meetings, and let the luggage and camera equipment arrive in India on a later flight. It was just before 2:00 a.m. when he — and we — arrived at the steamy and dusty Palam Airport outside New Delhi with our bags back in Bangkok. Thus was born the legend of the "Lost Luggage Tour" — and so began Clark's international ordeal.

If Clark's people had explained the plan in Bangkok and offered reporters a choice: stay behind with your luggage, or stick with the story and join Clark, we would have understood the need to stay with Clark and the story. We did it anyway, not thinking of bags, and got a royal reception at the five-star Maurya Hotel. Green had thoughtfully provided snacks and toiletries for the travellers, who eagerly fell into bed after some fifteen hours of travel.

The next day, Clark's strange interchanges began. In the village of Sidhrawali, an hour southwest of New Delhi, Clark wandered through a barnyard, startling one farmer with the question: "How old are the chickens?" With no major events on the itinerary to cover, reporters began shadowing Clark and recording each and every one of his stiff bons mots.

On a farm in rural India: "What is the totality of your acreage?"

In the Jordan Valley: "You have a lot of rocks here."

In the Holy Land: "Jerusalem is a very rich city."

By day twelve, when the Israelis escorted Clark to Camp Ziouani on the Golan Heights to inspect a twelve-man honour guard of Canadian United Nations peacekeeping troops, Clark was either so jet-lagged or so uncertain that he mistakenly swerved between two soldiers instead of walking to the end of the short line. CP reporter Doug Small filed a story back to Canada reporting that Clark had "collided with a Canadian soldier and nearly cut his head on a rifle bayonet." That story struck with the force of the football that slipped from Robert Stanfield's hands during the 1968 election. It created an image of Clark the klutz — and that was unfair.

In an excellent research project for Carleton Journalism School in 1983, student Chris Staples quotes Green saying that the bayonet incident was "a case of reporters looking for stuff that would match their own bias. The gaffes had become the major news.... They decided to do a job on Joe." Lowell Murray, Clark's friend and éminence grise, added: "It was the worst case of pack journalism I have ever seen."

According to Clark's chief of staff in 1979, the late Bill Neville, "Small alone made the bayonet story. Nobody else saw it. It just did not happen." From my vantage point, Clark's head was twenty to thirty centimetres from the bayonet. The next week *Maclean's* ran a close-up of a soldier with a bayonet and Clark in the background, but my story did not mention the incident. Sergeant Kent Metke of Penhold, Alberta, had the best view. "Mr. Clark had his head down while he was walking," he told Carleton student Staples. "I guess he just turned too soon. He bumped into my right side. He never came close to the bayonet. He apologized and that was that. I really think they made too big a deal out of it."

My friend and colleague Small, for his part, said, "Looking over the file, I can't find a story I wouldn't write again. I can't find one story I'm sorry I wrote. I can't find one that I can't justify. And I take some pride in the fact that I beat the ass off other reporters singled out for 'praise' by Joe Clark and the Conservative Party." Ouch.

The incident that gave several of us pause was Clark's meeting with Shimon Peres, at the time Israel's opposition leader. Until that session we had been given very little access to Clark except for the occasional scrum after his meetings. When we arrived at the Israeli parliament I appealed to an Israeli official — citing the nation's record of open democracy — to let us attend Clark's meeting with Peres. To my surprise, Peres invited reporters to stay behind after the photo op. Clark was clearly uncomfortable, no less so when Peres indicated that Clark was ill informed about the Palestinian issue. With that, a secretary handed Peres a note and he bolted from the room, leaving Clark to wonder, "Is he coming back?"

As I wrote the next week: "The image of the 39-year-old Albertan, dwarfed on the world stage, was inescapable. Clark's uncertain and awkward performance symbolized his misdirected adventure through four world capitals which ended, mercifully, last week as Clark was driven by Cadillac limousine from Montreal to Ottawa after faulty party planning caused him to miss a plane in New York." Jeffrey Simpson, whose reporting Joe Clark praised, also concluded that "Clark did not demonstrate to me that he had a very good grasp of the issues that he was being asked to learn about."

———————

Four months later, Charles Joseph "Joe" Clark was sworn in as Canada's sixteenth prime minister. He was, at thirty-nine, the youngest in history. But ultimately, to borrow from an infamous slogan used years later, he proved himself not yet ready. His time would come in the 1990s when he served effectively as minister of foreign affairs and then of constitutional matters during the government of his old political foe Brian Mulroney. In his subsequent role as an elder statesman, global adviser, and happy grandfather, Clark earned the respect he deserved.

Joe Clark and Robert Lewis at Pearson Airport: coffee before an early morning flight to Vancouver.

Chapter 20

JOHN TURNER: GREEK TRAGEDY

John Turner always seemed like a man of destiny in federal politics — as an Olympic track star from the University of British Columbia who became a Rhodes Scholar; a handsome Montreal lawyer with an Oxford degree who danced with Princess Margaret at a Government House ball in 1959; an MP at thirty-three, a junior minister in Lester Pearson's government at thirty-six, and, at forty-two, the youngest justice minister in a century; and, above all, an outstanding retail politician.

No gesture was too small. When the newspaper carriers of the *Montreal Star* came to Ottawa and met Pearson on the lawn outside the Parliament Buildings in 1965 — the *Star* assigned me to cover this unremarkable event — Turner posed with the prime minister in the photo that ran in the Saturday paper. Later there were more significant stories: his activism as minister of consumer affairs under Pearson, his effective advocacy in western Canada for official bilingualism, his reform of judicial appointments and the criminal code in justice under Pierre Trudeau — the man who stole the throne from him. When he resigned as minister of finance in 1976, it was clear Turner was going off to wait Trudeau out.

I followed Turner on that voyage. One result was an early 1977 profile for *Maclean's*, "The Turner Campaign. Never mind what he says. Watch what he does." What he did was one step short of overt campaigning. "He shook hands with more people than I know," one Toronto lawyer who strolled five blocks with Turner told me. In Calgary he burnished his image among western conservatives as the headliner at a political roast for Tory MP Jack Horner to help him pay off his leadership campaign debts. With Trudeau's party growing restive, Turner loyalists were poised for a comeback. "Look," said one supporter, "we Liberals were born to govern. If that birthright is threatened, watch out."

The watch took eight years, during which the Clark government went down to defeat and Trudeau made his remarkable resurrection. But when Turner's time came it was clear he was not ready. "I was rusty," Turner conceded in a mellow interview with CBC after his retirement. "I wasn't completely abreast of the issues."

Or the times. He was, in the words of historian Allan Levine, "more like a relic that belonged in a Grit museum than a leader for the 1980s." He was a backslapping jock in the age of feminism. His was the vernacular of the locker room. "Greed makes the world go around, baby," he liked to say. In the summer election of 1984 the TV cameras twice captured Turner patting the derrières of women at campaign events.

On July 13 in Edmonton, the target was Liberal Party president Iona Campagnolo, who patted Turner's bum right back. "That's known as *mano a womano,*" she quipped.

Turner: "You've been waiting some time to do that."

Campagnolo: "No, I haven't."

Later Turner tried to dismiss the incidents: "I'm a very tactile politician."

Grilled by Roger Smith of CTV, Turner responded: "I say hello to men the same way."

City TV's Colin Vaughan interjected: "Women find that offensive. It dates you, John."

Turner: "I don't think they find it offensive at all."

The travelling press corps named Turner's plane "Derri Air."

Equally revealing was Turner's failure to grasp the new morality on the press bus. Gone were the days of the quiet off-the-record chats. "It's all on the record now," said *Vancouver Sun* columnist and Turner friend Marjorie Nichols after returning to the Hill from an absence of several years.

Turner discovered how true that was after a chat with a small group of reporters on his campaign bus on May 10, 1984. In the conversation he blamed Trudeau for not backing him when, he said, it appeared he could get voluntary wage restraints from big labour. That led to his resignation as finance minister from Cabinet. When the *Globe*'s Thomas Walkom decided to report the disclosure, the *Star*'s Val Sears and the CBC's Bill Casey followed.

Turner was shocked when he read Walkom's story the next day. "In the bus, for God's sake," he exclaimed, as if referring to a Catholic church confessional. He did not blame Sears or Casey for breaking the story. "Those guys are all right. But that Walkom! I've never had a thing broken in a bus in my life."

What ultimately did Turner in was losing the TV debate to Mulroney from a true knockout blow delivered over patronage. How ironic it was that Mulroney won that one. He had said that he would appoint Liberals only "when there isn't a living, breathing Tory without a job in this country." Now, in casual conversation with reporters on his campaign plane, a journalist asked how he could then criticize Turner for patronage appointments. Mulroney replied: "I was talking to Tories then and that's what they wanted to hear. Talking to the Canadian public during the election campaign is something else." Mulroney then compounded the issue by volunteering that Liberal Bryce Mackasey was right to accept an ambassadorial appointment. "Let's face it," he quipped, "there's no whore like an old whore. If I'd been in Bryce's position I'd have been right in there with my nose in the public trough like the rest of them." Mulroney thought the conversation was off the record. Neil Macdonald, then of the *Ottawa Citizen,* printed it. "Mulroney Admits Altering Patronage Stand for Election," blared the headline.

In the debate later that month, Turner opened the skirmish by chastising Mulroney for the patronage comment. Big mistake. Turner had just made seventeen appointments, mostly Liberals including Mackasey and Gene Whelan as ambassadors — honouring a written undertaking that Pierre Trudeau insisted he make before retiring. Mulroney couldn't believe his good fortune. He wheeled on Turner. "I've apologized to the Canadian people for kidding about it," he boomed. "The least you could do is apologize for having made those terrible appointments."

Without invoking Trudeau, Turner replied, "I had no option."

Mulroney retorted: "You had an option, sir, to say no, and you chose to say yes to the old attitudes and the old stories of the Liberal Party.... You could have done better."

Game, set, match.

Turner recovered his footing for his rematch with Mulroney in the 1988 election debates. His assault on the prime minister's free trade plan set Mulroney back on his heels. "With one signature of the pen," he charged, Mulroney had "thrown us into the north-south influence of the United States." An effective Liberal TV ad depicted the border being erased. It was one of his finest hours.

But the Tories launched a fierce advertising barrage, as Turner put it later, "an unprecedented personal attack on my character, on my sincerity, and on my confidence." In the words of Tory strategist Allan Gregg, "We saw the bridge between the message and the messenger, and we had to blow up the bridge."

Turner, a man who believed in civility in politics and played by conventional rules, could not survive in the new world of political hardball.

Part IX

———————

OUR TIMES

Chapter 21

GEOFFREY STEVENS:
ACCIDENTAL CORRESPONDENT

Geoffrey Stevens was an accidental Ottawa correspondent. He was working in the *Globe and Mail*'s Toronto newsroom on Easter Sunday in 1965 when managing editor Clark Davey called him over. Davey said he had just remembered that he had to fill a vacancy in the paper's Ottawa bureau. Would Stevens be interested? Stevens asked when he'd have to be there. Davey replied: "Tomorrow." Although Stevens had "no particular interest in Ottawa" and had never been to the capital, he said yes and bought a road map.

So are stars created in the journalism business — or so they used to be. Davey had one piece of advice for the twenty-five-year-old: "For the first couple of months I want you to sit in the House every night and listen to what people are saying. And if you don't understand what they are doing, go and ask them." The lessons Stevens learned proved invaluable. In fifteen years in the Parliamentary Press Gallery he became one of the most respected journalistic voices on the Hill, a reporter who took the trouble to cultivate sources and learn the ins and outs. Ultimately, he proved a worthy successor to George Bain when he took over the valued page 6 editorial column in 1973.

But first came reporting on the Ottawa beat. In his first big story he revealed that Liberal health minister Judy LaMarsh was about to introduce legislation paving the way for a national medicare plan. The day the story appeared LaMarsh denied it. On her way into a Cabinet meeting she told a clutch of inquiring reporters: "Mr. Stevens and the *Globe and Mail* better guess again." Later that day, LaMarsh introduced the bill.

Stevens attributes his success to following Davey's advice. By working the corridors day and night, he said, "you learned and met people because you were around." The most important people were the enthusiastic young ministerial aides to the most powerful figures in Pearson's inner Cabinet. Among them: Michael McCabe for Mitchell Sharp, Bill Lee for Paul Hellyer, and Bill Neville for LaMarsh. They were a band of brothers, cultivating their networks and promoting their ministers with judicious leaks of inside information. "They were happy to do it," said Stevens. "There was no centralized control." In fact, the Pearson Cabinet did not leak like a sieve; it spilled from the top. The most famous story about leaks from the Pearson era was when the great man confided to his Cabinet that he was about to announce his resignation. After Pearson left the room, Jack Pickersgill stood in the doorway to prevent his Cabinet colleagues from hitting the phones to call reporters before Pearson could break the big news himself.

Government ministers gave reporters same-day access. "You'd call in the morning," according to Stevens, "and ask if you could see the minister after Question Period. The answer usually was, 'Sure, come on up.' And you could sit down and talk about policy. Often they would bring in a deputy minister or another official." Stevens said there was "less a sense of hostility between reporters and the politicians, a sense that we are all in this together."

Not that Stevens went easy on governments or parties — especially during elections. In the closing weeks of the 1979 election, Stevens delightfully sent up all the parties by giving voice to a fantasy: that instead of flying around the country, the leaders, their supporters, and the press would file into a studio at the Ottawa airport every day to hear set pitches and never leave the capital. The reason for Stevens's pique was his conviction that journalists covering the campaign "are less political reporters than they are stage props for the evening news." Detailing the inane itineraries of the party leaders, Stevens wrote:

Does Mr. Clark actually know anything more about the problems of small business than he did before he strode, rapidly, through a box company in Kitchener? Is Mr. Broadbent's understanding of the complexities of food pricing deepened because he was able to pose in front of the produce counter at a co-op in St. Boniface? Is Mr. Trudeau more sensitive to the diversity of the Canadian soul because he lit a string of firecrackers on a street in Chinatown in Vancouver?

Yet, Stevens went on, the fiction that these campaign stops somehow test a leader's ability to become prime minister must be maintained. In the words of the headline on his story, it was an "election trail made of plastic."

These confident judgments and wit were not a fluke. Stevens, thirty-nine at the time, had already paid his dues: two years as city reporter, including

Robert Stanfield in his Ottawa office with (left to right) Clark Davey, Geoffrey Stevens, and Martin O'Malley, January 22, 1976: same-day access.

the all-night police shift, two years covering city hall, four years in the *Globe*'s Ottawa bureau, two years as bureau chief in the Ontario legislature, three years in the Ottawa bureau of *Time,* and a leave to write the political biography *Stanfield* on the Tory leader.

His debut as a journalist was classically inauspicious, however. After graduating from the University of Western Ontario, he told his father he was thinking of a career in journalism. "He looked disappointed and said, 'Couldn't you get a decent job?'" Undeterred, Stevens signed on at the *Globe* at seventy-seven dollars per week — having rejected an offer from CP because it paid two dollars less.

His first big break came when a massive fire erupted in the Balmy Beach district of east Toronto. Stevens hustled to the scene with a photographer, interviewed the neighbours, and worked up a story. It ran on page 1. "The next day I started getting congratulations from all sorts of people. I said, 'It's just a fire story.'" Not exactly. Editor Dic Doyle lived in the neighbourhood and had been calling the desk to make sure the blaze was covered in his paper.

A similar accident of fate brought Stevens to one of his all-time favourite subjects, the Law of the Sea. The topic had been almost a fetish of *Globe* editor Doyle and his editorial board. But the man Doyle had assigned to cover the Third International Law of the Sea Conference in Caracas in 1974 had disappeared on him. Doyle sent Stevens off to find out why and to write about the global effort to set rules for use of the high seas and coastal waterways. The *Globe* reporter, Stevens reported, had set fire to his hotel room in an unguarded moment and had been put in jail. Stevens took over the assignment.

For the next seven years, as the conference moved from Caracas to Geneva to New York, Stevens dutifully recorded its progress — its lack of progress, in fact. Readers threatened to stop taking the paper if Stevens kept writing about the Law of the Sea. The *Toronto Star*'s acerbic writer Val Sears once said that "the two most dreaded words in the English language" were "more tomorrow" at the bottom of a Stevens column on the Law of the Sea. He took to numbering his columns, Law of the Sea I, II, III, and so on. In a fitting acknowledgement of his quiet obsession, on April 30, 1981, Stevens labelled one of his last efforts "Law of the Sea (CCCLXVI)."

Stevens left Ottawa for corporate journalism at the *Globe* before sea law made it onto the books in 1982. He lost track of how many columns he wrote on the subject. "All I know," he said, "is that I wrote quite a lot."

Mainly, Stevens wrote about national affairs and the prime ministers: wage and price controls, five elections, the first Quebec referendum, and the fates of Pierre Trudeau, John Turner, and Joe Clark. Inevitably, there was the uncertain fate of the Trudeau marriage to deal with. Stevens knew Margaret Trudeau from casual meetings at cocktail parties on the Ottawa circuit and her occasional visits to the Press Club. When she was in Venezuela at a state dinner with Pierre Trudeau and performed an impromptu song for the wife of the president, he wrote a column about her "erratic and unpredictable" behaviour, based on eyewitness reports from a source at the dinner.

His editors did not print the column because Dic Doyle first wanted to make sure that Stevens intended to comment on Margaret Trudeau's mental health. Assured that he did, Doyle ran the column the next day. "She seems to enjoy public attention," Stevens wrote, "but not the pressure and discipline that go with it." The column title was "Mrs. Trudeau, rebel." Margaret Trudeau was furious and confronted Stevens, insisting on her right to be herself.

Like so many journalists covering public figures — and sometimes aspects of their personal lives — Stevens had his own private challenges. His son Christopher, the eldest of three children, died tragically, eliciting a thoughtful note from Prime Minister Trudeau. His marriage to his first wife, Danny, ended, too. He eventually moved back to the *Globe* in Toronto where he served as the distinguished managing editor under Norman Webster, edited a newspaper for snowbirds in Florida, and in 1996 became my managing editor at *Maclean's*. His award-winning *The Player: The Life & Times of Dalton Camp* is one of the finest political biographies of its time.

Stevens, along with his second wife, Lynn, and their family, eventually moved to Cambridge, Ontario. There he continued to write a sprightly political column for the *Record* and teach on a subject about which he is an expert: corruption, scandal, and political ethics.

Chapter 22

MARJORIE NICHOLS: DEFYING THE ODDS

When Marjorie Nichols graduated from high school in Red Deer, Alberta, in 1962, she was determined to become a journalist. She headed for the nearest journalism school, the University of Montana at Missoula. There, upon graduation in 1966, she elaborated on her ambition in the yearbook: "Marjorie Nichols wants to work as a reporter for an Eastern Canadian newspaper." By the end of the year she had what she wanted, tapping out stories as a cub reporter in the Dickensian newsroom of the *Ottawa Journal*. Two years later she was in the *Journal*'s parliamentary bureau.

Journalist Jane O'Hara, the pen behind Nichols's telling 1992 autobiography, *Mark My Words*, recalls that Marjorie joined a bureau with two entrenched senior male colleagues. "She figured these guys would never leave," says O'Hara, "and so she started doing what she called the 'crumbs.' She basically did good, down-to-earth, hard reporting, reading the order paper, the orders-in-council, all this stuff that nobody did." The result was a regular diet of front page stories that launched her into orbit as one of the top political reporters of her generation — and plunged her into a hurly-burly life of alcohol and late nights.

Marjorie Nichols was always a determined, stubborn, and angry person. Her brother Sydney recalled: "She was a wild kid, terrible, absolutely nuts.

She and Dad were always at war. Everyone in our family was pretty well scared of her." As a journalist she continued the tradition. She fought with editors if they changed a comma in her copy. She once defied orders that she had to join the union, agreeing only to pay dues as long as she was not a member. As O'Hara wrote in her notes to *Mark My Words*, "She gave editors ulcers. She gave everybody else hell." But Nichols also loved politics and respected politicians. She made her mark in the pre-Watergate era when reporters could be critical of public people but still enjoy their company after hours. After her death from lung cancer in 1992, former Liberal leader John Turner, who had suffered Nichols's lance, called her "the ultimate professional." Former prime minister Brian Mulroney observed: "She was able to do her job in a critical way, but never with malice." Her friend, former Liberal Cabinet minister Judy LaMarsh, once said, "Marjorie is the clearest eye that ever held a pen."

Nichols was old school. Although she was the only woman in the press gallery for a time after her arrival, she insisted that she never felt any discrimination. "Nor have I ever been treated as an inferior by anybody," she wrote. "It wasn't that there was [no] discrimination against women. It was that there were no women." She railed about the then-fashionable New Journalism, with its personal opinion and edginess. "Reporters today think that scandal-mongering is journalism," she wrote in *Mark My Words*. "They're wrong. The art of journalism is the art of synopsis, and that art form has been lost."

Along the way, Nichols paid her dues. The *Ottawa Journal* archives bulge with her sprightly reports of humdrum city council meetings, public-service union negotiations, profiles of local achievers, and seemingly endless interviews with visiting heads of state during Expo 67. But by the fall of 1968 she had moved to the Hill as a sub for the ailing bureau chief, Dick Jackson. By October 1971 she was the star. Her analysis of the federal budget was the main story on page 1, a report about a massive stimulative package that she labelled a "winter works budget."

Nichols never looked back. She realized that mind-numbing pages of statistics or the auditor general's annual report on government misspending could yield fodder for countless columns and interpretive pieces. In a typical day Nichols would write five different stories. She covered the FLQ crisis, federal-provincial talks on the future of Confederation, and the evolving

Trudeau prime ministry, all with thoughtful and penetrating analysis. She became the first woman to serve as president of the press gallery and unofficial host to visiting firefighters. In that role she met and became close friends with BCTV star Jack Webster and, later, columnist Allan Fotheringham. Norman DePoe of CBC, and Charles Lynch of Southam became mentors and drinking buddies. She met and befriended Pat Carney, later to become a minister in the Mulroney government and a senator, when she spent a year in the gallery for the *Vancouver Sun* as economics correspondent.

It was a time of long days, late nights, hard drinking, gin rummy in the Press Club, and heavy smoking (at least two packs a day). Former senator Joyce Fairbairn, the lone woman in the gallery when Nichols joined, recalled: "Those were times when we'd go to all-night sittings and everyone was pissed as newts. Some of the politicians would get absolutely blotto and start punching out members of the press gallery. When Marjorie arrived, I showed her around, explaining all the lunatics to her."

In her autobiography, Nichols had "total recall of the first time I had a drink during a workday." Ironically, it was after she had called in on a tight deadline to dictate the details of the Le Dain Commission report on the non-medical use of drugs in 1972. Two colleagues at CP, Dave McIntosh and Stewart MacLeod, invited her to join them for a beer in the press gallery workroom: "I still remember how it relieved the tension. I had drunk to excess many times, starting as a teenager, but never before had I used alcohol as a palliative for the pressure of work. I discovered how well it acted. I would use it again and again almost to the point it destroyed me."

In 1972 Fotheringham helped lure Nichols to editor Stu Keate's *Vancouver Sun* as bureau chief in Victoria. The provincial press gallery was never quite the same again. As a sign that she rejected the "pack mentality" of the locals — several of whom were on the government's payroll — she moved her bureau out of the legislature into a suite at the stately Empress Hotel, filled the bathtub with beer, and hosted regular pizza parties. By day her column defined the agenda. When Premier Dave Barrett doubled his salary to fifty-two thousand dollars, Nichols reported that he was then the third-highest paid elected official on the continent. Barrett asked Nichols later if her story was true.

"Didn't you check this?" she demanded.

To his chagrin, Barrett had not.

Webster on radio and Fotheringham in print would often scalp a Marjorie Nichols piece and amplify and extend its punch. "In the 1970s, the three of us ran Vancouver," noted Fotheringham ruefully. Added Nichols: "The three of us worked together and we drank together. We had lunch and we had dinner and we partied. And we ran up big expense accounts."

Nichols admits candidly in her memoir: "I led a very promiscuous life. Promiscuity is one of the main symptoms of heavy drinking." She added:

> God, if I were to tell you whom I've slept with, you'd fall off your chair.... Obviously there were some people in journalism, but there were a lot of politicians too. I've slept with husbands of some friends. Hell, I've even slept with senators. I never kept count, but I guess I had at least twenty-five such relationships.

O'Hara told me that Nichols's account of a three-way tryst with two male friends was removed from the book at the demand of a man who threatened a libel suit.

After two years in Victoria, Nichols, then thirty-one, headed back to Ottawa as the *Sun* columnist with a mandate to write for the other dailies in the FP Publications chain, jointly owned by Victor Sifton and Max Bell. Importantly, that gave her an Ottawa voice in the *Journal*, as well as regular outlets in Vancouver and Winnipeg, among other western cities (but not in FP's *Globe and Mail*).* She became a regular on Barbara Frum's popular *As It Happens* show on CBC Radio and a frequent guest on CTV's *Canada AM*. She had sources all over town, including the prime minister's office — one of whom helped her find Margaret Trudeau during her New York escapade with the Rolling Stones.

Pamela Wallin recalled Nichols's thoughtful friendship when she was a gallery newbie in her midtwenties with the *Toronto Star* bureau. Although Wallin was a decade younger, Nichols knew Wallin as the affable chase producer on the telephone who had lined her up for her regular Friday

---

* At its peak in 1965, when it acquired the *Globe and Mail,* FP was the strongest Canadian chain, with total circulation of 780,000. The other FP papers were in Victoria, Vancouver, Calgary, Lethbridge, Saskatoon, Regina, Winnipeg, and Ottawa.

evening gigs on *As It Happens*. Wallin absorbed Nichols's lessons about the importance of federalism and the perils of an overly decentralized state during her coverage of the great constitutional negotiations. Nichols also taught her fellow Prairie colleague about freight rates and fiscal transfers. Nichols, always well dressed and conscious that appearances mattered, took Wallin to a specialty dress shop on the Sparks Street Mall where she bought her own clothes; there she steered Wallin to the sale rack. "She always believed it was always better to have one good dress than several bad ones," Wallin told me with a chuckle.

Party Central in those days was a house that Nichols shared with *Globe* correspondent Hugh Winsor on otherwise quiet Clemow Avenue in the comfortable Glebe neighbourhood, around the corner from the liquor store. It was the ribald party scene for reporters, politicians, and bureaucrats of every stripe. One morning Nichols discovered a "most unlikely" duo sleeping in her living room: veteran Liberal minister Bryce Mackasey and blueblood

Press gallery dinner, Ottawa. Left–right: Trudeau aide Paul Manning, Allan Fotheringham, Marjorie Nichols, and John Turner. Nichols's house was party central.

Tory Michael Meighen. Over time, other notable visitors included Margaret Trudeau, Adrian Lang, New Brunswick premier Richard Hatfield, B.C. premier Dave Barrett, and Justice Minister Ron Basford. At one legendary soiree during the Conservative leadership convention in 1976, someone reported breathlessly that the CBC's Norman DePoe was dead in an upstairs bedroom. In fact, after carefully laying his clothes over a bannister, DePoe had tried to crawl into a rollaway cot. Nichols wrote: "His head was hanging on the floor, and he was making those gurgling noises." Fotheringham, ever helpful, put DePoe's feet into bed and covered him up. "Of course," Nichols added, "that was a real mistake, because he was up, rip-roaring ready to go at six in the morning. He'd had his two-and-a-half hours of sleep."

Despite the carousing, Nichols took her work seriously. She liked nothing better than poring through a federal budget or plumbing the depths of the constitutional talks. At one point she became so concerned about the secretiveness of in camera negotiations that she joined Charles Lynch and the CBC's Ron Collister in a demonstration demanding that Trudeau open the sessions to the public. (He did, but the first ministers then did their real talking in private.)

In 1977, FP boss Brigadier Richard Malone assigned Nichols to Washington. It was in the wake of the Jimmy Carter election and Marjorie was a willing scribe, given the pro-American slant she had inherited from her father and her Montana schooling. But the assignment was an unhappy one. She tried to write different articles tuned to the interests of each FP paper and keep up her *Sun* column. She spent long hours covering Federal Power Commission hearings on the Westcoast Transmission Company gas pipeline, accurately predicting its demise and suffering the wrath of the company's executives and lobbyists. Chasing Margaret Trudeau around New York, she realized she was not cut out for paparazzi life. In May 1979 she jumped at *Sun* publisher Clark Davey's invitation to return to Victoria.

By day she covered Bill Bennett and his Social Credit government. By night, according to her own testimony, she retreated to her isolated cottage in the woods and drank until dawn. She would call friends at all hours of the night. Her mood swung wildly, often resulting in tirades directed at friends or editors. By 1981 she was taking Librium to calm her shakes. "The biggest story for me was my own alcoholism," she wrote. "I was drinking very heavily, almost uncontrollably.... I was an alcoholic. It was an addiction."

Fortunately, her old pals from Montana intervened — formally — and persuaded her to get help. She agreed to check into a Seattle rehab centre in November 1982. The thirty-nine-year-old political reporter was unimpressed with her surroundings. "Most of the people are old," she wrote to her friends. She was frustrated that she "couldn't engage a single inmate" in a political discussion. But she stuck it out for thirty days and returned to work, this time with a new crusade: temperance at city hall and in the city room. In 1987, still sober, she returned to Ottawa to write a column for the *Ottawa Citizen* at the behest of the new editor, Keith Spicer.

In the press gallery Marjorie discovered that you can't go home again. Parliament Hill and the beat had changed. Rivals resented her presence. She railed that television in the House had ruined Parliament. Most importantly, she was no longer "Queen of the Hill," in O'Hara's phrase. "The camaraderie, the friendships, just weren't there anymore," Nichols wrote.

Then she took the cruellest blow: having beaten alcohol, she got a diagnosis of inoperable lung cancer. Ever the fighter, she continued her thrice-weekly column while undergoing punishing bouts of chemotherapy.

Typically, within an hour of the signing of the Meech Lake Accord she wrote a fiery piece denouncing the pact, which declared Quebec a "distinct society" and gave the provinces a voice in federal appointments. There was nothing novel about the success of the meeting, she wrote: "The provinces demanded and the federal government acceded.… This is not co-operative federalism. It is co-operative provincialism."

When Nichols later changed her position after sitting through days of parliamentary hearings, critics accused her unfairly of falling to the blandishments of Mulroney. In fact, many opinion leaders swung in behind the accord — just not the people of Canada.

On December 6, 1991, Marjorie Nichols left Ottawa for the last time. She flew home to Red Deer with her brother Sydney. She died in his arms on December 29, her eyes open. A reporter to the end.

Chapter 23

MICHEL VASTEL:
FEAR AND LOATHING

When Marie Vastel's older sister visited Marie's office in the National Press Building shortly after she joined the Ottawa bureau of *Le Devoir* in 2011, it was an unexpectedly emotional moment. "This is Dad's old office," Anne exclaimed. Recounting the incident, Marie said: "I'm physically at the spot where my dad worked thirty years before. I didn't know until my sister told me. Sometimes I hope he is helping me, giving me a little push."

She should be so lucky. Michel Vastel was one of the most industrious, well-connected, and committed journalists of his day in the press gallery. His reporting and commentary over three decades were direct and authoritative. He was rambunctious and he was feared. He had a Rolodex that was the envy of his colleagues: office, home, and cottage numbers of premiers, Cabinet ministers, and senior officials. And, unusually for a Quebec journalist, Vastel strode the country, writing in depth about English Canada and its political leaders. He could sit down and talk the language of Ralph Klein in Calgary, and be the guest of reclusive billionaire Paul Desmarais at his exclusive Charlevoix estate. Journalists had to read Vastel to stay on top of his scoops.

Marie Vastel not only upholds the family tradition as a skilled reporter for *Le Devoir*, but she also represents a new generation in the

Parliamentary Press Gallery. At thirty-five she symbolizes an era of women and youth ascendant in the crusty institution, as well as the sweeping changes that are driving a new kind of journalism on the Hill. The scrum and the tweet are now paramount. While the sober *Le Devoir* accords its writers the luxury of spending time on a story, Marie Vastel also feeds the Twitter maw and does weekly TV and radio appearances: she is a regular on CBC's afternoon *Power & Politics* and on panels on the CBC's English and French networks.

In a conversation in the press gallery lounge in June 2016, Vastel reflected on the changing times. In 1979 her father wrote an article predicting that the Clark government would be defeated in the Commons, based on his reporting that the Créditiste Party was not going to support the minority government's budget. The article ran in *Le Devoir* the day of the vote.

"That would never happen today," she notes. "It would be online, everyone would kick on their cell phones, and [the Créditistes] would be convinced to vote differently. Everything is so instant now. An exclusive lasts, sometimes, ten minutes." The old two-day cycle of news flash, reaction, and follow-up now "happens in twelve hours and you have to fit it into six hundred words," said Vastel. "It's overwhelming. It goes too fast, not just for us, but for people to understand what is going on. I feel like you guys had more time, maybe, to think about the story."

"The story" was Michel Vastel's quest. He was relentless. He worked day and night, fuelling his drive with copious amounts of coffee, wine, and Gitanes cigarettes (and later, Camel Lights). A four-fingered typist, he pounded his typewriter with such force with both hands that he had to replace several keyboards. For thirty-two years starting in 1976 he covered politics for seven different Quebec dailies, did a regular column and blogged for *L'actualité* magazine, and was a frequent panellist on several French and English TV and radio shows.* He wrote seven books, usually during summer recess, including treatments of Pierre Trudeau, Jean Chrétien, and three

---

* He reported for *Le Devoir* (1976–83 and 1986–89) and *La Presse* (1984–85); was bureau chief for *Le Soleil* and columnist for *Le Soleil*, *Le Droit*, and *Le Quotidien* in Chicoutimi (1989–95); was Montreal bureau chief and columnist for *Le Soleil* (1995–2005); and was a political columnist for *Le Journal de Montréal* and *Le Journal de Québec* (2005–8).

Michel Vastel: fearless on the attack.

Quebec premiers. Jean Paré, the esteemed former editor of *L'actualité*, once asked him to interview every premier. Vastel turned in the assignment the next day. Brian Mulroney called him "Vastel Inc."

Most of us called him simply "Vastel." With his raspy voice and his rumpled, sardonic, ever-inquisitive demeanour, he looked like the archetypical B-grade detective. Some called him names as well. The CBC threatened a lawsuit over a critical article about network coverage. A bartender at the National Press Club threw him out after he started a fight with a colleague.

His disruptive behaviour got him dropped off in Mexico during a return flight from a prime ministerial mission to Latin America. "A guard told me he is the reason journalists are no longer allowed in the lobby of the House of Commons," said Marie Vastel. "Michel told me he had been thrown out of many places," Alberta premier Ralph Klein told journalism student Barbara Jobber of the *Ryerson Review* in 2009. "But I would never throw Michel out of my office." Nor did Paul Desmarais. In 2013 Vastel took readers behind the steel gates of the Power Corp. billionaire's retreat at Sagard in the Charlevoix region for an intimate portrait of the super-rich family at play for *L'actualité*.

Vastel was more at home in the hurly-burly of the political world. During the constitutional discussions in 1981, he eked out the behind-the-scenes story of the secret deal on patriation of the Constitution among justice minister Jean Chrétien, Roy Romanow of Saskatchewan, and Roy McMurtry of Ontario. That meeting in a conference room kitchen became known as "the Night of the Long Knives" after René Lévesque famously walked away the next day.

Vastel was fearless when he was on the attack. In 1988 when the retired Pierre Trudeau returned to Parliament Hill to urge the defeat of the Meech Lake Accord and spoke mainly in English, Vastel bellowed from the press gallery in the Senate: "*En français! En français!*" — and then was escorted from the chamber. On one celebrated occasion, when Trudeau walked away, refusing to answer a shouted question from Vastel, the reporter gave him the finger — and got one in return. Vastel summed up his ire about Trudeau in his illuminating book on the man: "Trudeau spent two decades in public life defying Quebec." And yet when someone called Vastel's home to say that Pierre Trudeau had died, Marie Vastel said her father "got really emotional. Obviously he had a certain affection for the man."

That was the point about Vastel — he actually liked politicians. And when he died of throat cancer in 2008, it became clear that many of them reciprocated. "We lost one of the best," said former Quebec premier Bernard Landry, the subject of Vastel's 2001 biography. Former Quebec premier Jean Charest said that Vastel wrote some of the nicest things about him but also some of the toughest.

———————

Michel Vastel was born in France's Normandy region in 1940 and grew up on a farm in northern Saint-Pierre-de-Cormeilles. After graduating in classics and journalism at the University of Lille, he did two years of compulsory military service in Algeria, a bitter and disturbing experience. He worked as a reporter at *Nord Éclair* near Lille from 1966 to 1970 but chose emigration to Quebec over pursuing his career in Paris. "He didn't like Paris, so he came to Montreal," said Marie Vastel.

He landed in the midst of the October Crisis. At *Le Devoir,* editor Claude Ryan told him he needed a better understanding of Quebec before he could work there, so he took a job as an executive assistant in the transport ministry then moved over as an aide at the Quebec Employers Council. Finally, Ryan hired him in 1976. In Montreal he met his future wife, Geneviève, also an émigré from France, who was a federal government translator.

Marie has fond memories of her father, although he was at the peak of his newspaper career and travelling extensively while she was growing up in Ottawa. "There was the Dad part and there was the work part," said Marie. "I remember him going on prime minister's trips to all these exciting places and bringing me back stuff — Russian dolls, jewels from China. He always loved to travel. My parents always took us a bunch of places." As for the work part, Marie often went with her father to TV shows when he was on a panel — including a Saturday morning gig on Radio-Canada that, years later, Marie also did.

At home after his return from an out-of-town assignment, Michel loved to cook dinner and have people over to their bungalow in Ottawa's east end. "It was," said Marie, "a busy house." One room was reserved for music. Marie, Anne, and Violaine played the piano. Michel worked in a large home office overlooking the backyard with its vast vegetable garden. After moving back to Montreal in 1995, Michel realized his dream of going back to the farm: he bought a vineyard in the Eastern Townships near Bolton and kept an apartment in Montreal.

After Marie graduated in journalism from the Université du Québec à Montréal, she parlayed her summer internships at *L'actualité* into an entry job with *La Presse Canadienne* wire service. At the beginning she did translations of the service's English stories, and covered local events and the Quebec election. Her election coverage impressed her superiors, and they posted her, then twenty-six, to the Ottawa bureau in 2009. After the 2011 federal election she moved to *Le Devoir*.

As she makes her daily rounds on Parliament Hill, Marie Vastel is conscious of her father's legacy. He was a proud Québécois who fumed when critics doubted his understanding of the province. "It was the worst thing you could tell him, that he wasn't a Quebecer," said Marie. And yet he also relished the opportunity to report in English Canada. "Very few people had that capacity to talk to everyone and know what was going on in every part of the country. He was one of the rare ones." Reflecting on the relentless flow of stories, she added poignantly, "There are a lot of times when I wish I could call him." So do Vastel's old Hill colleagues.

Chapter 24

JEFFREY SIMPSON:
THE LONG-DISTANCE RUNNER

When Jeffrey Simpson first went to Ottawa in 1972 as a twenty-three-year-old parliamentary intern fresh out of Queen's University, he rotated through the offices of a Liberal, an NDPer, and a Créditiste. He became an admirer of Liberal Barney Danson, ended up in Ed Broadbent's campaign headquarters for the election that year, and attended meetings of House leaders planning the daily business for his unilingual Créditiste MP. The grounding served Simpson well. After eight years on staff at the *Globe and Mail* in Toronto and Ottawa, he took over the prized real estate at the bottom of the *Globe* editorial page. When he retired on July 1, 2016, he had established the record for most seasons as the *Globe*'s Ottawa columnist, going out on top in his thirty-second year on the job. He was only the fourth, following George Bain — who set the gold standard — and the illustrious Geoffrey Stevens and Michael Valpy. Remarkably, his tenure embraced eight prime ministers, from Pierre Trudeau to Stephen Harper, and he served with distinction throughout.

Simpson formed his world view early in life. He grew up in a very political family. His American-born father, a conservative advertising executive, rejected Democrat Franklin D. Roosevelt because he delayed entering the Second World War; and his suffragette grandmother, an ardent Democrat, wrote her Republican sister out of her will.

The family moved from New York City, where Simpson was born, to Canada when he was nine. At the exclusive University of Toronto Schools, he excelled in English while being tutored by a drill sergeant of a grammarian who taught him all about gerunds and split infinitives. He also discovered that journalism was his future. "I was one of those lucky, lucky rare persons who knew when I was in high school that this is what I wanted to do."

At Queen's he was a top student. There he was exposed to one of the great political science faculties of the era. He developed a strong commitment to inquiry and the pragmatic value of education. His thinking about Canada also was shaped by the great Bruce Hutchison and his 1942 book, *The Unknown Country.* "The French-English dimension of Canada was central to his understanding of the country, which made him a rare observer in those years," Simpson wrote in an admiring *Queen's Quarterly* piece on the journalist.

Appropriately, Simpson's first Ottawa beat was national unity: the election of René Lévesque's Parti Québécois, a referendum in Quebec, and Pierre Trudeau's fight to patriate the Constitution. Even when Simpson transferred to the *Globe*'s London bureau for three years, the dreaded Constitution story followed him all the way to Westminster. Back in Ottawa there was plenty of columning fodder: the Clark interregnum, the second Trudeau retirement, the prime ministries of Turner, Mulroney, Campbell, Chrétien, Martin, and Harper — in addition to the rise of Lucien Bouchard and the Bloc, Preston Manning and Reform, and referendums on the Constitution and Quebec independence. Those were the days when Ottawa reporters immersed themselves in the minutiae of amending formulas, notwithstanding clauses, and federal powers. *Meech* and *Charlettetown* became code words for confrontation and impasse.

Simpson came away from it all convinced that he had seen the enemy in his own mirror — it was us. As he put it in a speech to journalists in Halifax in 1988, "Increasingly entrenched cynicism of journalists toward all politicians and governments is feeding the disrepute in which political men and women are held by the public." Not a popular sentiment among many journalists, most political people welcomed it.

Simpson dispensed his even-handed criticism across the board. His book on the brief prime ministry of Joe Clark, *Discipline of Power*, which won the Governor General's Award for non-fiction in 1981, was a devastating

Jeffrey Simpson: "Are we going to hold together?"

analysis of why the Conservatives fell after less than nine months in office. Stephen Harper's Tories used the book as a road map for how *not* to run a government. His sixth book, *The Friendly Dictatorship* in 2001, detailed Jean Chrétien's emergence as de facto ruler of a one-party state. As for the secretive Harper regime, as he said in an interview, "It was like a cloud that came right down to the horizon."

In his later years Simpson took on some of the bigger subjects that had him ranging beyond the narrow confines of Parliament Hill. In 2007 he tackled climate change in a full-length book. "This," he said, "is the most complicated public policy question I have ever dealt with. It can't be dealt with unless there is an international response, because it is the global commons that is at peril." In 2012 he published an analysis of Canada's health-care system that dared to question why the country was spending so much to be only a "middle-of-the-road performer." And in columns and speeches he challenged the notion that Indigenous Peoples, because of costs and small numbers, can realistically become self-governing once again.

One of the biggest stories on his watch was nothing less than the future of Canada — or so many of us believed and proclaimed. From the time he went to Ottawa in 1976, the role of Quebec in Canada dominated the news. Said Simpson: "The great issues really of Canada are, are we going to hold together as a country? Are we going to remain separate from the United States? And how do we overcome all the challenges of distances and ethnicity and language and religion?" Historian Allan Levine faulted many of us for a "penchant for doomsday journalism that heightened the drama of each debate and meeting, and therefore raised the stature and significance of the messenger." But we got plenty of help from Trudeau and Mulroney. In fact, Allan Gregg's annual poll for *Maclean's* in 1995 revealed that one in three Canadians — and half the Quebecers surveyed — believed that the Canada they knew would not exist by the end of the decade.

But the country did more than survive. Although he spent forty years as a critic of government, Simpson allowed on taking his leave that Canada is "probably the best governed country in the Western world." While nothing is forever, he stated, "we have reached an equilibrium, an understanding that we are better off together." Simpson submitted that "the single biggest accomplishment of the country — almost unique in the world — is that we have managed to bring all these people here, in great numbers from all kinds of different places, and not have any political backlash or any discernable social tensions."

Simpson was in a mellow mood that day, June 1, 2016, the day after he announced his resignation. During two hours of conversation, he waxed eloquent about the accomplishments of his wife, Wendy, an expert in family law at the federal justice department, their three children, and their two treasured grandchildren. In a rare display of emotion, Simpson's voice broke as he recalled his last chat with Danson, the distinguished soldier and former defence minister, who had only days to live. And he was candid about the limits of the Ottawa columnist in the age of Twitter, blogs — and Stephen Harper: "I'm not saying this just to be falsely modest. I've had almost no influence on government. I may have influence on people outside government who read what I write."

———————

Simpson had a deeper connection with the Trudeau and Mulroney operatives, the men and women from Queen's and Laval, who were his contemporaries and contacts. He was in the thick of the action when Mulroney came within a feather of striking an agreement on the Meech Lake Accord. The concessions contained in the accord would have brought Quebec into the Constitution as a distinct society. But then the prime minister's own hubris helped cause the deal to unravel. MLA Elijah Harper, the first Indigenous member of the Manitoba legislature, held up a vote long enough for Newfoundland premier Brian Peckford to decide not to hold one at all, contrary to his promise. Lacking unanimity, Meech failed.

What piqued Peckford's ire was an interview that Mulroney granted to Simpson, Graham Fraser, and Susan Delacourt of the *Globe* after the leaders reached a tentative Meech agreement late on Saturday, June 10, 1990. In the interview on the following Monday, Mulroney boasted that a month before, in a meeting with his advisers, he had secretly laid out his plan for dealing with the premiers: "I told them when this thing was going to take place. I told them a month ago when we were going to start meeting. It's like an

election campaign, you count backwards. You've got to pick your dates and
you work backward from it ... and I said that's the day that I'm going to roll
all the dice. It's the only way to handle it." Peckford, who had committed
to a ratification vote in his legislature, felt that Mulroney's confession was
the ultimate manipulation.

The irony, of course, was that no one was as conscious of his image and
press relationships as Mulroney. "Brian," said Simpson, "was a guy who
really liked to be liked." He was the little guy from Champlain Street in
Baie-Comeau on the North Shore, who rose to the pinnacle of the business
and political worlds. I always felt that Mulroney hid his humble roots when
he ran for the Tory leadership in 1976. That was a campaign marked by
bands, booze, and bundles of cash. The high style betrayed his natural pride
in having arrived, but gave little sense of where he had been. He was at the
summit of the political and social scene. Four Mulroney biographers sought
to capture his pride in moving up with different versions of the same anecdote — one that made the rounds after I told some friends. It dated from
the time I was his guest for lunch at the stately Mount Royal Club shortly
after his defeat in the leadership race and he was very bitter about losing to
Joe Clark. To change the subject I asked: "Where are you living now?" He
fixed me with a defiant look and responded, "You know the mountain? On
top, right on the fucking top."

In the darkest days of Conservatism in Quebec in the 1970s, Mulroney
was the Quebec Tory party for those of us covering politics. He was ever
available, always ready with the fast quote, the telling thrust: no reporter
ever had a better source. In opposition in Ottawa he quickly turned the
tables on the Liberals, badgering English-speaking ministers with questions
in French and, as Simpson observed, "reversing the Tories' usual linguistic
dynamics in Ottawa."

The mood changed quickly when he became prime minister in 1984.
Facing the inevitable jostling during an early scrum, Mulroney exclaimed:
"Hey, wait a minute, we're all friends here." The assembled scribes groaned
in unison. Eventually, Mulroney's director of communications Bill Fox,
a seasoned former Hill reporter who became Mulroney's soul brother,

tightened the flow of government information and ordered civil servants to talk only on the record, which had the effect that they said very little. And Fox firmly believed in getting control of the prime minister's appearances. As he once said, "It's kind of *People* magazine journalism gone awry. I would really rather that the prime minister didn't do scrums. The media gets a snippet and it's just not reflective."

As scandals engulfed his ministry, Mulroney ceased having formal press conferences. Typically, he would pause on the stairs leading to his office from the Commons only if he heard a question from below that he wanted to address, producing one clip for the evening news of an ostensibly accessible PM before he sprinted away to his office. Then, in 1993, the government banned reporters from the members' lobbies of the Commons. In a letter of protest to the government, gallery president John Burke of Global News said, "It represents a grave restriction of a press freedom that is as old as Parliament itself." Even the Russian Parliament, Burke observed, allowed television cameras on the floor during sittings.

Brian Mulroney, whose own love-hate relationship with journalists was legendary, had always shared the conviction in Tory circles that the press held a massive bias against his party. He betrayed that sense of grievance in his memoirs when he recalled Diefenbaker's bad press. "My generation," he wrote, "had not yet learned that the media are relentless in their assault upon Conservative leaders who win, thereby depriving 'the natural governing party', the Liberals, of time in office… Joe Clark and I would one day find this out for ourselves."

The discovery came early. After his unsuccessful run for the Tory leadership that Clark claimed in 1976, Mulroney was incensed when the *Globe* published Richard Cleroux's account of a campaign worker paying for the rooms of delegates from Quebec so they would stay in Ottawa to vote. Later, when he was prime minister, journalists Stevie Cameron and Philip Mathias wrote about Mulroney's relationship with German lobbyist Karlheinz Schreiber and allegations that Schreiber doled out money in connection with Air Canada's purchase of Airbus planes. To this day, even close Mulroney advisers know he took three hundred thousand dollars in cash-stuffed envelopes from Schreiber but they cannot understand how he could chance his reputation for such a tawdry scheme. In 2007, during an inquiry ordered by the Harper government, Mulroney claimed that the money was for consulting services for Schreiber's armed vehicle businesses — and that taking the cash was his "second biggest mistake in life," the first being meeting Schreiber.

In power, Mulroney did not hesitate to correct the record. He regularly called anchors and editors to complain about their reporting. Journalist John Sawatsky detailed one typical incident when Mulroney concluded that the CBC News had underestimated the size of a crowd at a campaign kickoff. He called anchor Knowlton Nash twice in his Toronto studio during the show and once at home to voice his protest, with mounting anger each time. A week later he summoned CBC reporters Peter Mansbridge, Mike Duffy, and Jason Moscovitz and complained again about unfair CBC coverage.*

He also kept a close eye on suspected leakers. After Simpson wrote about Mulroney's unhappiness with some of his Quebec ministers, the PM's adviser Allan Gregg got a pointed call from a senior Mulroney staffer demanding to know why Gregg had talked to Simpson. When a puzzled Gregg checked later with Simpson on his source, it turned out the information had come from a private meeting with the prime minister himself at his 24 Sussex residence — the only such session he ever attended, Simpson hastily pointed out. Mulroney also was ever conscious of his image. He loved signing photographs of himself with visitors taken by a staff photographer of their meeting — prompting his staff to give him the photo book for signatures *after* he left the office for home at the end of a day.

Mulroney pursued an activist, at times unpopular, public policy agenda: sanctions against South Africa (opposed by Margaret Thatcher), abolition of capital punishment (in defiance of public opinion), liberalized immigration laws, introduction of the GST, better relations with Washington, the Canada-U.S. free trade deal, and an acid rain treaty. In addition, as Simpson noted, he "kept Canada largely out of the Reagan administration's nutty Star Wars antiballistic missile scheme." His support for linguistic minorities outside Quebec was unflagging. His grand coalition of *bleus* and *rouges* in Quebec produced an administration that pursued the integration of Quebec

---

* John Sawatsky, *Mulroney: The Politics of Ambition* (Toronto: Macfarlane, Walter and Ross, 1991), 473–74.

in the Constitution with a passionate obsession, and a prime ministerial office where Mulroney personally made sure that the dominant working language was French.

Despite his government's accomplishments in various policy areas, it was the many scandals implicating Cabinet ministers for bad judgment or conflicts of interest that dominated the later years of his tenure. They resulted in the resignations of several front-benchers.

One of Mulroney's staunchest media defenders, George Bain, accused the press gallery of "systematic groupthink," adding, "In the Mulroney years, correctness demanded not just that opposition to the government be maintained but that, like justice in the courts, it be seen to be maintained."

There were exceptions, most notably his close ties to *Globe* editor William Thorsell and (for a while) columnist Peter Newman. Simpson notes that he also benefited from extensive CBC News reporting led by "the impeccably balanced David Halton." In fact, there was wide support from journalists for both the Meech Lake and Charlottetown Accords. Beth Haddon, the accomplished journalist who was bureau chief in Ottawa for CBC's *The Journal*, likened the atmosphere to Stockholm Syndrome: "We all wanted Meech to succeed. We were all out of touch with the mainstream."

Simpson recalled that he had a telling formal interview with Mulroney in 1985 that spoke volumes about his years in power. What he found revealing was that Mulroney, who had studied Ronald Reagan, admired how the U.S. president was able to establish a "comfort zone" where he would get the benefit of the doubt when he made mistakes. Mulroney said he hoped he could establish the same safe space for himself.

"As time went on with Mr. Mulroney, particularly after he left power," Simpson said, "the exact antithesis occurred. He never established a comfort zone with the Canadian people. Things stuck to him in a negative way. He almost became the Velcro man for all the things that people didn't like. He tried so very hard. It was a bit of a tragedy." When he beat his retreat in 1993, the man who had delivered the first Conservative majority in twenty-six years, and only the second Tory government in fifty-four years, had become one of the most unpopular leaders since polling began. He had been done in by an economic slump, by the unpopular GST, and by his old friend Lucien Bouchard over the failure of Meech. The Bloc and Reform parties were on the rise.

In contrast to Mulroney, his successor Kim Campbell was a youthful, spirited forty-four-year-old lawyer with a glib phrase and a promise of "doing politics differently." In the Mulroney Cabinet she had a string of firsts for a woman in Canadian politics: they included minister of Indian affairs and northern development, and minister of national defence. When she was sworn in later as prime minister on June 25, 1993, she was the first woman in Canadian history to hold the post. But Mulroney had left her a scant two months to call an election. That summer she held her own at the G7 summit of world leaders in Tokyo and in a one-on-one session with U.S. president Bill Clinton. By September her Gallup Poll numbers were the highest any Canadian prime minister had scored in thirty years, seemingly banishing memories of her unpopular predecessor.

It quickly came to a crashing halt. Stepping out of Rideau Hall after calling the election on September 8, Campbell took a question from *Toronto Star* reporter Edison Stewart. He noted Canadians' acute concern about the lack of jobs, and asked: "Can you tell us realistically, how long do you think they will have to wait before the unemployment rate is below 10 percent?" It was a question that launched a thousand slips. In a two-minute-and-eighteen-second answer that was theoretically correct but politically malapropos, Campbell said:

> Realistically, all the developed industrialized countries are expecting what I would consider to be an unacceptable level of unemployment for the next two or three or four years…. We can adjust to the changing world economy in a way that will get that unemployment rate down and I would like to see, certainly by the turn of the century, a country where unemployment is way down.

Make that seven more years. The reaction of senior Campbell campaign adviser Gregg said it all: "Whoa! That was hardly on strategy." Later, however, Gregg conceded that Campbell's statement "while off strategy, was essentially true…. So, how could we have come to a point in politics," he wondered, "where telling the truth is considered a mistake by all elements of society?"

Gregg shares some blame for that state of affairs. He and Campbell campaign manager John Tory were the architects of negative campaign ads aimed at Jean Chrétien in the closing days of the 1993 campaign, when their polls pointed to a Chrétien victory. As he had when he "blew up the bridge" on John Turner, Gregg advocated an assault on Chrétien's credibility. The infamous spots featured close-ups of Chrétien's face distorted by a chronic facial paralysis, with the headline, "Is this a prime minister?" The wily Liberal leader seized on the apparent mockery of his facial defect, which Gregg insists was unintentional. "God gave it to me — when I was a kid, people were laughing at me — but I accepted that because God gave me other qualities and I'm grateful."

Gregg insists to this day that the ads were working to erode Chrétien's lead. But the backlash in the country, and among disillusioned Conservatives, caused Campbell to pull the spots. Gregg conceded the campaign was "a uniformly unpleasant experience for me." Author Ron Graham concluded: "The professionals had undoubtedly screwed up, in other words, but they had only been allowed to screw up so badly because of Campbell's amateurism."* As Simpson noted, Campbell displayed "an uncertain political touch" on the campaign trail and fielded "the weakest cabinet in a generation, a Triple A team trying to cut it in the big leagues." In the end, the Tories plunged from 151 seats to 2 seats as Chrétien swept to a majority. It was the worst defeat in Canadian history. In a reflective post on his website in 2013, Gregg had changed his view of attack ads:

Of course they work. They play to — and I believe feed — the public's general cynicism towards the political system and distrust of politicians. Sad but true, a message that states "politician A is a crook" is far more likely to be believed than one that claims "politician B is a paragon of virtue." But using this justification implies that the only practice of politics and role for politicians is to secure short-term electoral gain over your opponent.

---

* Ron Graham, *All the King's Men: Politics Among the Ruins* (Toronto: Macfarlane, Walter and Ross, 1995), 136.

Jean Chrétien was an unlikely populist. He had been part of the governing elite in Ottawa for more than thirty years. Even so, as Fox noted in his
1999 exploration of media and politics, Chrétien's media managers "successfully maintained the prime minister's image as '*le petit gars de Shawinigan.*'"*

Familiarity, in this case, bred content. Even his excesses were excused,
such as the time he attacked a protester in 1996 with a chokehold and
people in English Canada laughed it off as his "Shawinigan handshake." As
Chrétien's communications director Peter Donolo explained to Fox in an
interview in 1998: "It's like your mother or your uncle. If they say something
stupid, you can be angry with them over it, but it doesn't change your core
view of them based on a lifetime of shared experience. It's the same with
Chrétien — you feel as if you have known him forever."

His unaffected style was enduring. Before he won the Liberal leadership,
Chrétien was my guest in a foursome at the Peter Gzowski Invitational, an
annual golf tournament to raise money for Frontier College's literacy programs. Our honorary caddy was the great Canadian cellist Shauna Rolston.
As they headed down the first fairway, Chrétien compared notes with a
fellow musician: "So, I hear you play the cello? I play the French horn
myself" — a youthful legacy from boarding school in Joliette. For the rest
of the round the two of them jabbered away, clearly engaged in each other's
company. Rolston finally approached me near the end of the round and
inquired about her friendly companion, "Who is this guy?" Informed that
he was the leader of the official opposition in the House of Commons, she
was gobsmacked. "No shit!" she stammered in disbelief.

Maclean's Ottawa bureau chief Anthony Wilson-Smith was very
tight with the Chrétien people and persuaded Donolo to get Chrétien
to be our first guest when the magazine staged a live online forum (on
the CompuServe network, a name people who were alive in the pre-web
era may recall). He could barely type. At one point, trying to fashion a
Merci, he inquired, "Where's the *M*?" But here he was, the first head of
government anywhere to go online in a live chat, answering questions from
four hundred and sixty subscribers. As reporter Warren Caragata wrote in
Maclean's, "It became apparent that Chrétien's skills as a politician had not
been overwhelmed by technology."

---

* Bill Fox, *Spinwars: Politics and New Media* (Toronto: Key Porter, 1999), 102–3.

Jean Chrétien, my guest at the Briars for the Peter Gzowski Invitational, with
Shauna Rolston. Left–right: Tony Wilson-Smith, Robert Lewis, Jean Chrétien,
Shauna Rolston, Allan Gregg, and Heather Peterson: "Who is this guy?"

Such skill on the big stage enabled Chrétien to win three back-to-back
majorities and establish a legacy that included eliminating the deficit
and presiding over a period of constitutional peace. Admittedly, he
was helped by the skill of his tightwad finance minister, Paul Martin,
and hectoring from the right by Preston Manning, other members of
the Alliance-Reform movement, Bay Street, and the growing chorus of
right-wing business columnists.

As well, he was the beneficiary of a splintered opposition consisting of a
devastated Conservative Party, Lucien Bouchard's disruptive Bloc Québécois,
and the insurgent Reform Party. His accomplishments included legalizing same-sex marriage, reform of election spending, support of the Kyoto
Accord, and major funding of scientific research. In what Simpson called "an
ironic legacy for a Prime Minister not known for cerebral interests," he also
poured billions into the university sector — from millennial scholarships to
Canada research chairs. His "clarity act" set tougher conditions for future
independence referendums. Yet it also was on his watch when one of the

biggest scandals in Canadian history took place — the sordid sponsorship scandal of illicit spending in Quebec that eventually contributed to the defeat of the successor government of Paul Martin. Andrew Coyne, writing in *Maclean's* in 2008, concluded bluntly that "the 'culture of corruption' of the Chrétien years flowed seamlessly out of the corruption of the Mulroney years," indicating that "you could get away with just about anything in this country." Both the Airbus and sponsorship scandals led to damning commissions of inquiry that besmirched the records of both prime ministers.

The sponsorship affair came to light through the dogged reporting of *Globe* reporters Daniel Leblanc and Campbell Clark starting in 2002. By the time they had finished, more than three hundred stories later, the facts were documented by the federal auditor general and a judicial inquiry. It was a tale of massive spending by Ottawa for federalist advertising at cultural and sporting events, kickbacks to the Liberal Party by suppliers, and massive fraud by Liberal organizers. At least six people were found guilty, the latest in November 2016 being former Liberal organizer and Chrétien intimate Jacques Corriveau, who masterminded a scheme to enrich himself and associates to the tune of more than six million dollars. In his memoirs, Chrétien minimized the affair. He said he was sorry that "a few rogues had broken the rules." He insisted: "The slurs on my character didn't succeed, I think, because the public felt they knew me to be an honest person."

Le petit gars also was a street fighter who had an uncomplicated view of his trade. "Politics, for me, it's a sport," he told journalist Lawrence Martin. "You know, it's a very important endeavour, but … it's scoring points. It is winning seats and winning votes." He had scored his victory based on an appeal for open government in his so-called Red Book. Yet his administration was as secretive as all the rest. In February 1994, after Chrétien had been in office more than a hundred days, gallery president Giancarlo Ciambella, backed by the signatures of thirteen bureau chiefs, wrote to the prime minister requesting restoration of the pre-Mulroney access to the Commons lobbies. The signatories included Kirk LaPointe (CP), Bob Fife (Sun News), Christopher Waddell (CBC), Rosemary Speirs (*Toronto Star*), Denis Lord (Radio-Canada), Edward Greenspon (*Globe and Mail*), Craig Oliver (CTV), and Jean Dion (*Le Devoir*). "It has been more than 60 years since there was a conflict of this sort between a government and the Gallery," wrote Ciambella. But the Chrétien answer was consistent: Go away.

In the end, Chrétien was brought down after a decade in power by MPs in his caucus who supported Martin. This was the kind of thing that usually happens to parties in opposition, not parties in power with a majority government. "No prime minister with a parliamentary majority had ever been unseated by his party," Simpson wrote in 2003. Although technically he quit, "it had become evident" that a majority of his MPs and party members "did not want him to run again."

Tensions had existed between the two men since Chrétien whopped Martin in the 1990 leadership race. They surfaced again when Martin wanted to introduce major pension reforms in his first budget as finance minister in 1994 and Chrétien opposed them. Reporters Edward Greenspon and Anthony Wilson-Smith detailed the outcome in their excellent book on the early days of the government: "It got to the point where Chrétien had no choice but to draw a line in the sand and say, 'I'm the prime minister and you're the finance minister. I am saying no,' commented one observer close to the standoff."

It ended brutally in 2002 when Chrétien pre-empted Martin's resignation by appointing John Manley as the new finance minister. Martin was in his car on his way back to Ottawa from his Eastern Townships farm when he heard the news on the CBC show *Cross Country Checkup*.

It was one of those classic cases of two strong individuals failing to communicate. The late political strategist Mike Robinson best explained the phenomenon to author and press gallery veteran John Gray, who quoted him in his book *Paul Martin: The Power of Ambition*:

> They're not people who could have a social conversation and want to talk about the same things. It's very hard to get Mr. Martin to talk about politics; it's easy to get him to talk about policy. The opposite would be true with Mr. Chrétien. So they never bonded in a personal way; they never formed a friendship; they never formed a relationship that would give them something to fall back on when their paths started to go in different directions.

The irony, as Simpson noted, was that "plenty of Liberals would have preferred someone else other than Jean Chrétien as their leader and the bubble of that unhappiness burst when he expelled Finance Minister Paul Martin from Cabinet in early June 2002." At one point Chrétien planned to challenge his opponents at a leadership review, but dropped the idea when he realized he couldn't win it. Just as the Chrétien forces had worked to topple Turner before him, the Martinites proved able foes of the prime minister inside the Liberal tent. Journalists were willing recipients of leaks that damaged Chrétien from within. In effect, his party deserted him.

Knowing the fragility of the party leadership, Martin launched himself on an ambitious agenda. From bold moves to create a national child care program and shorten hospital wait times; from the historic Kelowna Accord on Indigenous rights to a national cancer strategy, there seemed no limit to his aspirations. "Everything," as Simpson noted, "was transformational change, so many ambitions built up in him, everything was a priority." Yet Martin was haunted by his own indecision — the *Economist* called him "Mr. Dithers" — and the sponsorship scandal. In the 2004 post-Chrétien election his Liberals were reduced to a minority government with 135 seats, to 99 for Stephen Harper's newly reunited Conservatives, 54 for the nettlesome Bloc, and 19 for Jack Layton's NDP.

That Parliament lasted only eighteen months, until the opposition combined in a non-confidence vote and forced another election. It began in the wake of the Gomery report on the sponsorship scandal. While the report cleared Martin and Chrétien of any complicity, it hung like a dark cloud over the Liberal Party, especially in Quebec. "I simply could not believe, emotionally and intellectually, that anyone thought I had anything to do with this mess," Martin said later in his memoirs.

Simpson summed it all up: "Governments actually operate according to the personality of the prime minister. There was no discipline. There was a severe case of indecision all the time. It's too bad. He is a wonderful man. And he was a good finance minister."

For many Canadians, the legacy of Paul Edgar Philippe Martin, deficit slayer and visionary, would begin to look better in the seasons ahead. The long winter of Stephen Harper was about to begin.

Part X

DEFINING
MOMENTS

Chapter 25

STEPHEN HARPER: NEWS-MANAGER-IN-CHIEF

John Willison was not amused. He could not pry any information from the government on important policy. "It was difficult, if not impossible, to secure information from the public departments," he lamented. John Willison was the Ottawa correspondent for the *Globe and Mail*. The prime minister was Sir John A. Macdonald.

News management in Ottawa is as old as the country. Until the late 1880s, parties controlled newspapers by owning them. Well into the 1950s, successive Conservative and Liberal governments depended on loyal members of the Parliamentary Press Gallery to convey their message. In the 1960s, Lester Pearson restricted the press gallery's access. In the mid-1970s, Pierre Trudeau began a trend to strong central control of all government information by a small group of insiders, continued by his successors into the new century.

Enter Stephen Harper. In his ten years in power he went to greater lengths to control the message than any prime minister in Canadian history. Secrecy and control were part of his DNA. How Harper wove his web and how the press gallery, in a fierce, uncoordinated counterattack, evened the score, combine to tell a cautionary tale for government: not because reporters suddenly all became partisans of the Liberals or NDP, but because they rallied, convinced that what they saw happening before their eyes was wrong. As Tory senator Grattan O'Leary once observed, "The press gallery can't bring down a government all by itself, but it certainly can hasten the process."

The first confrontation between the Harper government and the press occurred immediately after Harper's election as prime minister in 2006. In effect, he declared a strike against Ottawa reporters, withdrawing his services from the usual hallway scrums and official news conferences. He rarely went in the front door of the Commons where he could be questioned — and he left his caucus meetings by the back door. Between 2006 and 2009 he held only seven formal news conferences in the National Press Theatre and for the next five years, not one. Ministers had to clear all speeches with his office. In the 2015 election several of his candidates refused even to attend all-candidates' meetings, let alone talk to the press.

Over the years his ministers and their departments were as scripted as Broadway plays. Senior public servants became policy eunuchs who sang from a common hymnal supplied by the Church of Harper. Instead of background briefings on policies and plans, the government bombarded Canadians with multi-million-dollar ad campaigns and pre-recorded sound bites. Conservative Fund chair Irving Gerstein conceded in a 2013 speech to party delegates: "It is a fact that money facilitates political discourse and that paid political advertising is the only way for parties to communicate with citizens en masse, without the filter of the mainstream media."

Ottawa reporters tried to fight back, once walking out of a news conference because Harper aides sought to control the list of questioners, another time dispatching a formal delegation to meet with his communications chief. It didn't work.

Revealingly, in an interview with Kevin Libin of the Harper-friendly *Western Standard* in June 2006, the prime minister insisted the protests had backfired: "I'm free to pick my interviews when and where I want to have them.... I've got more control now."

Harper's staff even started removing seats for reporters at news conferences with visiting dignitaries, prompting one Australian reporter travelling to Ottawa with Prime Minister Tony Abbott to exclaim: "At the White House, we get seats." The mania for isolating reporters reached an absurd level in 2014 when Harper's staffers erected bank-style crowd-control stanchions in remote York Sound during the leader's visit to the Arctic.

Harper's communications rope-a-dope with reporters was symbolic of a more disturbing trend: government by stealth. He abolished the long-form census, a valuable tool for research on public policy, on the grounds that counting bathrooms and the like was an intrusion on personal liberty. The Freshwater Institute in Winnipeg and the gun registry also disappeared — with no hard questions answered. The consequences were unsettling.

Major changes to fundamental Canadian policies — whether scientific research, environment, or criminal law — were buried in massive omnibus bills with little debate and precious little supporting information. More often than not, Harper passed major legislative changes under tight time limits or closure. Where once governments provided reporters with background, the Harperites offered a thin tissue of talking points. When reporters had questions about policy their calls often were not returned, and the replies came back in scripted emails.

Courtney Tower, a veteran Ottawa reporter and public servant, said bureaucrats were partly to blame. After sixty-two years in journalism he

Robert Lewis greeting Stephen Harper for editorial board meeting at Rogers Media.

was still working as an eighty-two-year-old freelancer in the gallery "hot room" when we met in the adjacent lounge in late 2014. "There was here a public service ready enough to accede to giving away as little information as possible to the media and the outside," he observed. Tower, a former *Time* correspondent who became a press adviser to Pierre Trudeau, added: "There is such a level of public cynicism about the press that the manipulation and extreme ruthlessness of this [Harper] government doesn't register."

Usually, the issues being concealed were important ones. Under protocols governing the Privy Council Office (PCO), the prime minister's department, official emails could be deleted in bulk after a mere thirty days with no public audit. Noted federal scientists were banned from addressing public meetings, including ones organized by foreign governments that requested Canadian expertise. Nothing was left to chance. In 2014 the government broadened the use of "Cabinet confidences" to prevent release of details on such mundane issues as the cost and distribution of Viagra to Canadian troops and such major matters as inadequacies of railway safety rules.

In early 2015 the Harper government buried a provision in an omnibus budget bill that retroactively exempted the RCMP from culpability for destroying data in the federal gun registry — an action, said Information Commissioner Suzanne Legault, that contravened federal statutes. In May 2015 the government clamped a lid on details of a fifteen-billion-dollar arms deal with Saudi Arabia, despite federal regulations that require screening of sales to countries with records of persistent human rights violations. (The successor Liberals were no more transparent on the issue.) In 2012 pollster Allan Gregg, a former top election adviser to Brian Mulroney and Kim Campbell, blew the whistle during a lecture at Carleton University. The government's use of facts and evidence in decision making was on the decline, he said, "and in their place, dogma, whim, and political expediency are on the rise. And even more troubling, Canadians seem to be buying it."

———

The Harper crackdown began almost immediately after Harper formed a minority government following the 2006 election. Craig Oliver, the ebullient

CTV parliamentary correspondent and former host of the *Question Period* news show, had developed friendly relations with Stephen Harper during his opposition years. He was chuffed when he learned that he would get the first interview with the new prime minister. But the offer came with a catch: he could only ask questions about Canada's mission to Afghanistan, from which Harper had just returned. Oliver declined the interview on grounds that Harper was trying to control CTV's journalistic agenda. Looking back in his memoir, Oliver wrote: "They intended to change the rules, to challenge the influence of columnists and reporters, and to subject them to the same centralized control they would exert on the Conservative caucus and on government bureaucrats."

While Oliver's access to Harper subsequently improved, that was not the case for most members of the press gallery. In short order the prime minister's office (PMO) banned reporters from the traditional post-Cabinet scrums on the third floor of the Centre Block; instead the PMO picked which ministers went down to microphones outside the Commons. If a reporter had a question about the Atlantic fishery, but the only minister to show was from the ministry of defence, tough luck. If a journalist wanted to talk to the minister of agriculture about tainted meat, but the government was pushing a crackdown on crime that day, too bad — some junior in red suspenders would send an email addressing the journalist's questions. For press conferences, reporters who wanted to ask questions had to submit their names in advance and a PMO official used a list to recognize them. That defied the long-standing practice of having those sessions chaired by a member of the press gallery executive in the National Press Theatre.

On March 24, 2006, three months after Harper's election, a delegation from the press gallery had an on-the-record meeting with director of communications Sandra Buckler to voice journalists' concerns about PMO news management. The press gallery posted the transcript three days later. Buckler made it clear that Harper preferred keeping "The List" as well as the more magisterial setting in the corridor in front of the main doors to the House of Commons. He wasn't about to be cornered in a sit-down, press-theatre setting. "We're a different kind of government," she told the reporters without irony, "and we place a heavy value on communications, and we like the visuals and the ability to present the

Parliament to Canadians, which is one of the main reasons we like going in front of the House."

In fact, Buckler pretended not to know about the National Press Theatre across the street from the Hill: "That's the [place with the] big long table with the flags?" she ventured. As for objections about the PMO press office making a list of questioners — and an attendant boycott and walkout by two dozen reporters — Buckler insisted: "Some people have told us they enjoy the fact that they get to get on a list." And then this: asked if the PMO would publicize the dates of Cabinet meetings, Buckler responded, "Not sure yet."

Jason Kenney, the closest the Harper Cabinet had to a press gallery favourite, observed accurately: "The communications director for the prime minister does not believe in communicating."

Jennifer Ditchburn, a former CP parliamentary correspondent, documented what she calls one of the "unintended consequences" of the Harper crackdown on information in an excellent M.A. thesis.* She detailed how, in effect, he turned press gallery members into a bunch of Izzy Stones, the celebrated U.S. muckraker who disdained official Washington and based his scoops on prodigious mining of public documents. In an interview in late 2014, Ditchburn said: "People are doing more data reporting and using documents. They are much more diligent about looking at the public accounts. I never used to look at spending estimates or the strategic plans. You were really so busy. In the past you got a lot of information given to you, and you had access to ministers all the time." As Ditchburn noted, "Reporters have had to look for other ways to get their information. That's why you see so many scandal-driven stories."

An example was the work of her CP colleagues Mike Blanchfield and Jim Bronskill, who disclosed the extraordinary measures the Harper government took to script every announcement, every speech, and every response to press inquiries, no matter how trivial. The device was a so-called message event proposal (MEP) complete with the following

---

* Jennifer Ditchburn, "Journalistic Pathfinding: How the Parliamentary Press Gallery Adapted to News Management Under the Conservative Government of Stephen Harper" (master's thesis, Carleton University, 2014).

checklist: "event, event type, desired headline, key messages, media lines, strategic objectives, desired sound bite, ideal speaking backdrop, ideal event photograph, tone, attire, rollout materials, background, strategic considerations."

Based on almost one thousand pages of documents acquired under the Access to Information Act, the stories detailed how even the most experienced public servants had to seek permission to respond to reporters' questions, give press conferences, or make speeches. A special species singled out for extra adult supervision were the seasoned members of Canada's once-proud foreign affairs ranks, who were brought to heel like so many cypher clerks. When Robert Greenhill, former president of the Canadian International Development Agency (CIDA), was preparing for a high-level panel at the United Nations, CIDA sent a query to Ottawa with the demeaning request for "your authorization for President Greenhill to respond to questions." Clearly, everyone had to sing from the same Tory hymn book. As columnist Paul Wells observed in his 2013 book on Harper, *The Longer I'm Prime Minister*, "Harper's press office became a centre, not for disseminating information, but for containing it."

By 2014 control over the news agenda accelerated — and so did the reportorial use of the Access to Information Act and unofficial sources. Sun Media's David Akin used the act to acquire "House cards," the draft answers to possible opposition questions in the Commons prepared for government ministers, which often contained useful background on policy. Akin would digitize those cards, creating his own library of key policy issues. *La Presse* hired an extra bureau person just to launch access to information requests — for information that could have been provided without a formal request. Anonymous sources were behind the efforts of Stephen Maher and Glen McGregor, who broke stories about the Tory use of robocalls in 2011 to disrupt election day, and Bob Fife's disclosure of the Nigel Wright payment of ninety thousand dollars to Mike Duffy as part of the Senate expense scandal.

In early 2014 the PMO started producing a daily web video report called *24/Seven*, purporting to cover Harper's activities in the style of a newscast. One segment included "coverage" of an upcoming trade deal with South Korea, although reporters preparing to travel with the PM to Seoul had no chance to ask questions about it.

In March, after Harper staged an unusual private swearing-in for new Cabinet ministers at Rideau Hall — including Finance Minister Joe Oliver — the new members mutely skipped away from waiting reporters outside who had been barred from the ceremony. It was an elevation to Cabinet befitting a banana republic. The only commentary the new ministers offered was to the unchallenging interlocutors from *24/Seven*. (Keeping Oliver sequestered was probably a good idea. While facing real questions after delivering his first budget in April 2015, he raised eyebrows among PMO operatives when he suggested that any burden from tax changes could be left to "Stephen Harper's granddaughter to solve.")

At a Canadian Journalism Foundation (CJF) panel in 2014 — "Does the Press Gallery Matter?" — Akin, then of Sun News, described with mounting anger how his network spent some twenty thousand dollars to cover Harper's January 2014 trip to the Middle East, only to be shut out of some key moments. He was irate that the PMO did not notify journalists that Harper planned to greet Syrian refugees at the Jordanian border. A Harper aide actually tweeted clips shot by PMO cameras to reporters — aired later exclusively on *24/Seven* — of Canadian MPs hard by the border, receiving refugees and putting them on a truck. "Not a single journalist was notified this was happening, let alone got a chance to film it," said Akin angrily.

Why does any of this matter? Who cares if reporters in Ottawa, or anywhere, were having a difficult time getting information? Doesn't the public dismiss the lamentations of reporters as bellyaching? Didn't several Ottawa reporters refuse to join their colleagues in boycotting Harper press conferences? In an age of Twitter and *24/Seven*, does the press gallery even matter anymore?

Not as much to the parties, as it turns out. At the CJF panel, Harper's trusted Cabinet minister Jason Kenney said the press gallery has "always mattered as an institution to hold us elected guys accountable." But there were now other avenues for governments to get their message out, including social and ethnic media. As for message control, Kenney noted that all governments around the world do it — a point illustrated in Ditchburn's research. Kenney went on: "I'd like to believe there is an audience — a paying audience — for substantive coverage that's actually interested in finding interesting policy stories that go deep; that it is not just political journalism as fight promotion."

The problem was, there was precious little opportunity for Ottawa reporters to dig or go deep during the Harper years. Many of them were running breathlessly to stay on top of a 24/7 news cycle, filing news reports, shooting video, tweeting. Besides, as Ditchburn noted in 2014, before Harper's defeat the next year:

> What we are seeing now is a real crisis of government infor-
> mation, in the sense that reporters can no longer talk to
> bureaucrats. When I came to the Hill in 1997, I could call
> up somebody who was drafting legislation and get him to
> explain it to me. That's what you need to do substantive
> coverage. That stopped in 2006. The lines into the bureau-
> cracy just shut down.

Paul Wells argued that the origin of the MEP actually went back indirectly to the 2004 campaign, when Harper's message was sabotaged by undisciplined remarks by his own backbenchers — so-called bozo eruptions from candidates with too much time on their hands and too little party policy in their heads. These eruptions usually had to do with social and moral issues, ranging over abortion to same-sex marriage and evolution.

One of the most vibrant of the cast was former B.C. Reform MP Randy White. Before the 2004 campaign he gave an interview to filmmaker Alexis Fosse Mackintosh, who explicitly told White she wanted someone from the "no" side for her documentary on the appropriateness of same-sex marriage. He obliged, speaking, as she put it, "very clearly and articulately" for "the feelings of his constituency." What he felt was that the controversial "notwithstanding" clause of the Constitution could be used to overturn same-sex marriage laws. As a parting shot, he added: "To heck with the courts, eh."

Trouble was, it was the eve of the 2004 election. The Mackintosh film found its way to the Liberals and Prime Minister Paul Martin gleefully screened it at a press conference. "White's interview was enormously damaging," wrote Tom Flanagan, then Harper's campaign manager, in his book, *Harper's Team: Behind the Scenes in the Conservative Rise to Power.* "The interview was perfect for the Liberals because it seemed to show that Harper had a secret agenda." As part of a series of gaffes, the bozo eruptions helped

Martin to a minority government victory. And they steeled Harper's will to ban the eruptions, if not the bozos.

————————

In Ye Goode Olde Days, there was absolutely no subtlety about managing the news. Prime Minister John A. Macdonald helped raise funds — and contributed personally — to start the *Toronto Mail*, a Conservative newspaper that would compete with his archrival George Brown and his *Globe*, the bible of Ontario Liberalism. When the *Mail* failed to live up to Macdonald's idea of Tory partisanship, the prime minister became an investor in the *Toronto Empire*. Near the end of the century, Prime Minister Wilfrid Laurier raised money to launch *L'Électeur* and installed his friend Ernest Pacaud as editor. The paper was the prime minister's most consistent voice in the province; it later became *Le Soleil*. Wealthy Tory leader R.B. Bennett organized the loans that launched the *Regina Daily Star* in 1927 — $40,000 from his Calgary bank, $105,000 from his law firm.

Historian Minko Sotiron has documented the many ways governments of both stripes routinely rewarded their papers in the early days: there were contracts for printing ballot papers and other official material, as well as bailout loans. Bulk subscription buying of issues by politicians to promote favourable coverage was standard practice. Ottawa Liberals once bought forty thousand copies of the *Free Press* for distribution because it contained the text of a Laurier speech. Knighthoods and Senate seats were distributed to elite supporters like candy at Halloween. In 1902, A.J. Magurn, a press gallery veteran who had preceded John Dafoe as editor of the *Free Press* — and worked in Liberal campaigns — went so far as to defend his demand for a seat in the Upper Chamber on the grounds of his long-time loyalty to the party:

> The newspaperman is generally a politician and can expect nothing from the other side after he has compromised himself seriously year after year.... It is nothing unusual or out of the way if I say to the party whose battles I fought in season or out of season for many

years: "I helped you when you needed it most, now I want you to help me."*

Harper's staff-produced web show, *24/Seven*, was not the first attempt to fool unsuspecting voters. Historian Allan Levine, in his authoritative book on prime ministers and the media, *Scrum Wars*, traces the roots of deception back to the 1930s. The pioneer of the genre, actually, was "Bible Bill" Aberhart of Alberta. His *Man From Mars* radio shows, begun in 1934, portrayed citizens deploring economic conditions in the province, complete with a "Martian" asking why Albertans weren't smart enough to support Social Credit policies. The next year, the federal Conservatives used six dramatizations featuring "our friend and neighbour Mr. Sage," who savaged Liberal leader William Lyon Mackenzie King and plumped for Prime Minister R.B. Bennett. The Sage shows, conceived by a Toronto advertising executive, were not identified as Tory propaganda. When they returned to power the Liberals managed to pass a ban on dramatized election programming.

Managing the news was a specialty of Clifford Sifton, who served as Laurier's interior minister and right hand. He not only owned the powerful *Manitoba Free Press* but published a series of newsletters that friendly Liberal papers were expected to run. "The object of a Party newspaper," he proclaimed, "was to 'get the public mind saturated with its own views and ideas.' … The theory that you want the elector to read both sides and trust to him that you are right, is not practical politics."

Within a few years of his coming to Ottawa, Levine wrote, "Sifton's machine had established an 'efficient propaganda network' that published biased editorials and slanted news articles." Later in the decade a Tory backroom committee adopted the idea and churned out party propaganda faithfully recorded in some seventy newspapers.

On the surface, the classic prime ministerial clam was William Lyon Mackenzie King. Although Canada's twelfth prime minister had been a reporter in Toronto during and after university, he showed little sympathy for the needs of the press. When King arrived back in Ottawa from a trip, members of the press gallery would go down to the train station and line

---

* Minko Sotiron, *From Politics to Profit: The Commercialization of Canadian Daily Newspapers, 1890–1920* (Montreal: McGill-Queen's University Press, 1997), 106–12.

up — according to seniority — to greet him. As was his custom, King would greet "the boys" warmly and invite them to come to his office later for a briefing where he would hand out some tidbit — with emphasis on "bit" — of news. After waiting outside an East Block Cabinet meeting for most of a hot July day in 1937, reporters stood as King emerged to say: "I don't think I can give you anything today."

In actual fact, King cultivated close relationships with key members of the press gallery, including Grant Dexter of the *Winnipeg Free Press*, Bruce Hutchison of the *Vancouver Sun*, and especially Charles Bishop, a Conservative-leaning columnist for the *Ottawa Citizen*, whom he later appointed to the Senate.

Grattan O'Leary of the *Ottawa Journal* had no qualms about being *parti pris* either. He was an unabashed admirer and long-time friend of Arthur Meighen when he was Tory leader and, briefly, prime minister. "I am a party man. I am a partisan. I am a Conservative without prefix or qualification," O'Leary boasted in his inaugural Senate speech in 1962.

John Diefenbaker, the dishevelled Prairie populist, was one of the first leaders to bring the emerging advertising and marketing sensibilities to political campaigning in the late 1950s. His agent of change was Allister Grosart, who had formed the Canadian Publicity Bureau in 1934 to promote American movies and pop songs in Canada. Later, while at McKim Advertising, Grosart went to work on Dief's leadership campaign and then became the party's national director. From that post he planned the Chief's election campaigns with a level of detail Stephen Harper would embrace five decades later.

On the eve of the 1958 election, as reported by Peter Newman in *Renegade in Power*, Grosart advised all candidates how to pose with their families for campaign photos: "The ideal setting is the Candidate and family in his own backyard, setting off to Sunday morning church, hand-in-hand with wife and children. An ordinary back fence is a good background; a split-level $25,000 ranch house is not." Grosart also devised a ditty designed to encourage the correct, soft pronunciation of the leader's name as *DiefenBAYker*, instead of the then commonly used Germanic-sounding *DiefenBACKer*.

The first move against open access in modern times came in 1965 when Lester Pearson decided to end the tradition of reporters waiting at the door for ministers to emerge from the second-floor Cabinet room of the East Block. Ironically, Pearson had always had solid relationships with reporters as a civil servant and external affairs minister, built mainly on his penchant for off-the-record briefings and studied leaks of information. "It was a technique Pearson used at the U.N. and in Ottawa," his former press secretary Dick O'Hagan told me. "He was skillful and had a lot of good relationships with a lot of reporters." But as prime minister, he objected to the scrums outside his office. Instead, Pearson agreed to brief reporters after Cabinet meetings in a basement meeting room. Reporters were upset. In an attempt at mollification, O'Hagan sent a memo to the gallery executive: "Our purpose is not to impede but rather to expedite, hopefully through clearer channels, the free flow of information." Right. But when scandals and controversy enveloped the government, Pearson gave up on regular press conferences.

There was no doubt about Pierre Trudeau's views on reporters. Heading into an election in 1978, and trailing Joe Clark in the polls, the Liberals turned once again to O'Hagan, bringing him back to Ottawa from the embassy in Washington. Funny thing: Trudeau objected to the scrums of reporters, and O'Hagan negotiated an agreement with the gallery types to end them. In return they got a commitment to regular news conferences in the National Press Theatre chaired by a member of the gallery executive. But after two years the PMO moved the sessions to the Conference Centre with a Trudeau staffer in the chair. Then Trudeau tired of the weekly confabs, especially during his nasty public breakup with Margaret, and ended the sessions.

The Trudeau era also ushered in a much more central control of communications. A subcommittee of Cabinet under two former journalists, Gérard Pelletier and later Roméo LeBlanc, reviewed all policy announcements and plans through the lens of how they would play in the media. Each Cabinet document had to contain a section on the communications implications of the decision. The journalist who wrote the strategy scripts was an experienced reporter and my former *Time* magazine colleague Courtney Tower. "I was an agent of spin, absolutely," he concedes with a smile. Still, the Liberals continued to release the Cabinet policy documents that explained the rationale behind their decisions.

Much of the prime ministerial posturing over the years has been self-protective. Harper believed that rigid control would allow his government to keep the focus on his top priorities — tougher crime laws, a GST cut, child-care allowances, an accountability act, and health-care wait times. On one level, his strategy was a winning one: he did win three elections, including a majority in 2011.

It is little wonder that so many leaders court allies in the media, and all of them have surrounded themselves with an army of communications specialists. Today they talk only in political parables and fables. They dare not go off script. The message is the massage for a public that has stopped listening. In the 2015 campaign, when CBC chief correspondent Peter Mansbridge asked the leaders one by one what personal quality best defined them, no one had an answer — at least nothing unscripted that they wanted to volunteer.

Acts of political self-immolation or party fratricide have haunted generations of politicians. In a heated Commons debate, William Lyon Mackenzie King once rejected demands from Conservative MPs for unemployment funding with the unfortunate barb, "I would not give them a five-cent piece." In the 1962 campaign Pearson dug himself a hole by appearing to threaten yet another election if Canadians elected a minority government. Similarly, Pierre Trudeau was cast as a villain in western Canada when he was tagged with the quote, "Why should I sell your wheat?" In fact, Trudeau gave a thoughtful, five-hundred-word response to a pointed question, Pearson had merely stated the obvious, and King did not want to fund provincial governments opposed to his policies.

And the damage list goes on down through recent history: Liberal Prime Minister John Turner patting the bums of two female colleagues in front of CTV cameras; Brian Mulroney boasting in an interview about the climax of the Meech Lake Accord in 1990 as the day he would "roll all the dice"; or Tory PM Kim Campbell insisting in the 1993 election that a campaign was no place to discuss complicated issues like unemployment.

In a private moment, the late Ron Basford, the former justice minister under Pierre Trudeau, once told me astutely: "Every politician is one sentence removed from oblivion." Truer words were never spoken — off the record.

Chapter 26

CELEBRITY JOURNALISM: TWELVE FEET TO STARDOM

To its critics, the Parliamentary Press Gallery has always been something of a Star Chamber, mysteriously dispensing arbitrary judgment on the conduct of Canada's rulers. That it may be. But the gallery in modern times also has been a star machine, launching careers into orbit and turning certain journalists into A-listers with wealth, influence, fame — and, sometimes, notoriety. Peter Mansbridge, Pamela Wallin, Mike Duffy, Wendy Mesley, Allan Fotheringham, Jeffrey Simpson, Chantal Hébert, Andrew Coyne — the list goes on. They are what Charles Lynch, who did much to invent the breed, called "celebrity journalists." Certainly the anglophone edition of this breed is pervasive. Norman DePoe, the legendary CBC TV reporter, and CTV's Duffy would often attract more attention at campaign stops than the prime minister or leader of the opposition. Today's cast is omnipresent on TV panels, even if they are not hosting them, and they rake in the cash for speeches to conventioneers or lectures at universities. Three of the most successful happened to become friends: Mansbridge, Wallin, and Fotheringham.

It was a long, steady climb for Peter Mansbridge from the day in 1968 when the manager of the CBC station in Churchill heard him announce: "Transair flight 106 for Thompson, The Pas, and Winnipeg is now ready for boarding." The next night, after one hour of training, the twenty-year-old newbie was on the air at CHFC as a disc jockey.

From the beginning he wanted to do news. He used his shortwave radio to learn from experienced broadcasters in other cities and signed up for CBC training courses. He paid his dues for twenty years as a reporter in Winnipeg, Regina, Ottawa, and around the world. For the better part of his last twenty-nine years with the CBC, he sat twelve feet from the lens in the broadcast studio, not so much dispensing the news as sculpting his distinct vision of the country as anchor of *The National*. Looking back, he said, he has no regrets — not about passing up the offer to host the CBS morning show in New York in 1988 (beating out Charlie Rose, who later won the job and then lost it amid a flurry of sexual harassment allegations in 2017); certainly not about taking over *The National* from a gracious Knowlton Nash who stepped down to keep Peter at the CBC; not even about the attacks from his voluble critics. "Look, I did *extremely* well by staying here," he said in an early 2017 interview. And he vowed to do even better after he stepped away from the anchor's seat on July 1, 2017, for a new life. After a relaxing summer, he resumed a lucrative sideline of paid speeches, which CBC management had cut short after a public controversy, although it was part of his original contract.

His first big break came when he got a job with CBC News in Winnipeg and was assigned to co-host the local coverage of the 1972 federal election. He was twenty-four, and, he confided, "my heart was pounding through my chest." Before they went on the air he commented that the hands of his co-host, Bill Guest, were shaking under the desk. "If you are not nervous before a big show," Guest told him, "then you are in the wrong business." Mansbridge said, "He was right. All these years later I still feel that way before an election night or big story."

Big stories have been a Mansbridge specialty since he arrived in CBC's Ottawa bureau on Labour Day, 1976. Even after he moved to Toronto in 1981, he kept his hand in doing coverage of special events and hosting live specials.

In 1984 he broke the controversial story about an abortive plot by senior Liberals to unseat leader John Turner in the midst of the election campaign and install Paul Martin. In the interview, I asked him, "How solid was that story?" His reply:

> One hundred percent. The sourcing was ironclad. The issue was, are we interfering with the campaign by telling this story? That became an issue which cost us a day. They didn't deny it because they couldn't deny it. Let's put it this way: the people who were involved knew it was going on and had happened. The people around and closest to Turner knew it happened. So there was a pool to choose from to have multiple sources — and we had multiple sources.

Since his first live special in 1981 on the Supreme Court decision on the Constitution, his calm, measured demeanour during major live events earned him a reputation as one of the best. From the 1995 Quebec referendum to the 9/11 attacks and the shootings on Parliament Hill in 2014, he guided viewers through the major events of our times, never shying away from saying what we *did not yet know* about the event.

One of the most controversial calls by the CBC was the decision to go with ongoing coverage of Mulroney's efforts over five years to redraw the Constitution and bring Quebec into the fold. The CBC relentlessly cast its spotlight on the failed 1987 Meech Lake negotiations and the defeat of the subsequent Charlottetown Accord in the 1992 referendum. After it was over, said Mansbridge, "it caused a lot of consternation at the CBC about, Did we do too much? Did we make it sound like the world was going to come to an end if they didn't get everything done in a certain period of time?"

One thing is clear, the so-called elites favoured the accommodation with Quebec and were surprised by the 55 percent "no" vote. As with the Trump victory in November 2016, most of us in the media failed to detect the uprising against Charlottetown. "That was the discussion that took place at the CBC: what did we miss and how did we miss it," said Mansbridge. "It came down to, we missed the people. We spent a lot of time covering old guys in suits walking in and out of a room. Meanwhile there was an outraged public out there that we didn't understand or that we dismissed." The result was that the CBC and other news organizations started involving citizens in panels and specials. CBC, CTV, and *Maclean's* convened televised retreats with typical Canadians struggling to produce solutions.

Mansbridge recalled with some fondness the early days in the bureau, which head of news Trina McQueen and her deputy, Vince Carlin, had seeded with a new, younger — and all male — breed: Mark Phillips and John Blackstone, both now with CBS News; Mike Duffy, now of Senate fame; Brian Stewart; and Ken Colby. "It was a different time," recalled Mansbridge. Usually once a week, "we used to go down to the old Prescott and have great lunches that would last all afternoon. John Drewery would enthrall us with stories about what it was like when he was a kid reporter. We used to do a lot of drinking in those days."

The biggest change Mansbridge saw on Parliament Hill — and it was overnight — was the arrival of TV in the House of Commons in 1977. "Suddenly," he says with a grin, "all the guys who used to turn up in suits that looked like they were made from seat covers of a '56 Chevy started to dress better. Their comments became punchier." But with that came

Peter Mansbridge with Mike Duffy (left): Watergate changed the business.

a decline in spontaneity. "A lot of what we considered the fun moments disappeared. As that change became more firmly embedded over the next decade," Mansbridge added, "journalism changed. It was never friendly, but it certainly became less friendly and more aggressive, looking for a scandal around every corner."

The turning point was the fall of Richard Nixon. "Watergate changed the business," said Mansbridge. "My start in journalism could not have happened after Watergate. After Watergate everybody wanted to be a journalist. I got my start because nobody wanted to be a journalist. There would have been two hundred people lined up for that job after Watergate."

It was a good run. His third marriage, to actress Cynthia Dale, has made him the proud dad of a son now in university. (He has two grown daughters from his first marriage.) Around CBC News his word on coverage and personnel was the law. The well-watched *At Issue* panel usually did not take place if he was out of town. He won dozens of industry awards for his work over forty-nine years with the CBC, in addition to being named as an Officer of the Order of Canada. As someone who never went to university, he relishes his nine (and counting) honorary degrees and his stint as chancellor of Acadia University. He has friends across the country and around the world, and hangs out with Canada's rich and famous (Bobby Orr, Jim Balsillie, Gerry Schwartz, and Heather Reisman). As if to underline the point, an old friend who noshed with him before he left CBC said to him jokingly, "So, Peter, is this the first time recently that you have had lunch with someone who isn't a billionaire?" He laughed heartily. All the way to the bank.

When twenty-seven-year-old Pamela Wallin reported for work in the Ottawa bureau of the *Toronto Star* in 1980, she admits, "I had absolutely no qualifications, except a willingness to work hard." What Wallin also had was a fierce interest in federal politics, a passion for journalism, charm, and guile. Plus a restless, burning ambition. In the short span of fifteen years those qualities took her from tiny Wadena, Saskatchewan — "Where Big Dreams Grow" is the town motto — to the pinnacle of Canadian journalism.

Her life has been a study in contrasts. She was a girl from a small town of thirteen hundred souls who ended up with a handsome flat in midtown Manhattan, which she occupied while representing Canada as consul general in New York. She started broadcasting in a small Regina station and ended up hosting CTV's premier morning show. She began life as a left-wing social worker and ended up in the Senate as one of Stephen Harper's fierce acolytes.

But when she approached the *Star*, the only newspaper article she had ever written was a test piece for the paper's national editor Lou Clancy. And in her memoir, *Since You Asked*, she disclosed that she did it with help from her friend *Star* journalist and author Alison Gordon, and colleagues at the CBC show *As It Happens*, where she was, appropriately, a chase producer.

It was not entirely a con job. She did know and understand the capital. In 1975 she had moved to Ottawa from Regina, where she was producing a radio show for CBC, to be a story editor at *CBO Morning*. Importantly, in Ottawa the host was the indomitable Elizabeth Gray, who became her mentor. She and her husband, journalist John Gray, swept Wallin into their wide orbit of Hill power brokers and journalists. Two years later, in Toronto at *As It Happens*, her focus was the Ottawa beat, using her contacts on the Hill to line up stories and guests for Barbara Frum on the popular evening radio show. (Disclosure: She paired Bill Fox, then with Southam News, and me on a regular gossipy Friday evening gab segment.) When she walked into the *Star* bureau in Ottawa, where Fox was then working, she was ready to take on the capital.

She said in a 2016 interview that the first thing she noticed was that "guys went to lunch with sources. The males asked me for *dinner*. They didn't take me seriously." Big mistake. "They told me things they wouldn't tell Bill Fox and the other guys in the bureau." Wallin shared her intel with her colleagues and ended up with contributions to several stories each day. But she had an unusual writing technique that bemused the boys: typing her stories on a long role of teletype paper threaded into her machine, then rearranging the paragraphs by cutting and pasting the copy into a story. She also tapped a wide circle of "smart and creative women friends," including Elizabeth Gray, political aide Terry Kelleher, and journalists Mary Janigan, Carol Goar, Stevie Cameron, and Sandra

Gwyn. One of her closest friends was the tough and able *Vancouver Sun* bureau chief Marjorie Nichols. Wallin, typically, was with her through her struggle with cancer to the very end.

She said that the constitutional debates of the late 1970s were "the most formative journalistic assignment I had." Nichols took Wallin under her wing, teaching her about the importance of the division of powers in a federation — and about freight rates. She put that and her Saskatchewan roots to good use when she covered western outrage about the Liberal government's National Energy Program, scoring an exclusive interview with Alberta premier Peter Lougheed — and landing a piece on freight rates for her *Star* readers in Toronto.

Another key development was her emergence as a star on TV under the aegis of the late Bruce Phillips of CTV. In addition to his pithy "Brucegrounders" on the evening news, Phillips was host of the Sunday show *Question Period*, which then featured a panel of journalists asking questions of prominent political people. After her first appearance, Phillips pulled her aside and asked if she had been nervous. "I told him, 'No, I wasn't nervous because I was prepared.'" After getting the same assurance a second time, Phillips pronounced: "You have a future in television."

And how. After less than two years with the *Star* she moved to CTV as an Ottawa-based host of the national morning program, *Canada AM*. In December 1981 she took over as the co-host of the show in Toronto with Norm Perry, following the retirement of Gail Scott. It was her eighth move since leaving hometown Wadena in 1975. In a decade at CTV she covered the Falklands War, and fell in love and later married her cameraman, Malcolm Fox. In 1984 she went back to Ottawa as bureau chief and host of *Question Period* when Mulroney appointed Bruce Phillips to the Canadian embassy in Washington.

That was when Wallin started commuting to Toronto every week "to maintain some semblance of a personal life" with her Toronto-based husband. Finally, in 1988, she moved back for good, where she anchored the weekend news, hosted special events, and filled in on the *AM* show. But the stress of making a marriage work "in the glare of the public spotlight" proved too challenging for their ten-year relationship (five of them as a married couple). She also grew unhappy with life at CTV.

Pamela Wallin interviewing Margaret Thatcher: a passion for journalism.

An offer to jump to CBC was timely. The masterful Barbara Frum, who presided over *The Journal*, the forty-minute segment that followed the national news, had died of leukemia. Merging the two shows to create *Prime Time News*, CBC planned to team Wallin with Peter Mansbridge as co-hosts in a new 9:00 p.m. slot (instead of the traditional 10:00 p.m.) They would alternate reading items and doing interviews. But first some air had to be cleared. Peter was "convinced I had made a cruel comment about his all-too-public marital meltdown with CBC journalist Wendy Mesley." Wallin, at the time in the midst of her own public marital breakdown, assured Mansbridge that the report was unfounded.

Still, it was an uneasy time. A demanding workaholic, she was known by some critics around the newsroom as "Pamatollah." The ghost of the popular Barbara Frum hung over the show, and the ratings slumped as viewers resisted the move to 9:00 p.m. Despite a three-year contract, Wallin had the feeling that "it just wasn't working out." Before the end of her third season she was told her contract would not be renewed. She left the show that day.

Mansbridge admitted that *Prime Time News* was one of the low points of his career. "It was never about friction with Pam," he insists, "it just didn't work for a lot of reasons." In her first speech after the firing, Wallin joked that her chapter on the *Prime Time News* saga would be titled "None of This Would Have Happened if Only I Had Played Golf" — a reference, in part, to Mansbridge's love of the game.

After *Prime Time News*, Wallin linked up with her old friend and CTV producer Jack Fleischmann to start their own company. It produced a weekly show, *Maclean's TV*, that ran on CTV; a successful interview show, *Pamela Wallin Live*, for Newsworld, the CBC's twenty-four-hour cable network; and the Canadian version of *Who Wants to Be a Millionaire*. In 2001 she helped organize and promote the "Canada Loves New York" rally after the 9/11 attacks, and the next year Prime Minister Chrétien appointed her consul general in Manhattan with an official residence on Park Avenue. From there, it was a steady march forward — to several corporate boards, dozens of honorary degrees, the naming of Pamela Wallin Drive in Wadena, and, finally, the fateful appointment to the Senate by Prime Minister Harper.

Friends saw changes over those years. In the Senate, the travel in airplanes and limos that had become such a part of her life as a star did not stand up to the glare of public accounting. Friends warned her to be careful. But she developed a hard, partisan edge promoting the Harper line that many found disturbing. For three years after the Senate suspended her pay pending investigation of sloppy expense account claims in 2013, she was in limbo. She was vilified in public, even in the streets of Wadena. She repaid some $150,000 in expenses that had been challenged. Finally, in the wake of Mike Duffy's acquittal on similar charges, the RCMP dropped its investigation of Wallin's expenses in 2016. She was free, at sixty-three, to return to life as a senator, this time as an independent, still bitter about the betrayal in the Conservative ranks that caused her downfall, still determined to make a difference.

In the course of my days as managing editor and editor-in-chief at *Maclean's*, I once calculated that I had authorized more than three million dollars in payments to our back page columnist over two decades.

Allan Fotheringham liked to boast that using expense accounts from his many outlets — *Maclean's*, a national newspaper syndication, *Front Page Challenge* on the CBC, speaking fees, and eight books — he had travelled to ninety-one countries and never had to use his own money for lunch or a drink. Not that there were any tag days. In one year, in fact, his income was $492,000, making him the most highly paid columnist in the country. Or so he says in his memoir, *Boy from Nowhere: A Life in Ninety-One Countries*. I do know that he made more than I did, but he sold seats in the stadium.

He started out in Hearne, Saskatchewan, about a three-hour drive south of Wadena, fifty miles south of Regina. "All the great ones come from Saskatchewan," he once observed. As he must have said a thousand times in speeches, "the town was so small it couldn't afford a village idiot. Everyone had to take turns." Also this: "People from Hearne are called 'Hernias.'"

His mother, a widow with four kids, ran a post office out of her home. Fotheringham developed his love of reading and travel by borrowing magazines that came in the mail. "I would get in deep trouble for not remembering which slot they were supposed to go back in," he recalled during an interview at his Toronto home in early 2016.

When his mother remarried and the family moved to British Columbia, the owner of the local paper, the *Chilliwack Progress*, saw his writing in the high-school paper and asked him to be a columnist. He submitted a piece about kids feeding Coke and junk food to rats. "We all know the resulting conclusions," he wrote in his memoir. "A stiff-necked Coca-Cola lawyer threatened to sue for patent violation. (I was in high school, for Christ's sake!)"

"Foth" made a practice of goading the powerful the rest of his career. At the University of British Columbia, where he became editor of the *Ubyssey*, a mock issue spoofing the downtown dailies infuriated the editors but prompted publisher Donald Cromie to offer him a job at the *Vancouver Sun*. He was good. In four months, when he was twenty-four, the boss tapped him to be the sports editor. Never lacking in self-confidence, Fotheringham said, "I knew I had made it." He then promptly took off for Europe where he "bummed around, chased girls and drank wine for three years." When he got back, he did better than sports editor: he landed a general column at the *Sun*. As the years passed he became great friends with broadcaster Jack Webster and Marjorie Nichols, at the time Victoria bureau chief for the *Sun*. "Marjorie was the first terror in Canadian journalism," he said, unabashedly repeating a favourite phrase: "Marjorie, Jack Webster, and I used to run the town."

In 1975, at forty-three, Fotheringham signed on as a columnist for *Maclean's*. When he picked up the first issue, his oversized ego was crushed when he did not find his piece in the first few pages of the magazine — but on the last page. That turned out to be a brilliant stroke by editor Peter C. Newman. The "back page" became one of the best-read features in the magazine, a column placement later emulated by *Time* and *Newsweek*.

Through the late 1970s and '80s, Fotheringham commuted between Vancouver and Ottawa, churning up conflict and consternation. He tangled once at a party with "Pierre Easily Trudeau" over bilingualism, and the PM did not speak to him for years. He led the mocking coverage of Joe Clark on his fateful world trip in 1979, coining the term "Jurassic Clark" to describe his leadership style. He insisted that he "invented" Brian Mulroney, "the

Allan Fotheringham in the Southam office on Parliament Hill.

jaw that walks like a man." He said he once asked Mulroney, "When did you decide to run for leader?" The answer came back, "The second time I read it in your column."

So tight with Mulroney did the self-styled "Dr. Foth" become that he and his friend Pierrette Lucas were guests of the prime minister and Mila at the government retreat at Harrington Lake on several occasions. They gave the Mulroneys a croquet set on one of their anniversaries. The Mulroneys gave him gifts as well: one Sunday at midday a speedboat hove into view with a waiter carrying "smoked salmon, scrambled eggs and champagne" to the guest house.

Among people in the press gallery who encouraged him to move on was fellow Southam columnist Charles Lynch, who shared the limelight with "Dr. Foth." Fotheringham said he realized Lynch and friends were right: he was far too close to Mulroney, "and it was hurting my reputation (such as it was)." With that, Fotheringham transferred to the Southam bureau in Washington. Upon his return, Foth recalled, "My columns apparently were no longer regarded as amusing." Mila Mulroney took a mallet from the croquet set and mailed it to Fotheringham's boss with the note: "Please tell Mr. Fotheringham to stick this up his yazoo."

In Washington he enjoyed insider status with Canadian ambassador Allan Gotlieb and his wife, Sondra, friends from their Ottawa days. He was a regular at what became one of the most desirable tables in town. "On any given evening at the Canadian embassy," he wrote, "I might find myself sitting down to dinner with Henry Kissinger across the table, Defense Secretary Caspar Weinberger beside him." Foth noted that the Gotliebs tended to invite each of the twenty Canadian correspondents in town to one dinner each year. "But I was there every single night at their dinner parties," he boasted with Trumpian bombast. "Which of course is why I was hated by all the Canadian reporters in town."

His insider status backfired once during the biggest Gotlieb party — in honour of visiting Prime Minister Mulroney and President George Bush Sr. in 1984. Seated inside with the other guests, Fotheringham missed a major diplomatic incident outside where the rest of the reporters were assembled: in a fit of pique, Sondra Gotlieb had slugged her social secretary. Fotheringham only learned about the infamous "slap flap" the next day from a CP report. "I missed the biggest scoop of the year," he admitted ruefully.

He gloated that he had attracted "more libel suits than any journalist in Canadian history." He claims that of twenty-six libel cases he won twenty-four. The two losses he suffered were the result of suits filed against *Maclean's* for columns he had written. One was awarded for libel against two Liberal back-roomers offended by Fotheringham's jocular reference to their neighbourhood as "wife-swapping" Shaughnessy (where the judge also lived). The other was awarded for libelling Sir Ranulph Twisleton-Wykeham-Fiennes, who took umbrage at Fotheringham's skepticism about his image as a noted world explorer. *Maclean's* had to pay five and six figures, respectively. There may have been a third, unannounced out-of-court settlement after Fotheringham accused Trudeau adviser Jim Coutts of being less than truthful whenever "his lips moved"; thereafter, Coutts relished inviting guests to his Toronto home to play "Fotheringham's grand piano."

Still, despite his irreverence and penetrating jabs at politicians, Foth became part of the official fabric wherever he went — whether his subjects liked it or not. He was on a friendly first-name basis with prime ministers and moguls. His personal files bulge with cloying letters to, and personal greetings from, the high and mighty: the boy from Hearne had made it in the big leagues. There are handwritten notes from prime ministers and premiers in those files, typed invitations from Kissinger and Bobby Orr, get-well messages during a serious illness in 1998 from Bill Clinton on White House stationery and from Jean Chrétien.

In a letter wishing him well on his Washington posting, Maureen McTeer took the occasion for a gentle rebuke about rumours circulating among Ottawa gossips like Foth about the state of her marriage to Joe Clark. "Of course, what disappoints me the most," she told Fotheringham, "is the fact that most people still refuse to accept that two strong people with different views, opinions and careers can make a go of any long term relationship…. Age-old stereotypes of marriage relationships still exist, even in 1984."

Fotheringham himself went through a painful and costly divorce after seventeen years of marriage. He remained bitter about the "bad decision" to hire lawyer Peter Butler to represent both himself and his wife. "To this day," he wrote in 2011, "I send my ex-wife a monthly cheque. More than 30 years later." He remains close to his two sons and daughter and lovingly celebrated his five grandchildren in his memoir. But he was devastated when his oldest son, forty-seven-year-old Brady, died of a heart attack in South Korea where he was teaching.

In his later years tears came easily to Foth when he talked about family. This vulnerable side is one that the public did not see. In private he is a good listener. He is not the wisecracking spirit known to his readers. "I can be funny on a typewriter," he once said. "I'm not terribly funny in person. Most humourists are inherently troubled people, or very sad inside."

For all his muckraking, he is also a true reformer and an idealist. "I believe in democracy," he told Richard Ouzounian in a TVO interview. "And you know the basis of democracy? It's the secret ballot, and I vote every election."

After seventeen years of playing the field, Fotheringham had the good fortune to meet and marry Toronto art maven Anne Libby. Three weeks after the ceremony Fotheringham got a diagnosis of prostate cancer — "a great gift to the bride." He recovered, went public in *Maclean's* at my urging, and became a poster boy for the disease. Then, in 2007, Fotheringham went into hospital for a routine colonoscopy. Five months later, after poor care, attacks by superbugs, and administration of the last rites, he emerged, battered but battling. Anne had saved his life by sitting with him day and night, confronting the medical establishment, and keeping Fotheringham's spirits up.

He was frail and forgetful when we last had lunch, but he knocked back a martini and some white wine and delighted in trading gossip. In 2016, at eighty-four, he and Anne went off to winter on the Costa del Sol in Spain. "Allan has five British papers every day," Anne told me in an email. "He has about 230 English-speaking channels to choose from. All is good." Especially being with the lady he calls "the gem."

Chapter 27

THE MAKING OF NEWS

Making news in Ottawa changed dramatically as governments hired legions of press agents and consultants to spin, prevaricate, and deny, deny, deny. People like CP reporter Dave McIntosh were the prime reasons for the change. He once described his modus operandi during his nineteen years in CP's Ottawa bureau during the late 1950s and '60s simply: "Of course what you are looking for is something that embarrasses the government." You didn't take the side of the opposition, he added, "but you never gave the government any help."

It's a stance that comes naturally to most trained reporters. The good ones have a nose for finding a story. Some exploit access to information laws. Others work their sources. Some make their breaks. Some just get lucky. The best stories are always the ones the government doesn't want told.

———

"What do you have?" Doug Small asked the caller. As the reporter listened, it became clear that his informant had details of the April 1989 federal budget, scheduled for presentation the next day by Conservative finance minister Michael Wilson. Small, then forty-seven and an experienced Hill veteran, knew the ramifications. A budget leak is one of the biggest Ottawa scoops going, a cause for scandal and possible dismissal of the minister. It was 5:58 p.m., two minutes before Small was scheduled to go on air for Global News.

He wrote a short bulletin saying that parts of the Wilson budget were in the public domain, and delivered it with no details. "I went off the air," said Small, "and the phone rang again."

Caller: "It's me again. Why didn't you report all the stuff I told you?"

Small: "I can't, unless I have some proof."

Caller: "I can sell it to you."

Small: "No, no. We don't buy news."

With that, the caller gave Small the address of a gas station in the city's west end. "I'll give it to you. Can you meet me there?"

Small's wife, Brenda, was waiting outside to take him home. Instead, they sped to the gas station, picked up a brown envelope and, while Doug drove, Brenda read the document to him. It was a summary, the customary "Budget in Brief," and it presaged major spending cuts and a massive tax increase. Global News was still on the air. Small raced into the studio in the National Press Building and delivered the details. When the show ended, he was mobbed by colleagues from other news organizations.

It turned out that copies of the "Budget in Brief" brochure had been retrieved from a waste bin where they were tossed after some of the pages had been printed upside down. Prime Minister Mulroney was so angry about a "criminal act" that he ordered an RCMP investigation. Wilson gave an impromptu delivery of his budget that night at a press conference. Small was hailed and attacked and, later, charged with theft. Judge James Fontana subsequently threw the case out and said that Small had performed an "important public function" by preventing speculation. Throughout the ordeal, Small was sanguine about the charges. "If you are worried about that, you shouldn't be a reporter. I was uneasy about the fact that I was going to be the story, rather than covering it."

———————

Twenty years earlier, swinging bachelor Pierre Trudeau certainly was the centre of the story when he attended his first Commonwealth Conference in London. Although Rhodesia was a top issue, it was meeting with a mystery woman that dominated coverage of Trudeau. After he boasted about having had a private lunch with a "blonde," reporters crawled London looking for her.

The *Toronto Star*'s Val Sears was one of the first reporters to strike gossipy gold. It came in the form of one Eva Rittinghausen, and Sears nursed it lovingly into a large front page story and photo in the January 6, 1969, *Toronto Star*:

> New girl in Trudeau's life
>
> She claims love, he denies it

Sears described her as a "shapely, 35-year-old blonde divorcee" who had met Trudeau around the pool at Murray Bay on the St. Lawrence the previous summer. He wrote: "The lady tucked the hem of her clinging green dress under her excellent legs and murmured: 'When I saw Pierre dive into the pool it was, well, love at first sight.'" For further salacious emphasis, Sears wrote that Eva was "strikingly attractive" and "frequently appears in glossy magazines devoted to the activities of the rich." She told Sears that Trudeau liked the fact that she was "an outdoor girl," and added: "I am, I think, *sportif*."

At the rival *Toronto Telegram*, the heat was on. Political editor Fraser Kelly had come to London with orders from owner John Bassett to beat the competition. As well, Bassett planned to pre-empt CTV's flagship *W5* with his own show on his own station, Toronto powerhouse CFTO, as part of his ongoing feud with CTV boss Murray Chercover. "I want you to beat CTV," he said. Kelly had already secured a promise of an exclusive interview with Trudeau. He also had received an official reprimand for arranging to sneak a photographer into the grounds at Buckingham Palace for an exclusive photo of Trudeau's arrival — the fellow was disguised as a dignitary in a black limousine that swung in undetected behind the official party. And now he had to find Eva Rittinghausen.

"I got clobbered the first day," Kelly admitted. "I was determined to find this woman. By this time, this is a big story. Everybody is wondering, Is this going to be Canada's new First Lady? We had a guy in London named Dennis Eisenberg who was working for the *Daily Express*. I said, 'I want you to spread the word that I've got several hundred dollars. I am prepared to give it out to anyone who can produce that woman.'" After a short while Eisenberg returned from Fleet Street with an address. "I never did have to give out the money," Kelly said. "I decided to go and see her."

A man at the door greeted Kelly and disappeared to ask Rittinghausen if she would see the visitor. "He goes into the bedroom," Kelly continued, "comes back and says, 'She'll speak to you.' I go into the bedroom and there is this woman lying on the bed in baby doll pyjamas. She says, 'What can I do for you?'" At this point in the retelling, Kelly was close to speechless with mirth. "And I said, 'You can tell me the story.' We did the interview sitting side by side on a leopard skin love seat."

When Kelly checked in with Trudeau's press secretary, Roméo LeBlanc, he learned that his interview was still on — with one condition: no questions about Eva Rittinghausen. No deal, Kelly responded, passing up the interview, knowing that Rittinghausen would be the top bill on his show. When Trudeau learned about that decision, he told LeBlanc ironically, "Aha, at last a journalist with principle."

Trudeau expressed his outrage about the coverage in an extraordinary lecture to the travelling press corps as the London conference ended. He lashed into the "crummy behaviour" of the English-Canadian reporters who "pester the girls I have been seen with," and reworked one of his famous phrases: "The nation has no place in the bedrooms of the state, and certainly not the press." Pointedly, Trudeau exempted the francophone reporters who "rarely meddled in my private or personal life," while the English press "behaved in a perfectly disgusting manner." So much for the Trudeau-media honeymoon.

Some critical pieces about Trudeau's performance inside the Commonwealth heads of government meeting followed.

———————

Dan Turner was part of the "swat squad" investigative unit when the *Ottawa Citizen* asked him to look into a tip about a Canadian federal minister and a visit to Tiffany's, a strip club in Lahr, West Germany. What he and his team found was bluntly stated in the first paragraph of a February 12, 1985, exclusive:

OTTAWA — Prime Minister Brian Mulroney's office has been advised of an early morning visit last November by Defence Minister Robert Coates and two of his chief aides to a West German nightclub that featured prostitutes, nude dancers and hard-porn movies.

The story went on to say that Coates, on a four-nation swing through NATO countries, "spent about two hours drinking and chatting at the bar with one of the strippers while his two aides disappeared with two other women to another part of the establishment." The *Citizen* quoted "a very senior former Canadian intelligence officer" that Coates "made himself a perfect intelligence target."

In the morning Coates was gone from Cabinet, despite his assertion that the report was "wrong and libellous."

"I never did get a complete second source," Turner said in a 2015 interview. "But if Coates had not gone into hiding, he might have talked his way out of it because we just weren't dead certain." But the story left little room for doubt. Neil Macdonald, Turner's colleague, travelled to the bar where "a 38-year-old woman who called herself 'Micki O'Neil' told the *Ottawa Citizen* she talked to the minister, who she identified by name from a photograph."

In fact, back in Ottawa, Coates's chief policy adviser, Duncan Edmonds, had already raised questions about his minister's behaviour with Mulroney's top bureaucrat, who in turn had briefed the prime minister. Turner said he got the story from Edmonds. Edmonds left Coates's office a few days before he blew the whistle and effectively became *persona non grata* in Mulroney's official Ottawa. The Coates affair was the start of a series of ministerial scandals that befell Mulroney's young government. Eventually Coates, who died in 2016, sued the newspaper and the two sides settled out of court.

Sometimes the big scoop came — inadvertently — out of the mouth of the top dog. In the 1979 election campaign, an aide invited Andrew Phillips, then with CBC, and Mary Janigan of the *Star* for a coffee aboard Pierre Trudeau's campaign jet. They came away with a flash that Trudeau said he planned "to put our program to the test" in the Commons even if the Liberals trailed the Tories by five or ten seats in a minority Parliament.

That was what Prime Minister MacKenzie King had done after the 1925 election when Arthur Meighen's Tories won more seats.

Trudeau's plan on a replay ignited a firestorm and contributed to Joe Clark's election victory.

———————

For reporters confronting tight-lipped Canadian officialdom in Ottawa, Americans often were the best sources. When Christopher Waddell was covering the trade beat for the *Globe and Mail* in 1986, he cultivated sources on both sides who came to trust him. In 1986 the U.S. side gave him the real story behind the settlement of a long-festering dispute over lumber exports — an issue that festers to this day. The Mulroney government had secretly made major concessions that allowed Washington to control compliance with the agreement — a step that Canada had adamantly refused to accept only two weeks earlier. When they found out, the Canadian industry and the official opposition denounced the agreement as a sellout that would cost lumber companies millions, while allowing Americans to run the Canadian industry.

Waddell noted with a touch of glee that he broke the story on New Year's Eve 1986 and followed with a more detailed report. The government trotted out spokespeople on New Year's Day to denounce the story. But Waddell had it cold, including a private letter from U.S. trade officials to the lumber lobby detailing restrictions on Ottawa's ability to assist the industry in Canada. "There were a couple of loopholes the Americans were happy to point out," said Waddell. "The United States will tell you things Canadians won't."

———————

In January 2002 the *Globe* carried a series of stories detailing how the Liberal minister of public works and government services, Alfonso Gagliano, and his staff tried to influence the work of the Canada Lands Company and obtain jobs for their pals. Daniel Leblanc's January 9 story said the former chairman of the agency, established to dispose of Crown assets, "was appalled by the political interference he witnessed" in his six years on the job. What established the authenticity of the story was that the one-time chairman was a leading corporate executive, Jon Grant, who allowed his name to be used.

Behind the headline were lengthy personal connections between a *Globe* reporter and his source. "That came about because we had a relationship," said former Ottawa correspondent Hugh Winsor, who encouraged Grant to speak out. "He called me because he knew me through previous policy discussions." At first Grant preferred to give the *Globe* the information anonymously. Said Winsor, "I remember saying, 'No, they'll just deny it. But if we put you on the front page and you don't have any axes to grind and you're prepared to name names, that will cause the shit to hit the fan.'" And so it did. The articles got the *Globe* an honourable mention citation in that year's Michener Awards and caused Gagliano's exit from politics.

———————

By the late 1990s investigative journalists embraced new technologies. Reporting had entered a world beyond spreadsheets and calculators, to sifting through metadata for information and historical trends. At CP in Ottawa, bureau chief Rob Russo placed a heavy emphasis on breaking news and data mining. "I would never say, 'What are we covering?'" Russo explained. "Our news meetings would begin with me asking, 'Who's got news? Who's going to tell me something I don't already know?'" Usually that would be reporters Jennifer Ditchburn, Heather Schofield, Joan Bryden, or Jim Bronskill, or data guru Dean Beeby, who conducted seminars on freedom of information legislation for other journalists.

During the Harper years Ditchburn used the Access to Information Act to reveal International Cooperation Minister Bev Oda's expensive switch of hotel rooms in London and her purchase of a sixteen-dollar glass of orange juice. She also unearthed details about how bureaucrats from Citizenship and Immigration Canada staged a fake ceremony by posing as new immigrants for a Sun TV network broadcast.

In 2008 CP and Radio-Canada teamed up to produce an important exposé of the misuse of taser stun guns in the wake of the violent death of Polish traveller Robert Dziekanski at Vancouver International Airport. Bronskill and his team, working with journalist Frédéric Zalac and his colleagues, mined some four thousand RCMP taser records acquired under the federal information law. What they found was that, contrary to warnings about the danger, multiple taser bursts were used in almost half the incidents, and that more than two-thirds of the victims were unarmed and 10 percent of the taser units were defective.

———————

Veteran Dave McIntosh, who parked his pencil and notebook in 1972, lived in a different but no less competitive era. He had great sources and a rare ability to beat everyone on the Hill with a scoop, although he toiled for the great grey news service, The Canadian Press. ("It insists on a capital T to distinguish itself from the *hoi polloi,* the Canadian press," he noted sardonically in the author's note to his memoir, *Ottawa Unbuttoned, or Who's Running This Country Anyway?*)

Launched in 1917 as a co-operative whose members shared stories, CP had a reputation for playing things down the middle. In 1940 the official guide defined the journalistic meaning of impartiality in a manner that most of us embraced: "Parties in controversy, whether in politics or law or otherwise, receive equal consideration. Statements issued by conflicting interests receive equal prominence." CP, in fact, was an important reason that the partisan political press in the Macdonald-Laurier era gave way to more rounded reporting in the mid-1900s. But by the late 1960s there was pushback. Member papers wanted more than just the facts, ma'am.

And the lanky, acerbic McIntosh, a native of Sherbrooke, Quebec, relished giving it to them — with a twist. When McIntosh arrived in the press gallery in 1953, he quickly devised a technique to thwart colleagues in the gallery who were given to "topping" a CP story with their own words, slapping their byline on it, and then instructing the desk, "Pick up CP" for the heart of the story. The McIntosh Twist was based on his intimate knowledge of the various deadlines for the big eastern papers.

In an interview Doug Small, a former CP reporter, fondly recalled what his colleague McIntosh would do:

> If he had a really great story he would write a "BULLETIN"
> and then an "URGENT" and a couple of other pages. He

would hand it to Tom Mitchell on the desk at the downtown office. He'd say, "Hang on to this for a couple of minutes; just need to check a couple of things." Then he would go up to the Hill, for all the world as if nothing was happening, wait until the bells started to ring [calling the Commons into session]. As soon as everybody was safely in the House, just as Question Period started, he would pick up the phone and say, "Tom, may want to move that now."

In the press gallery hot room there would then ensue a scene of total chaos. Phones would be ringing off the hook as newspaper main desks tried to get their Ottawa reporters to match the McIntosh scoop. But they were all in the Commons. And there was no instant messaging to connect reporters or share news in that pre-wireless age, so there was no reaction in the House. By the time the papers asked their befuddled reporters for a "matcher," the afternoon editions were on the press and McIntosh was already working on his "folo" (follow-up story) for the next day. For McIntosh it was not only the chase that counted; it also was important to build the CP brand. As detailed in his amusing memoir, "No self-respecting CP staffer was interested in making just the small papers: CP was often their only service. The proper test was to get a story into the big dailies. Besides," he added, "that was usually the best way to attract head office attention."

McIntosh, a pilot who received the Distinguished Flying Cross for daring exploits against Germany during the war, was deeply suspicious of authority, even including his Toronto bosses. CP had a practice of demanding to know reporters' sources on touchy stories. Inevitably, McIntosh would cite a fictitious colonel in the armed services. To cover his tracks, every couple of years McIntosh would promote the guy until, finally, he became Major General Maurice Code. "I don't know whether anyone in Toronto twigged," he confessed, "but nobody ever questioned the colonel's good name."

Chapter 28

TAKING A STAND

Over the years the dukes and duchesses of the Parliamentary Press Gallery employed their knowledge of parliamentary rules to good effect, often on their own affairs. The private archives of the gallery, maintained in unindexed boxes on shelves in the press gallery on Parliament Hill — near the place where the beer machine used to sit — bulge with minutes of endless general meetings, motions, and special pleadings. There are accounts of spending on parties and farewell ceremonial "muggings" in the lounge, and proposals for dealing with the space shortage and with the annual surplus (usually resolved by throwing another party).

Despite the gallery's knowledge of *Robert's Rules of Order*, some decisions it made were better than others. Two that backfired involved denial of membership to writer Sandra Gwyn of *Saturday Night* monthly and to Anthony Westell, then a weekly columnist for the *Toronto Star* in the late 1970s. The executive cited the shortage of gallery space as the reason, but there was an inherent bias against people who did not cover "hard news." The gallery later rescinded both rulings — against two talented journalists — after protests, including one from *Saturday Night* editor Robert Fulford who professed that he was "astounded, and outraged."

In a more sinister, anti-Semitic phase, between January and December 1938 the gallery repeatedly denied membership requests for correspondents of the Jewish Telegraphic Agency (JTA) and the *Daily Hebrew Journal* on the pretext of space shortages. Max Bookman, the

Canadian correspondent for the JTA, noted in protest that "outside of Nazi Germany and Canada, the JTA is officially recognized as a news gathering body for the Jewish press throughout the world." His editor, H. Wishengrad, wrote to the press gallery president, Charles Lynch, noting that Bookman's work was compromised because he had been "barred from the Prime Minister's press conference on the ground that he did not have the requisite Gallery privileges."

In the same era, the gallery prepared to play host to visiting members of the British press covering the royal visit of 1939 with a grant from Prime Minister Mackenzie King, as he put it, "to assist in extending courtesies."

The boxes of the archive also contain notes from members or their spouses, with thanks for flowers marking a health crisis or a death. The widow of one former member wrote to thank the gallery for a generous donation after her husband's death. The boxes contain invitations to free travel and accommodations. In 1939 members were treated to Trans-Canada Airlines demonstration flights to Vancouver and back. In 1964 there was a weekend in Montreal with wives as guests of Expo 67, hosted by corporations, complete with a Labatt's-sponsored lunch during the Grey Cup game. The itinerary included a dinner and stay at the Windsor Hotel, a helicopter ride over the site under construction, and dinner at Altitude 737 restaurant at Place Ville Marie.

But there is more than the stuff of social commentary in the boxes. They also yield information on great debates about the role of the press and an issue that obsesses journalists — access to the truth. Among those agitating for more information were reporters who later became gatekeepers for prime ministers themselves, including *La Presse*'s Pierre O'Neill (Pierre Trudeau), Jim Munson of CTV (Jean Chrétien), and TVA's Luc Lavoie (Brian Mulroney).

The restiveness started in the late 1970s. Heated arguments took place at annual meetings about the place of the press gallery in public affairs. Some members argued that the body existed solely to administer memberships and worry about things like parking and supplies. Others, led by president Bruce Phillips, insisted it was time for the gallery to take stands on issues affecting freedom of the press. One of the most hotly contested affairs was the strike by CP reporters in 1976 in support of a first contract.

Another was the inquiry by the TV regulator, the Canadian Radio-television and Telecommunications Commission (CRTC), into allegations that Radio-Canada had a separatist slant. Finally, there was the activist role the gallery played in the introduction of television to the House of Commons, a move that had unintended consequences for the way Canadians receive their news from Parliament Hill to this day.

The CRTC-CBC issue arose in the spring of 1977 when the Trudeau government called for an inquiry into perceived bias. The gallery executive, headed by Phillips, voted 4–3 to oppose the hearing "as an interference with the rights of a free press." At an emergency meeting of the 269-strong gallery on May 5, a mere minority of members voted 32–21 to support the executive.

The debate exposed divergent views of the place of the press gallery, according to minutes of the May 3 meeting. CBC reporter Mike Duffy argued that the "currency of journalists is devalued" when they take political stands. Supporting him were CBC reporters Terry Hargreaves and Vince Carlin, who argued that the gallery should stick to housekeeping. *Toronto Star* columnist Richard Gwyn and reporter Michael Benedict backed the executive. Benedict submitted that remaining silent was more dangerous than supporting the motion, while Gwyn affirmed the right of the gallery to take stands — along with the government's right to ask for an inquiry. In the end, the gallery position was a small bleat amid the noise, and the inquiry absolved Radio-Canada of bias while calling for improvements in coverage of French-English issues.

The gallery had already cut its activist teeth in 1976 after the CP reporters walked off the job and refused to cover Parliament when a new session began in October. Management, with a long history of blocking unions, had recruited non-unionized employees to report from the House and Senate. Gallery members, in solidarity with the strikers, refused to accredit them. The *Globe and Mail* formally protested that decision, ordering its own parliamentary reporters to refrain from voting on the matter.

The dispute escalated. The speaker of the House, James Jerome, ruled that the gallery had the right to exclude the "scabs," as they were denounced, and said they would not even be allowed to take notes in the public gallery. The *Globe* attacked the speaker. The prime minister and leaders of the other parties backed the strikers. The Commons censured the *Globe*. The stars of the gallery — TV reporters including Phillips — paraded on the picket line in sympathy, as did Cabinet ministers, MPs, senators, and reporters from other news organizations (including the non-unionized *Maclean's* bureau chief and staff).

The main issue was getting the union certified, with the right to automatic dues check-off. The day Ottawa reporters walked out, Prime Minister Pierre Trudeau was on his way to a news conference in the National Press Building and stopped to ask a CP reporter-turned-picketer if theirs was a legal strike. Informed that it was, Trudeau turned on his heel and declared: "Then I won't cross." One-time gallery member Carman Cumming, then a Carleton journalism professor, wrote: "For the CP strikers, the Trudeau incident marked a breakthrough." At issue, he wrote in *Content* magazine, was whether the press gallery's rights and responsibilities "flow from Parliament or from employers — or whether it has any rights solely its own."

Among the senior gallery members who disagreed with the vote was the *Toronto Star*'s Anthony Westell, a former chief of the *Globe*'s Ottawa bureau. Although he supported "the modest demands" of the strikers and opposed efforts by CP to "crush the CP union before it becomes established," it was, he wrote, more than a simple labour dispute. "It is access for press and public to Parliament, and that to me is more important than the struggles of the union — to which, incidentally, I belong." Westell added: "We members of the gallery have been granted in effect a monopoly — the exclusive right to report Parliament. It is a privilege entrusted to us by Parliament, and not a power we are entitled to use in another cause, no matter how worthy."

Lynch, the Southam News columnist who happened to be president of the press gallery once again at the time of the strike, wrote that the CP reporters "were putting collective bargaining ahead of the freedom to report events."

Columnist Doug Fisher of the *Toronto Sun*, a former NDP MP, took a different tack. Although he had been highly critical of the gallery's perks and privileges when he sat in the Commons, Fisher boldly noted that the strong vote by gallery members "to block any scabs" reflected the wide sympathy "of almost everyone in the news business" for the strikers. "Some of the sympathy is simply because no one knows better that our publishers are cheapskates, and the CP, a co-operative agency organized by publishers, is really run by them." Support extended beyond the ranks of reporters and columnists. Cabinet ministers Roméo LeBlanc and Iona Campagnolo joined NDP leader Tommy Douglas and other MPs for a march of support in the sub-zero temperatures.

By October 19 Speaker Jerome was involved. A formal Commons motion denouncing the use of "scabs" had fallen just one "nay" short of approval. Jerome told both sides that he had decided to respect the gallery's decision. The *Globe* unloaded its big guns in an editorial, denouncing Trudeau and Tory leader Joe Clark for siding with the strikers: "They cannot pick and choose which members of the press they want to have as their links with the reading and listening public." As for Jerome, the *Globe* said he had no right to "banish representatives of CP from the Galleries of the House of Commons." CP reporter Doug Small, who wrote a thorough research paper on the dispute, noted the irony that barring two skilled reporters "represented the kind of collective action normally shunned by the press gallery."*

The beginning of the end of the dispute came in late fall with the launch of mediation talks under Jerome's hand-picked deputy. On November 10 the parties made a deal, subsequently approved by a majority of CP staffers. It was, on balance, a weak contract that made no provision for automatic dues for any employees. But it was a first contract. CP staffers went back to work reporting on the affairs of the nation, while their boss, general manager John Dauphinee, curiously continued his attack on the press gallery and the speaker, accusing them of censorship — an unusual charge for a boss to be making about his own employees.

The *Globe* ratcheted up its assault on the speaker, calling him "a gambler who plays incredible odds for the popularity of his party." In the Commons, angry MPs rushed to the speaker's defence and unanimously approved a motion of censure against the *Globe*. The paper counterattacked.

Then John Diefenbaker, often highly critical of coverage — especially of himself — spoke out on behalf of the CP strikers during a speech at the annual National Newspaper Awards in Toronto. "What was done," he declared, "was entirely within the rights of Parliament and, in particular,

---

* Doug Small, "The Power and Jurisdiction of the Parliamentary Press Gallery" (research paper, Carleton University School of Journalism, 1977), 14.

the press gallery." Interestingly, the *Globe* carried the CP account of the speech, but excised that quote.

By then there was a general sense that the paper had overplayed its hand and the gallery collectively had lost the fire to install the no-scab rule in its bylaws. But the dispute did at least enshrine the role of the gallery in the affairs of the nation. As Speaker Jerome noted, "The Press Gallery function is more than a commercial news reporting service. It is an integral part of our work; a service which Parliament must safeguard for the Canadian public who are entitled as of right to the fullest information on activities here."

Television arrived in the House of Commons with the formal blessing of the press gallery. In a brief to Parliament, the gallery "enthusiastically and unreservedly" backed the proposal for an "electronic Hansard." It turned out that government House leader Mitchell Sharp's concept was not the same as the one endorsed by the gallery. "We were fighting for access and wider coverage of proceedings," recalled reporter Christine Hearn, a member of the gallery executive at the time. The government proposal reflected the concern of many members that roaming cameras might cast MPs in an unfavourable light — reading newspapers, dozing, or picking their noses. As a compromise, Sharp proposed that the camera would show only the MP who was speaking, not any of the sideshow. "It would not roam the House looking for sleeping or nose-picking MPs or empty chairs," he wrote in his memoir, *Which Reminds Me....* The gallery brief, in contrast, argued that viewers should be able to see "exactly what can now be heard and seen by a member of the public by sitting in the public galleries." If that did not happen, it would "inflict a competitive penalty upon broadcast journalists as compared to their colleagues operating in print." Intriguingly, the three presenters of the brief were broadcasters: gallery president Bruce Phillips of CTV, Paul Taylor of the private Newsradio chain, and one Michael "Mike" Duffy, then a promising reporter for CBC Radio.

By the time Parliament installed the cameras, radio and TV membership in the gallery had soared to a hundred out of two hundred and thirty members. Media had access to a basement interview studio where Cabinet ministers and opposition MPs would troop after question period.

As organizations established quarters off the Hill, the focus on the Commons declined. Now, if reporters went to question period at all, the daily ritual had become little more than a tip sheet for stories to be pursued during the scrum in the corridor. Ultimtely, TV in the House made it possible for reporters *not* to be in the House — all of them missing, for example, Justin Trudeau's dramatic dash across the floor of the Commons and his shoving match with opposition MPs in 2016.

In retrospect the CP strike proved to be the last hurrah for print in the press gallery. Today the membership is dominated by TV and radio reporters and the legion of camera and sound people. The members of the major outlets are dispersed around the downtown Parliament Hill precinct, tethered by fibre to sound at their desks from the Commons and scrums over a network run by Commons employees who work for the gallery. The old "hot room" on the third floor is mainly occupied by freelancers and solo practitioners. But still, one issue unites the disparate members of the tribe: even the hint that their access to news will be restrained provokes a call to the barricades.

Chapter 29

CLOSE QUARTERS ON THE HILL

Prime Minister William Lyon Mackenzie King described it as "one of the great agonies" of his life. King referred not to his trials during the Great Depression and the Second World War; no, this master strategist of government and Parliament for twenty-two years could not abide the annual rite of spring in Ottawa, the press gallery dinner, an evening of off-the-record drinking and irreverent song dating back to the mid-1800s.

King especially resented the one on a Saturday night in 1929 when, according to his diary account, "their publications and songs were very vulgar and I felt resentment at the cartooning and references to myself." He stayed on chatting with the boys until about 1:30 a.m., yet he was still seething when he got home and penned a note: "I dislike it more than any event of the year." Even after "a good night's rest," he remained indignant on Sunday. "The whole proceeding was wholly unworthy [to] thoughtful & serious minded men," he wrote. "As a matter of fact, it gives to press an idea of their power to destroy & to make reputations such as they should never be permitted to have." On top of that, King admits he made a "poor speech" — which might be the real point.

Over the decades, many politicians have shared King's view. Pierre Trudeau and Brian Mulroney both failed initially at the required art of self-deprecation and both stopped going, Trudeau during the public breakdown of his marriage and Mulroney during days of crisis for his administration. In the early 1990s the event disappeared altogether from the Hill calendar. One reason was growing discomfort with the off-the-record rule. In 1992 Southam's irascible scribe Don McGillivray told the gallery when he submitted his cheque, "I will attend as a journalist as well as a member of the press gallery, and will write about the event should something of interest to the public occur." Press gallery president Manon Cornellier of *Le Devoir* returned McGillivray's seventy-five dollars without a ticket, but the old ways were coming to an end.

There were mixed results when the event went public again. Stephen Harper attended when he was in opposition, declaring deadpan: "Actually, I'm really excited to be here. This is how I look when I am excited." But after he became prime minister in 2006 he boycotted the affair. Governor General Michaëlle Jean also cancelled that year. In her previous appearance in 2005 she created a stir in Quebec when she said of Parti Québécois leader André Boisclair, a one-time cocaine user, "He always follows the party line." After an overtly political speech in 1998 former Bloc Québécois leader Gilles Duceppe faced a hail of dinner buns; he never went back. Embattled Liberal leader Stéphane Dion got marks for effort in 2007 when he criticized reporters for calling him the worst Liberal leader in a century: "Why only in a century? I can't win anything with you guys."

In the early years the atmosphere was generally genteel, reflecting the warm relations between the gallery and politicians — especially if they were not in government. In 1938 the mock newspaper printed for the dinner, the *Mailed Fist*, bid the retiring Tory leader, R.B. Bennett, defeated by King in 1935, "long years of health and happiness and that leisure that he has so well earned." The same issue contained a hint in verse for King that he, too, was a mere mortal. The irreverent ditty, delivered after a meal of lobster and filet of beef, touched on his bachelorhood and declining fortunes to the tune of "Silver Threads Among the Gold":

> Yes, your [*sic*] getting on in life,
> Ain't it time you took a wife
> There are many in the land,
> Who'd accept your gracious hand,
> After all, you may not be
> Always young and fair to see.

Often, the so-called humour was blantantly racist by today's standards. *Humbug*, the "fake" newspaper for the 1931 dinner, offered up parodies of francophones speaking broken English and caricatures mocking an Inuit couple.

In his day, Liberal opposition leader Pearson actually seemed to enjoy the evening. In a letter signed "Mike" when he was leader of the opposition, he thanked the gallery for the gift of a canoe paddle and "just about the best press gallery dinner I have attended." One of the most popular speakers in the modern era, ironically, was Conservative Robert Stanfield, whose penetrating wit and self-mockery delighted the scribes and stood in sharp contrast to his dull public image.

The twists and turns of the dinner are symbolic of the generally complicated relationships between the governors and their watchers in the Fourth Estate. Invitations to the gala are prized among MPs and top officials. For reporters the dinner is a vehicle to cultivate relationships with key people. Such intimacy can be a ticket to exclusive information in a town where knowledge is power. But people on both sides can get too close to the flame, either burning good sources and losing friendships, or being taken in by the spin.

Susan Delacourt is a case in point. The award-winning political reporter found herself enmeshed in Brian Mulroney's suit against the Chrétien government over allegations he had received favours in return for the awarding of Air Canada contracts to Airbus.

The sting was that Delacourt had passed rumours along to her friend, Justice Minister Allan Rock, that became part of the government case against Mulroney. She had gotten to know Rock in 1993 while reporting what became a highly favourable piece on the new minister. Regular lunches or dinners with Rock and his wife followed.

The government settled the case, so the veracity of claims was not established. But Delacourt denies that she passed along rumours about Airbus and felt burned by reports in her own paper that Rock had alerted the RCMP, apparently based on information she had also shared in confidence with *Globe* colleagues.

"There are lessons here for all political reporters and the people who deal with them," Delacourt wrote in the *Globe*. Those included "lessons about the nature of friendships between journalists and politicians; and lessons about the continuing nonsense that plagues women on Parliament Hill." She added: "One's reputation as a journalist is never questioned if you write nasty, negative stories but it is severely challenged if you use the same critical skills to produce a favourable or positive story. Double the penalty if you are writing about a man."

———————

Writing about a woman — Margaret Trudeau — proved to be a challenge for most Ottawa reporters, including this one. Journalist Dan Turner first met Margaret when he was a reporter for United Press International and she hopped aboard the press bus in the 1972 election campaign. "I hear you have fun back here," she declared. What transpired over the next several minutes provided reporters with their first informal look at the prime minister's young wife. "I'm just Old Mother Earth," she declared at one point. At another: "I'm not my husband's property either." Turner rushed the story off to the wire first and it ended up on the front page of the *Star* — and led to a job offer from the paper in Toronto.

Turner returned to Ottawa two years later and Margaret Trudeau invited him and his wife, Gail, for dinner while Pierre was out of town. Turner and Margaret Trudeau became close friends. He had the direct line to 24 Sussex, and they were seen around town together. Yet he continued reporting on her deteriorating relationship with her husband, and in one famous 1980 local news show appearance he predicted Margaret and Pierre's separation.

———————

Sometimes real news breaks out behind the curtain of secrecy. In 1948 at the gallery dinner the featured song was about "Good King Willieslaus" clinging to power, after which Mackenzie King stood up and announced his plans to a startled room. Charles Lynch recreated the scene in his memoirs: "Willie rose to his feet and announced his retirement, to the great consternation of his listeners, all of whom were deeply into the sauce and unprepared for a news development of these proportions late on a Saturday night and at an off-the-record-dinner." The CP bureau chief Andy Carnegie later checked with King to inquire if he could print the report, and King agreed.

In 1979 Pierre Trudeau titillated his audience at the dinner when he allowed that he had discussed dissolving Parliament with Governor General Ed Schreyer. He taunted the crowd by saying they wouldn't really know whether this was another of his "lousy jokes." The next day his press secretary, Patrick Gossage, told inquiring reporters the PM "was spoofing" — although not entirely: nine days later Trudeau did call an election for May 22. It was the election that resulted in his defeat by Joe Clark.

In 1967 the gallery decided to honour John Diefenbaker at a special private dinner. It was meant to be an off-the-record affair, mainly because the boys wanted to relax over some drinks. But Diefenbaker ruminated that he would not be running in the next election. Bruce Phillips of Southam News decided that was news fit to print. With the support of bureau manager Charles Lynch, who wrote a column, and bureau staffers who signed their names, Phillips's piece went out across the country. Curiously, from among those involved the gallery singled out Lynch, suspending his privileges for three weeks.

At times, news intruded on the evening. In 1963 Prime Minister Diefenbaker's Cabinet was split on the nuclear issue, and there were hot rumours that Defence Minister Douglas Harkness and Trade Minister George Hees were about to resign. That February night, the song of the night, "People Love Me," sung by Bruce Phillips to the tune "Jesus Loves Me," included the lines:

> There were rumours from George Hees
> I had Harkness's disease.

Diefenbaker was outraged. Listening to the song without his hearing aid, he mistook "Harkness's disease" as a reference to Parkinson's disease, a sensitive subject given how his jowls trembled. Walter Grey, the *Globe* bureau chief and dinner convener, took the full brunt of Diefenbaker's wrath. As Grey told his boss, editor Dic Doyle: "He stood very close to me and shouted. I could feel his spittle on my face." Harkness resigned the next day, Diefenbaker's government fell two days later, Hees quit the Cabinet, and Diefenbaker never forgave Phillips.

————————

For all of that, Ottawa is a company town. Even in an era of bitter partisanship, the tribe rallies at special times to bury the hatchets. In the summer of 2016 hundreds of people from all parties gathered to bid farewell to the popular Liberal strategist Mike Robinson, a man who exemplified a commitment to politics without rancour. In his spirit, they — Grits, Tories, Dippers, journos, and lobbyists — lingered well into the night at his favourite eatery, the Métropolitain.

Several private events on the calendar also now feature the kind of gleeful non-partisanship of the days of yore. In the fall, pols from all parties mix with journalists for an off-the-record evening of song, skits, and fried food at the rustic Black Sheep Inn in Wakefield, Quebec, to raise money for the Jaimie Anderson Parliamentary Internship. The evening honours the memory of a popular young Hill staffer who died of cancer in 2010. The event, which raised two hundred thousand dollars in 2016, is organized by her uncle Bruce Anderson and her father, Rick, both political power brokers, and their families. It features Peter Mansbridge doing stand-up and musical cameos from Hill heavies. The hit of the 2016 show was Treasury Board president Scott Brison, whose same-sex marriage to Maxime Saint-Pierre took place in 2007, singing Tammy Wynette's "Stand by Your Man."

A highlight of the spring season is the annual Shaughnessy Cohen Prize for Political Writing, awarded at the Politics and the Pen gala by the Writers' Trust of Canada. The event, which enjoys the cachet that the press gallery dinner once had, attracts a who's who of journalism, politics, and business. And in fall a cross-party clan of politicians and journalists gathers for a fundraiser to support a fellowship in foreign corresponding in honour of James Travers, the popular *Toronto Star* columnist and *Ottawa Citizen* editor who died in 2011. The format features two debates, one on a serious topic (in 2016, the future of media), and the other, not so much (why heckling is good for democracy). The tone of the event reflects the style of a hard-hitting reporter and foreign correspondent for Southam News who liked to say, "Screw 'em if they can't take a joke."

Away from the lights, camaraderie between journalists and politicians in private moments is common. One example occurred during Mulroney's years as prime minister.

Ian Urquhart (left) and Doug Small on the campaign trail.

Doug Small of Global News had just quit drinking. A lengthy, gruelling trip to Moscow with the prime minister was over and, as the government plane lifted off the tarmac for home, out came the customary trays of booze. "Everybody has drinks going," Small remembers. "I thought, 'I'm not going to get through this. I couldn't see anyone who wasn't drinking.'" Then Small spotted Mulroney at the front of the plane, talking to Joe Clark, his foreign minister. Only six months before, a furious Mulroney had sicced the Mounties on Small for his unauthorized release of budget details. "I catch his eye. I walked right up to him and said, 'I need to talk to somebody about drinking.'"

Mulroney responded, "You've come to the right place."

With that, Small slipped behind the curtain into Mulroney's private section. For the next several minutes the reporter and the prime minister shared their "drunk stories" and Small went back to his seat.

"If you ever have to talk about this," said Mulroney, "you know where to come."

In 2018 Small marked his twenty-eighth year of sobriety, Mulroney his thirty-ninth. Fellowship across the great divide.

Chapter 30

IN CONCLUSION:
TRUTH AND CONSEQUENCES

From Sir John A. Macdonald to Justin Trudeau: twenty-three prime ministers, forty-two elections, forty-eight leaders of the opposition; a new country, the Riel Rebellion, the building of the CPR, the burning of the Parliament Buildings, national radio, two world wars, the Great Depression, the crash of 1929, television, Sputnik, the Cold War, Kennedy, the Cuban Missile Crisis, the new flag, medicare, Quebec bombings, separatism, the pollsters, Expo 67, Pierre Trudeau, the murder of Pierre Laporte, the kidnapping of a British diplomat, women's liberation, the internet, the BlackBerry, the iPhone, terrorism, 9/11, gunshots on Parliament Hill — and more gunshots in Iraq, Afghanistan, and Syria. And throughout, tragedy and triumph, calumny and honour.

Such is the sketch of political history for Canadians since 1867, and such is the arc of the Parliamentary Press Gallery and its works. Mackenzie King called it "an adjunct of Parliament," and veteran-Ottawa-correspondent-turned-senator Charles Bishop once observed, "Parliament simply couldn't function without the Gallery." Others had a different view. One of the leading detractors was historian Frank Underhill, who denounced gallery members as "intellectually lazy and unwilling to devote the time and effort that are needed for an adequate study of the complex issues which it is their duty to report." Whatever the view, the institution has endured. The lingering question: Does the press gallery matter anymore?

As we have seen in these pages, in the early days the gallery really was a partisan adjunct, at first supporting Liberal or Conservative parties depending on its members' provenance. Newspapers — and their Ottawa correspondents — were mere pawns in the hands of prime ministers. The gallery has come a long way since those early days. Its members are better educated, more agile on deadlines, and more independent — certainly compared to the cautious treatment afforded the powerful in the past by the men (usually) who shared the burdens of national governance.

When Mitchell Sharp joined the public service in the 1940s, newspaper reporters dominated the gallery. There were no accredited television or radio reporters and neither media was a major source of parliamentary news. As Sharp wrote in his memoir, *Which Reminds Me…*, print reporters "valued their access to officials and did not betray confidences when they were given information 'off the record.' They expected to be writing stories for a long time to come. They expected that the officials who could help them would also be around for a long time." He added: "In those days the media did not consider themselves the opposition to the government. That role was left to the political opposition in Parliament." Politicians and reporters were all part of the same club. When the influential Blair Fraser of *Maclean's* placed a newspaper ad advising that he had lost his Irish terrier, he was surprised to get a call from Prime Minister Mackenzie King, owner of three terriers, inquiring: "Have you found your dog?"

The end of the clubby atmosphere came in 1956 when C.D. Howe tried to muscle approval of the pipeline bill. Typical of the hostile press reaction was that of the *Telegram's* fiery Ottawa columnist Judith Robinson: "Clarence Decatur Howe has never shown any signs of liking Parliament. In the twenty years he has sat on a government front bench he has not learned to disguise his contempt for the slow and clumsy process by which Parliament exercises its control over the executive power."

As historian Paul Rutherford noted, "The twin notions of investigative and adversary journalism had gained increasing favour in press circles, ever since the furious pipeline debate of 1956 had converted the press gallery into the voice of an angered opposition."* That was a sentiment reflected by the irreverent Val Sears of the *Toronto Star* on the eve of Prime Minister John Diefenbaker's bid for re-election in 1962: "Come, gentlemen. We have a government to overthrow." (In a variation on that theme, in the 1979 election when Conservative leader Joe Clark came glad-handing through the press section of his plane in a yellow cardigan and asked Sears, my seatmate, how long he would be with the tour, Sears looked up and deadpanned: "Long as it takes, sir.") In the decade that followed, Canadians were served up a regular diet of investigative stories and scandals and, tellingly, rampant political instability — five elections in ten years, four of them producing minority governments.

It was the worst of times for government. George Brimmell, then with the *Telegram*, incurred Diefenbaker's wrath when his full-page feature disclosed the building of a massive underground complex by the Canadian Army at Carp, Ontario, where the government would move during a nuclear attack. He called it "the Diefenbunker" and speculated lightheartedly that "it's the place where our tax dollars are to be buried." An equal-opportunity assassin, Brimmell also brought down two Liberal Cabinet ministers with stories about how they had acquired house furniture on generous terms.

The nadir was "the Gun Fight at the Pearson-Diefenbaker Corral," in the words of the CBC's Larry Zolf. The Tories and willing allies in the media savaged a series of French-Canadian ministers in the Liberal government. Three of them were hounded from office for a crime no greater than showing poor political judgment. At the peak of the Cold War, the opposition accused the government of mishandling the case of a lowly postal clerk named George Victor Spencer, who had sold unclassified information to the Russians. Inexcusably, Pearson went on a fishing expedition for dirt on his opponent and persuaded the RCMP to hand over details of what became a retaliatory scandal that he pinned on Diefenbaker. He even went so far in a testy private meeting to threaten Diefenbaker — "that awful man," he once called him — with exposing the Gerda Munsinger case unless Diefenbaker called off the hounds. New Liberal MP Gérard

---

* Paul Rutherford, *When Television Was Young: Prime Time Canada 1952–1967* (Toronto: University of Toronto Press, 1990), 403.

Pelletier was so troubled that he called Parliament "an absurd nightmare, a Kafkaesque sort of labyrinth without any exit." *Maclean's* even indulged its readers in a limerick contest. The winner:

> There was a young lady from Munich
> Whose bosom distended her tunic
> Her main undertaking
> Was cabinet making
> In fashions bilingue et unique.

In his rollicking review of the Trudeau era, gadfly Zolf concluded: "The denizens of the Parliamentary Press Gallery had wallowed in a sea of scandal, growing fat off the avails of Rivard-Munsinger-Spencer. Journalistic careers were made by finding bail-jumping labour leaders or bed-hopping courtesans, or by proving that the Mounties were terrorizing a cancer-ridden old Commie." Hyperbolic? Not entirely: The *Toronto Star's* swashbuckling reporter Robert Reguly found union boss Hal Banks in the United States after he had skipped the country following criminal charges, and Reguly scored the Canadian scoop of the century by finding Gerda Munsinger alive and living in Munich. We were all told she was dead, but Reguly found her name in the city phone book and called her up. Then Richard Gwyn literally wrote the book, *The Shape of Scandal*, detailing the sordid stories of the era.

The other force shaping the new, aggressive journalism was the CBC's Sunday evening show, *This Hour Has Seven Days*. Invented by a pair of McLuhanites in their midthirties, TV producers Patrick Watson and Douglas Leiterman, the show became appointment viewing in the late 1960s, as a parade of public people submitted to their "hot seat" interviews and irreverent questions. They took their cameras into shareholders' meetings, smuggled equipment into prisons, and door-stopped reluctant politicians, all in aid of exposing malfeasance or corruption. Zolf famously confronted Pierre Sévigny during the Munsinger case, and the former Diefenbaker associate defence minister, who had lost a leg in combat, swung his walking stick at Zolf's head and chased him away in what Zolf remembers as his "Citizen Cane" moment.

"The very irreverence, the iconoclasm, that defined *Seven Days* had touched something in the Canadian soul," said TV critic Roy Shields.

CBC management tried to muzzle the show, provoking a parliament-ary inquiry and a national outpouring of support. But by early 1966 management canned the show — not the last time that the brass bowed to pressure from the power brokers on Parliament Hill. The other was the 1962 cancellation of a documentary, *Mr. Pearson*, by the promising filmmaker D.A. Pennebaker, which drew protests from Liberal insiders because it depicted an informal PM watching an afternoon World Series game in his office and a youthful aide, Jim Coutts, who appeared to be running the country. Richard O'Hagan, Pearson's adviser at the time, told me: "Pearson couldn't imagine — and I misjudged it — anybody taking issue with him putting his feet up and watching two or three innings of the World Series."

Television has played a seminal role in Canadian public affairs, for better and for worse, for years. Historian Paul Rutherford noted that in 1956 during the infamous pipeline debate "the CBC found itself acting as a conduit for the anti-government opinions of the press gallery on its assorted network shows."

In Quebec, Radio-Canada's popular *Conférence de Presse* aired a steady diet of anti-Duplessis government sentiments by journalists from *Le Devoir*, the premier's Union Nationale Party having decided to boycott the show. The panels, wrote Rutherford, "were one of the first agents of a liberalization that would pave the way for the collapse of the Union Nationale and the forthcoming 'Quiet Revolution.'" One of the leaders of that revolution, René Lévesque, came to public prominence on a weekly half-hour Radio-Canada show, *Point de Mire*, which challenged conven-tional thinking at home and abroad. (It is a tradition that continues in French Canada today in the popular Sunday show, *Tout le Monde en Parle*, an entertaining two hours of talk on politics and culture where NDP leader Jack Layton made a breakthrough appearance with Quebec voters in the 2011 election.)

National politics also has been heavily influenced by events and per-sonalities outside Ottawa. Behind the scenes, broadcast executives Trina McQueen, Tom Gould, Don Cameron, Bill Cunningham, and Mark Starowicz were among the leaders in the professionalization of news and public affairs on English radio and TV. A generation later in the same tradition, Radio-Canada news executive Jean Pelletier, a gallery veteran who broke the story of the American hostages who had been hidden at the Canadian embassy in Tehran, oversaw a remarkable series of investigations into corruption and police malfeasance that put the guilty in jail. They and others did it with swagger. There was a sense of journalism, as former *Fifth Estate* producer Ron Haggart put it, "in which journalists themselves decide what are the issues of concern and importance, a journalism in which the issues are established not by the politicians, but those who watch them with pencil and film."

For two generations CBC Radio shows like Peter Gzowski's *Morningside* and Barbara Frum's *As It Happens* helped set the agenda for English Canada with important interviews and informative panels. In television, Knowlton Nash with *The National* and Frum with *The Journal* gave political junkies their fix of national news and analysis. In print, Doris Anderson at *Chatelaine* drove the feminist agenda in "Middle Canada." In the West, Jack Webster ruled the airwaves. Editor Claude Ryan was a powerful voice for Quebec in the pages of his *Le Devoir*. Later, former gallery reporter Lise Bissonnette, who became editor of *Le Devoir* in 1990, shifted the paper to a more nationalist course and was a personable and outspoken advocate for the province's aspirations. Radio-Canada viewers had the irrepressible Denise Bombardier for pointed interviews and provocative thoughts, while publisher Jean Paré's *L'actualité* was a mirror of the modern Quebec during his twenty-five-year tenure.

———

After the disclosure by the *Washington Post* of the Nixon White House role in the Watergate burglary and cover-up in 1972, the hills were alive with imitation Woodwards and Bernsteins. In the heyday of the late 1970s and early 1980s, the CBC, the *Globe and Mail*, the *Star, Le Devoir, La Presse,* and Southam papers broke major stories on everything from Mountie barn-burning to organized crime rings.

Eric Malling was one of the finest investigative reporters of his day on CBC's *The Fifth Estate* and CTV's *W5*. Among his disclosures was a government cover-up of a two-billion-dollar loss — then the largest in Canadian history — at aircraft maker Canadair. His reporting of the tainted tuna affair in 1985 caused the resignation of the minister of fisheries who had authorized the sale of the fish over objections from his department. Malling also fronted a remarkable CTV special that celebrated efforts by New Zealand to reduce its deficit and debt with massive cuts to social programs and agricultural subsidies in 1980. Here in Canada, politicians began to wilt under the scorn of prominent business journalists and conservative think tanks that trumpeted the perils of deficit financing. These attacks ultimately gave rise to budget slashing in Ottawa and the provinces.

Yet, by 1991, slash-and-burn Malling was having second thoughts. He conceded that "Watergate envy" had caused many reporters to become contemptuous of all authority. "We have gone overboard in the notion that it's the media's job to criticize, to be the real opposition to whoever is in power," he said at a University of Regina journalism symposium.

The post-Watergate era also ushered in a new journalistic puritanism. The gallery beer machine was banished in the late 1990s, and the National Press Club closed for lack of customers. Reporters shied away from fraternizing with MPs and Cabinet ministers. "This adversarial journalism," lamented the talented Stewart MacLeod in a whimsical column for *Maclean's*, "is getting entirely out of hand. It's reached the point where you're afraid to be seen talking to backbench politicians, let alone the Prime Minister of Canada — unless, of course, you can play a tape of everything that was said."

Pamela Wallin also worried about the impact of television cameras trolling the halls of Parliament. "Words are never enough. I've got to have video," she noted. At the time she was the Ottawa bureau chief of CTV. And she knew that the politician who could serve up the best pictures would win the day. "There is no question our shots are visually dictated too often," she told the *Globe* for a 1988 piece on the role of TV on the Hill. Doug Small, the bureau chief for Global News, added that whoever could speak in "clips" and look comfortable would get the airtime. "It's such a crummy way to judge people," Small conceded.

It's also a crummy way to judge policy. The snippet became the norm. Conflict won out over content. Often, if a politician was quoted at all, it would be only a phrase to amplify the point the broadcaster was making. We often got the views of the reporter without ever knowing what actually happened at a news event. Coverage revolved around the scrums — "not a very civilized way of doing journalism," Roger Smith once observed when he patrolled the Hill for CTV News. Conservative leader Robert Stanfield echoed the sentiment. "How silly can grown men get?" he asked during a conference on politics and the media. "We are forcing politicians to be simplistic, impressionistic and, when they succeed, to manipulate." Patrick Gossage, the able communications director for Pierre Trudeau and an active political commentator, agreed: "There is a lack of gravity about the gallery, an unwillingness to take on big issues. It's a shame. It's partly manpower, and it's just so much easier to cover the trivia."

Author Roy MacGregor, who spent fourteen years in the press gallery before covering the NHL for the *Globe*, also argues there has been "a massive 'cheapening' of opinion." He blames "first, social media, second, all-news format. Social media has created a world where everyone thinks their opinion has merit with the best. The field has been levelled. Everyone is a columnist, everyone an expert. And mean-minded opinion wins daily over even-handed opinion. Then you have all-news channels and the increasing reliance on 'panels' to fill time and offer up talking heads."

In a paper published by the Centre for International Governance Innovation, digital expert Jesse Hirsh wrote that while legacy media made room for "opposing perspectives," social media "encourages people to connect with like minds and filter out opposing views. All space is taken up by a never-ending flow of posts and information, which makes it difficult for new or contrary ideas to emerge above the buzz of the usual suspects."

David Herle, a thoughtful backroom Liberal strategist and pollster, said that an obsession with the horse race, not the platform, dominated election coverage in 2011. The pollsters ruled. They "turned the election into just another sporting event during the NHL playoffs," he wrote. "The election turned from what do we want government to do to who's going to win the game."

After "Everywhere TV," the next major development in political reporting was the BlackBerry invasion. Christopher Waddell, former dean of journalism at Carleton and a veteran of the press gallery where he was a reporter for the *Globe* and bureau chief for CBC, argued that the device was as much a curse as a blessing for political coverage. He noted in a 2012 academic paper, "Berry'd Alive," that in advance of the 2000 election the BlackBerry's creator Research in Motion provided sixteen BlackBerrys to

CBC, in exchange for an assessment by reporters and editors of the new phone's performance. The devices allowed the network to plan coverage more efficiently and to share the latest news among its reporters on leaders' planes. By the 2004 election, however, political operatives also had BlackBerrys — and the email addresses of the reporters. Waddell argued that opening their systems to back-roomers "was a fateful decision since it meant that collectively, the media had handed over its communications tool to the political parties." What he called "BlackBerry journalism" thus became the channel for political spin 24/7, as operatives bombarded reporters with leaks, slants, and pitches.

The downside of the instant communications was that the "hacks and flacks" fell into a whirligig on Parliament Hill, chatting back and forth among themselves, often in isolation from what was happening in the country. Instead of analysis of policy, voters were treated to endless excited reports about "war rooms," "ground games," and "ballot questions" of little interest to the Canadian public. With the media's insatiable maw demanding continuous updates of blogs and online reports, parties were only too willing to fire statements across the digital platform into 'Berrys and iPhones. Waddell concluded that technology caused the media establishment "to turn its back on the public, forging closer links with the people reporters cover than the people who used to read, watch, and listen to their reporting."

Industry-wide cutbacks also had a major impact on the quality of reporting from Ottawa. The Canadian site iPolitics.ca reported in 2016 that the Parliamentary Press Gallery had shrunk to its lowest level in twenty-two years: as of December 7, 2016, there were 320 members — reporters, columnists, editors, technical staff, and camera operators — compared to the previous low of 314 in 1994. That represented almost a 20 percent drop from a peak of 379 members in only four years. But the devilish part was in the details provided by the press gallery. While the staffs of the CBC, CTV, Global, the *Globe, La Presse,* and *Le Devoir* had grown or were stable, in the twenty-two years since 1994 CP had lost eight of its twenty-six reporters. Important regional outlets that put the spotlight on their local MPs and local issues had entirely withdrawn their bureaus, including CFTO in Toronto, BCTV in Vancouver, CFCF in Montreal, and CJOH in Ottawa. Six newspapers had closed their Ottawa bureaus: the *Hamilton Spectator, Windsor*

Star, London Free Press, Regina Leader-Post, and Saskatoon *StarPhoenix* — along with the once-influential *Western Producer*. Ongoing cuts at Postmedia decimated its Ottawa ranks as well.

The news industry is in deep trouble right across the country. In a landmark report in early 2017, *The Shattered Mirror*, the Public Policy Forum estimated that 30 percent of the journalism jobs in Canada had vanished in the previous six years. Since 2010, 27 daily newspapers and 225 weeklies had disappeared through closings or mergers. Then, in a brazen move in late 2017, Torstar Corporation and Postmedia swapped 41 newspapers and carved out monopolies by closing 36 of them, including all but one of their small community papers. In the spring of 2018 the federal Competition Bureau initiated an investigation into this transaction.

One reason for the turmoil is that between 2006 and 2015, total advertising in newspapers plummeted $1.3 billion from an initial $2.75 billion. As digital innovations by traditional news outlets have stalled, Google and Facebook have gobbled up 82 percent of online advertising, while originating precious little original content in an ocean of disinformation. In a companion national online survey, Allan Gregg of Earnscliffe Strategy Group, in partnership with the Canadian Journalism Foundation, established that an overwhelming majority of respondents considered current affairs, and community and political news as important — more so than sports, entertainment, and celebrities. A majority said that democracy would be threatened without news from traditional or digital sources. Yet more than half had no idea that news media outlets were in crisis, and a third did not view the decline as a problem. Ominously, in early 2018 Torstar board chairman John Honderich, whose company publishes the largest daily in Canada (measured in overall weekly sales), warned in an interview with the *Globe*: "We have little time left. More cuts will be coming.… We are very close to the end." As if to seal the point, the Desmarais family abandoned ownership of *La Presse* in the summer of 2018, proposing that it become a charitable trust. The paper already had eliminated all its print editions in a bid to survive online.

Jim Poling Sr., a press gallery old boy who retired as general manager in 1979 after twenty-eight years with CP, offered a telling lament about the disappearing journalism in Canada's regions. He wrote in his 2007 memoir:

The shrinking of smaller newspapers has created huge
black holes that reduce the exchange of news between
Canadians. Almost all our news comes from, and is about,
urban areas. As a result, urbanization is smothering many
of the beliefs and traits of small-town and country life.…
The news is a one-way pipeline now: It is big city news
about big city life produced by big city people. And it is
news produced mainly for making some corporation in a
big city some money.

Even on the national level there are fewer people in Ottawa chasing
fewer stories. While organizations like CP once had "beat reporters" and
sent staff to committee hearings, now everyone is a generalist, posing
as an expert one day on the Trans Mountain Pipeline and the next on
right-to-die legislation. And feeding the beast with tweets, blog posts,
and online updates requires the dexterity of a Houdini. The *Globe* ran
an exclusive video of the 2014 Parliament Hill shooting on its website
and carried a front page picture because reporter Josh Wingrove shot
both on his BlackBerry, using his hostile-environment training from his
Afghanistan tour to duck away from the shots in the Hall of Honour. On
screens in major newsrooms, measuring systems like Parsley at the *Toronto
Star* and Chartbeat at the *Globe* post scores of which stories are attracting
the most attention online — a kind of perverse cheering section for the
race to the bottom of the clickbait bucket.

Today's gallery members are industrious — and sober. History may
not record the date that relative sobriety returned to the affairs of the
press gallery, but reporter Marjorie Nichols signalled its dawn in a piece
she wrote for *Weekend* magazine in 1979. It ran the day of the annual
press gallery dinner. "These days," she wrote, "Parliament Hill guards
are never called to scrape an errant scribe off the doorstep at 4 in the
morning; the gallery is mostly made up of serious-minded young men
and women who limit themselves to one martini and change into their
pajamas before *The National.*"

———————

The other observable fact is that since the late 1970s there has been a grow-ing cohort of well-educated women in the ranks, after a century of virtual male exclusivity. One of the best and brightest was award-winning Jennifer Ditchburn. A bilingual Montrealer, she wanted to be a journalist from the sixth grade. "When you are young and a teacher tells you that you are really good at writing, then you take it to heart," she explained in an interview in the press gallery lounge. At Concordia she supplemented her journalism studies with practical experience by becoming news editor of the school paper, the *Link*, and filing stories for the *Gazette* and the Sherbrooke *Record*. That got her a part-time position with CP in Montreal and eventually full-time work in Edmonton. In 1997, at age twenty-four, she moved to the press gallery in Ottawa by way of covering the federal election. Now a married mother of two girls, Ditchburn also found time to get an M.A. in journalism from Carleton. She is a three-time winner of the National Newspaper Award, and in 2015 she received the prestigious Charles Lynch Award for coverage of national issues. She left CP in early 2016 to become editor of the public-affairs magazine *Policy Options*; with Graham Fox, pres-ident of the Institute for Research on Public Policy, she co-edited *The Harper*

Jennifer Ditchburn (left) and Marie Vastel at launch of press gallery book, Ottawa, 2016: a critical mass of talented women.

Factor, a telling assessment of the former prime minister's legacy that came out in 2016.

Ditchburn celebrates "the real critical mass" of females as one of the best changes in the press gallery. As of June 2016, in fact, about 40 percent of the membership was female (130). Other veterans on the Hill included CP bureau chief Heather Schofield; Manon Cornellier, columnist for *Le Devoir* and blogger for *L'actualité* magazine, who came to Ottawa in 1985; *Le Devoir*'s Marie Vastel, a seven-year veteran; and Hélène Buzzetti, a correspondent since 1999 and a two-time president of the Parliamentary Press Gallery. Fully 35 percent of bureau chiefs listed on the 2016 website of the gallery were female.

As a further sign of gallery diversity, Huffington Post appointed Althia Raj as its first bureau chief in 2011. A McGill grad, she came to the position after several years of federal experience with the *National Post*, Sun Media, CTV, and the CBC, and a stint with the external affairs department. She is one of several new online journalists with gallery membership, including reporters for iPolitics, rabble.ca, Blacklock's Reporter, and the Tyee. (BuzzFeed shut down its Ottawa bureau in 2016, after just a little more than a year of operation.) She files several stories a day, is a regular on TV political panels, and is regarded as an important link to people who get their news mainly online by power players such as key Trudeau adviser Gerald Butts.

Whatever the gender, the men and women of today's gallery have their work cut out for them. In addition to the challenges of the digital age, they are facing governments that have become even more sophisticated about media management. From Pearson through Harper there was an evolving control of the message from the top. With the arrival of television in the Commons in 1977 and scrums in the hall, the focus shifted to the prime minister of the day. Centralizing the message replaced any desire to use reporters as intermediaries to explain government policy. Suddenly, no minister made a move without a communications expert and a press secretary. The army of spinmeisters totally overwhelmed the thinned-out ranks of the fourth estate.

John Ivison, the thoughtful Ottawa columnist for the *National Post*, said that during the Harper era "we got a perfect storm and it was pretty unproductive." Ivison recalled calling Harper's communications director Sandra Buckler, whom he had known as a lobbyist, to find out if it was true that the PM had poached the chef from the governor general's residence. "It was a pretty innocuous story," he said. "Her immortal words to me were, 'Off the record, I can't comment.'" He concludes, "Over the course of the ten-year reign, they went out of their way to pick fights with people which were needless. The gallery obliged them. Frankly, some of the people running the gallery at the time had animus."

Despite appearances, many experienced Ottawa hands don't see substantial deviation from message control under Justin Trudeau. "They're picking their times when they put shiny things in the window," said the CBC's industrious Hill reporter Chris Rands. "They throw out what is going to be the clickbait of the day." At the same time, there has been a return to quiet, selected background chats. The bureaucrats have opened the veil. "People will talk to you," notes CBC bureau chief Rob Russo. "You cannot last in this town as a serious reporter unless you have people who trust you."

Despite the odds, the current generation of gallery reporters has a solid record of investigation and analysis. Bob Fife of the *Globe*, Joël-Denis Bellavance of *La Presse*, and Murray Brewster of CBC, among others, have consistently broken stories of import. Gallery members know that their audiences gravitate to quality and information they need in their lives, and retreat from the superficial. Celebrated columnist Chantal Hébert personifies the breed. While fearless in her criticism, she has said that the purpose of journalism has nothing to do with "making people angry." The need for substance was a point echoed by Goldy Hyder, president and CEO of the Ottawa lobby firm Hill+Knowlton Strategies and a veteran Joe Clark Conservative. As he told the journalists attending a 2014 panel on journalism in the National Arts Centre: "Some of the navel gazing that you do needs to be more about ... looking much more for content, much more for insight, much more for storytelling that may or may not be handed to you." It was a kind of get-over-it moment. "Political parties," added Hyder, "are all playing the same game, and I wouldn't expect them to change any time soon."

And that is the problem. Playing the same game starves the system of information citizens need to make thoughtful decisions about key issues. After covering professionl hockey for fourteen years, the *Globe*'s Roy MacGregor points to a striking parallel between the sport and politics: "the intensity of the media managing." He added: "Players, like politicians, now have talking points. If they go off-script, a media handler will cut it off or yell out 'Last question!'"

———————

An informed media can, in Byron's metaphor, cause "a small drop of ink, falling like dew upon a thought" to make millions think, but only if there is access to solid information. In turn, reporters chasing sensation over substance, the horse race over policies, contribute to declining faith in the legitimacy of government.

Elly Alboim, a veteran of sixteen years in TV news, including a decade as CBC's parliamentary bureau chief, and a partner with the powerful Ottawa consultancy Earnscliffe, paints a glum portrait. In a 2014 policy paper he wrote: "These days in Ottawa, competent communications advisors try to stay away from the mass media whenever they can.... They have learned that there is seldom a win to be had, that playing for ties is as good as it gets." In an interview in spring 2016, Alboim took note of the declining investment in Ottawa news and a drop in salaries because of cuts in overtime. "People in the gallery know there is less interest at head office in what they do and less interest among the public. Covering Ottawa was once the pinnacle of a journalistic career. No longer. It is a three- or four-year stepping stone to something else."

Torstar Corporation board chair John Honderich supports that view. Recalling with great fondness his five years in the gallery starting in 1976, he said: "Going to work in Ottawa no longer has the cachet it once had. When I was there, being a parliamentary correspondent was the top of the pecking order. That was something you would aspire to. Not so today."

Does the decline have any impact? It is certainly true that as consumption of news has declined — and it has — there has been a striking drop in political participation. Since Pierre Trudeau was elected in 1968 and

75 percent of eligible voters went to the polls, there has been a steady erosion. The low point was the vote of 2008, which returned a Harper minority government, when voter participation fell to 59 percent. (In the 2015 election the combination of anti-Harper feeling and Justin Trudeau's effective campaign moved the needle up to 68.5 percent, the highest since 1993.)

Christopher Waddell of Carleton University provided an additional clue when he examined election results in six Ontario communities over seven federal elections between 1979 and 2000. It so happened that newspapers in three of the cities — Windsor, Hamilton, and London — closed their Ottawa bureaus between 1993 and 1996. The other three community newspapers — Niagara Falls, St. Catharines, and Sault Ste. Marie — did not have Ottawa bureaus. Waddell noticed that voter turnout in the three communities whose newspapers shut their Ottawa bureaus "fell more quickly than the provincial average in the elections after their bureaus closed." In cities with papers that never had Ottawa bureaus, the decline in turnout was less dramatic. In the 2016 national poll, Earnscliffe's Allan Gregg found a direct correlation between those who followed the news and civic engagement in local charities or causes.

People decide not to vote for different reasons, Waddell acknowledged. But "declining coverage of national politics appears likely as one explanation." Tellingly, Waddell asked, "Would as many people go to an Ottawa Senators hockey game, a Toronto Blue Jays baseball game, or a Calgary Stampeders football game if all the local radio, television, and print media in those communities simply stopped covering the sport with their own reporters, instead using occasional stories written by wire services?"

––––––––––––

Thus we end with a lament — not for a press gallery that might have been, nor for some mystical golden age. To be sure, we can regret the spontaneity that has long been gone from our public affairs. And we need to admit that we media hounds are partly to blame. The post-Watergate trend to "gotcha journalism" has had a negative impact on the naturally risk-averse breed of politicos. There is an endless loop of confrontational questions and evasive replies. As academics Mary Anne Comber and Robert S. Mayne observed in their book on news distortion, *The*

Newsmongers: "The overall effect of this cat and mouse game between politicians and the press is to reinforce what can only be called a siege mentality on the part of politicians once they are in power."

Ink-stained wretches, to borrow from columnist Murray Kempton, are the kind of people who come down from the hills after the battle is over and shoot the wounded. The great Ottawa columnist George Bain observed in his 1994 book on media distortions the beginnings of "the current prosecutorial style of political reporting." Nothing exemplifies the trait more today than the roving bands of shouting reporters with their armadas of cameras, microphones, iPhones, and lights — and inane questions of the have-you-stopped-beating-your-wife variety. They have invited taming.

On the other side, the fixation with control of the message has become all-consuming. As former Liberal leader Bob Rae observed in his 2015 gem, *What's Happened to Politics?*, "Political leaders are coiffed, dressed, managed, scripted, controlled, and presented to the public not so much as real people but as packaged products. The character and courage of the past is desperately needed today."

It is also unsettling to observe a climate of constant confrontation — and constant electioneering — that drives too many good men and women away from the political arena, and turns many incumbents into unattractive bullies intent on manipulation instead of leadership. It took Donald Trump to unite the parties in a rare display of unanimity in condemning U.S. trade policy in the summer of 2018.

In his farewell to the Commons after his defeat in 1938, a mellow R.B. Bennett acknowledged the shortcomings of "the rough and tumble of political life," adding: "It is a tiresome task. It is a wearying task. It is an ungrateful task."

In his autobiography, journalist Anthony Westell said one reason he decided to leave his *Toronto Star* political column to go into academia was the damage he believed adversarial journalism was doing to democracy.

In my frequent returns to the press gallery during my research before the 2015 election, I was struck by how dysfunctional Parliament Hill had become. It was all about the clip, not the substance. The reporters, arrayed in fenced pens at selected spots around the corridors, leaned in as leaders emerged to deliver their pre-rehearsed barbs. The whole place is wired for sound, yet the information flows in a trickle over the "uni-mics" — as in, unidirectional messaging. Insults and invective fly through the air, producing a corridor parody of question period. Parties slag each other across our TV sets, the participants all talking at once. Truth is muted. Bombast rules. A presidential-style government has reduced Cabinet ministers to nobodies on Parliament Hill.

The cattle pens and the slagging continued after the change of power. The challenge for government, opposition, and the media is to change that, perhaps to revive values from an earlier time. There was a day in this country when our politicians had profile and standing in their communities before they landed in Ottawa. Cabinet ministers had national reputations. You could actually name ten of them. Government MPs engaged in policy formation. If the election of 2015 meant anything, it was a clarion call for change. It highlighted the need for reporters to operate with civility, thoughtfulness, and a modicum of humility — along with skepticism — and for politicians to give up the bullhorn and the lash, if they truly believe that actions and words have the power to do good. The election year of 2015 was a time to end the politics we abhor and to restore the politics we deserve. We are still waiting.

As for the question, *Does the press gallery still matter?* Now, more than ever.

ACKNOWLEDGEMENTS

The germ of the idea for this book came on a golf course and in the stylish Le Salon of the National Arts Centre in Ottawa. My golfing friend Allan Gregg first suggested there was a book to be done about Canada's notable journalists. In Ottawa the debate at a panel sponsored by the Canadian Journalism Foundation, which I chaired at the time, was: "Does the Press Gallery Matter?"

For the next four years, I was able to rely on journalists, politicians, and historians to help me with answers to that question, especially the ones mentioned in these pages. The dedicated and efficient staffs of Library and Archives Canada, including the Library of Parliament, spared no effort in pointing me to books, documents, photographs, and, importantly, the transcripts of oral histories by press gallery journalists — recorded by veteran Hill correspondents Peter Stursberg and Tom Earle. Press gallery head Terry Guillon, a friend to all reporters, generously provided access to the minutes and documents in the informal archive kept in boxes near the site of the old beer machine.

The good people of Toronto Public Library, especially the shining Reference Library on Yonge Street and my own Deer Park branch, provided an endless flow of books, papers, and photos to flesh out the stories of the journalists who covered twenty-three prime ministers and Parliament for the past 150 years. From the trove I rediscovered the insights from excellent journalistic and academic histories, most notably historians John English,

Richard Clippingdale, and Allan Levine, whose *Scrum Wars,* published in 1993, was the first major examination of the press gallery.

I'm especially indebted to editor emeritus John Macfarlane for encouraging me to write this book and to Charlie and Nancy Gordon who provided shelter, sustenance, and inspiration during several trips to Ottawa. I owe a special debt to my many colleagues from the *Montreal Star*, *Time*, and *Maclean's* who were my partners during more than a decade in the press gallery. I am also grateful to the book publishers — many now gone, alas — and talented writers cited in the bibliography whose work stands the test of time; and to photographers Peter Bregg and Fred Chartrand who were generous with their advice and help.

Beverley Slopen, a friend for almost forty-five years, worked her literary agent magic to find the manuscript a home, all the while calming my jitters that it would ever happen. At Dundurn, Scott Fraser had the confidence to acquire my manuscript, although it was my first crack at a book. Dominic Farrell had the patience to edit it — carefully and with tact, a grace every newbie author should have. Project editor Elena Radic, copy editor Cy Strom, proofreader Ashley Hisson, and Dundurn's publicity department were welcoming and dedicated in making sure the words worked — and that the word got out on the street.

On the eve of publication, people heard me refer to "my London producer." Actually, he was our son Tim, a freelance editor at CNN, who lent his many media talents to the final push and joined his brother Chris in New Zealand in sending good vibes. My greatest debt is to my loving and inspirational partner. Sally O'Neill not only is an uncanny proofreader and critic; she is the very special person I have been blessed to have at my side for fifty-one years — and counting.

SOURCES

MEDIA

Books in Canada
Brandon Sun
Canadiana historical publications (canadiana.ca)
CBC Archives (cbc.ca/archives, ici.radio-canada.ca/archives)
CPAC.ca
Gazette (Montreal)
Globe and Mail
La Presse
Le Devoir
Le Soleil
Montreal Star
Ottawa Citizen
Ottawa Journal
Policy Options
Quebec Daily Telegraph
Radio-Canada news (ici.radio-canada.ca)
Ryerson Review of Journalism
Vancouver Sun
Weekend magazine
Winnipeg Free Press
Winnipeg Tribune

PRIMARY SOURCES

Canadian Parliamentary Historical Resources (parl.canadiana.ca)

Charles Lynch papers (Library and Archives Canada [LAC])

Duncan Cameron papers (LAC)

House of Commons debates

John D. Dafoe papers (Queen's University)

Library and Archives Canada oral history project:

    Tom Earle interviews: Charles Lynch, Dave McIntosh, Douglas Fisher, Tom Earle (by Doug Small), Joyce Fairbairn, W.A. "Bill" Wilson

    Peter Stursberg interviews: Clement Brown, Victor Mackie, Lubor J. Zink

Norman DePoe papers (LAC)

Parliamentary Press Gallery archives

Robert Lewis papers (Clara Thomas Archives and Special Collections, York University)

Ted Grant papers (LAC)

University of Manitoba Archives

Vic Mackie papers (LAC)

AUTHOR INTERVIEWS

Elly Alboim, George Brimmell, Helen Brimmell, Clark Davey, David DePoe, Susan Dexter, Jennifer Ditchburn, Luke Fisher, Allan Fotheringham, Bill Fox, Graham Fraser, Patrick Gossage, Allan Gregg, Terry Guillon, Richard Gwyn, Beth Haddon, Christine Hearn, Jesse Hirsh, John Honderich, John Ivison, Fraser Kelly, Collin Lafrance, Allan Lutfy, Peter Mansbridge, Jim Munson, Blair Neatby, Peter C. Newman, Richard O'Hagan, Jane O'Hara, Chris Rands, Rob Russo, Robin Sears, Jeffrey Simpson, Doug Small, Rosemary Speirs, Geoffrey Stevens, Courtney Tower, Brian Trepanier, Dan Turner, Ian Urquhart, Marie Vastel, Christopher Waddell, Pamela Wallin, Anthony Westell, Les Whittington, Frederica Wilson, Josh Wingrove, Hugh Winsor, Sandra Woods, and Bernie Zukerman.

BIBLIOGRAPHY

Adair, Robin. "Parliament and the Press." *Canadian Liberal*, Spring 1951.

Alboim, Elly. "On the Verge of Total Dysfunction: Government, Media, and Communications." In *How Canadians Communicate IV: Media and Politics*, edited by David Taras and Christopher Waddell. Edmonton: Athabasca University Press, 2012.

Anderson, Antony. *The Diplomat: Lester Pearson and the Suez Crisis.* Fredericton: Goose Lane, 2015.

Bain, George. *Gotcha! How the Media Distort the News.* Toronto: Key Porter Books, 1965.

Bélanger, Claude. *Quebecers, the Roman Catholic Church and the Manitoba School Question: A Chronology.* Marianopolis College, 2000. faculty.marianopolis.edu/c.belanger/quebechistory/chronos/manitoba.pdf.

Bercuson, David. *Maple Leaf Against the Axis: Canada's Second World War.* Toronto: Stoddart, 1995.

Bilkey, Paul. *Persons, Papers and Things: Being the Casual Recollections of a Journalist with Some Flounderings in Philosophy.* Toronto: Ryerson Press, 1940.

Brennan, Patrick H. *Reporting the Nation's Business: Press-Government Relations During the Liberal Years, 1935–1957.* Toronto: University of Toronto Press, 1994.

Bridle, Augustus. "Ottawa the Unusual." *Canadian Magazine*, January 1911.

Buzetti, Hélène, and Josh Wingrove, eds. *Sharp Wits and Busy Pens: 150 Years of Canada's Parliamentary Press Gallery.* Ottawa: Hill Times, 2016.

Cahill, Jack. *John Turner: The Long Run.* Toronto: University of Toronto Press, 1984.

Chrétien, Jean, with Ron Graham. *My Years as Prime Minister.* Toronto: Knopf Canada, 2007.

Clippingdale, Richard. *The Power of the Pen: The Politics, Nationalism, and Influence of Sir John Willison.* Toronto: Dundurn Press, 2012.

Cook, Ramsay. *The Politics of John W. Dafoe and the Free Press.* Toronto: University of Toronto Press, 1963.

Crone, Kennedy. *The Press Gallery (Ottawa), 1937–38.* Montreal: Beaver Hall Press, 1936.

Dafoe, Christopher. *In Search of Canada: The Early Years of John Wesley Dafoe.* Winnipeg: Great Plains, 2014.

Dafoe, John Wesley. *Sixty Years in Journalism.* Address delivered in Winnipeg, October 16, 1943. peel.library.ualberta.ca/bibliography/6562.html.

Davey, Keith. *The Rainmaker: A Passion for Politics.* Toronto: Stoddart, 1986.

Dean, Misao. "Duncan, Sara Jeannette (Cotes)." *In Dictionary of Canadian Biography*, vol. 15. Toronto and Laval: University of Toronto Press / Presses de l'Université Laval, 2003. biographi.ca/en/bio/duncan_sara_jeannette_15E.html.

Delacourt, Susan. *Shopping for Votes: How Politicians Choose Us and We Choose Them.* Vancouver: Douglas and McIntyre, 2013.

Dempson, Peter. *Assignment Ottawa: Seventeen Years in the Press Gallery.* Toronto: General Publishing, 1968.

Desbarats, Peter. *Guide to Canadian News Media.* Toronto: Harcourt Brace Jovanovich, 1990.

Ditchburn, Jennifer. "Government News Management and Canadian Journalism." In *The Harper Factor: Assessing a Prime Minister's Policy Legacy,* edited by Jennifer Ditchburn and Graham Fox. Montreal: McGill-Queen's University Press, 2016.

———. "Journalistic Pathfinding: How the Parliamentary Press Gallery Adapted to News Management Under the Conservative Government of Stephen Harper." Master's thesis, Carleton University, 2014.

"Does the Press Gallery Matter?" Canadian Journalism Foundation, *CPAC online,* podcast, 2014.

Doyle, Richard J. *Hurly-Burly: A Time at the* Globe. Toronto: Macmillan of Canada, 1990.

Duncan, Sara Jeannette. "Diogenes on Bric-a-Brac." *Canada Monthly* 4, June 1880.

———. *Selected Journalism.* Edited by T.E. Tausky. Ottawa: Tecumseh Press, 1978.

Eggleston, Wilfrid. *While I Still Remember.* Toronto: Ryerson Press, 1968.

English, John. *Just Watch Me: The Life of Pierre Elliott Trudeau, 1968–2000.* Toronto: Knopf Canada, 2009.

———. "Pearson, Lester Bowles." *In Dictionary of Canadian Biography*, vol. 20. Toronto and Laval: University of Toronto Press / Presses de l'Université Laval, 2003. biographi.ca/en/bio/pearson_lester_bowles_20E.html.

———. *The Worldly Years: The Life of Lester Pearson, 1949–1972.* Toronto: Knopf Canada, 1992.

Flanagan, Tom. *Harper's Team: Behind the Scenes in the Conservative Rise to Power.* Montreal: McGill-Queen's University Press, 2007.

Ford, Arthur. *As the World Wags On.* Toronto: Ryerson Press, 1950.

Fotheringham, Allan. *Boy from Nowhere: A Life in Ninety-One Countries.* Toronto: Dundurn Press, 2011.

———. *Fotheringham's Fictionary of Facts & Follies.* Toronto: Key Porter Books, 2001.

Fox, Bill. *Spinwars: Politics and New Media.* Toronto: Key Porter Books, 1999.

Fraser, Blair. *The Search for Identity.* Toronto: Doubleday Canada, 1967.

Fraser, John, and Graham Fraser, eds. *Blair Fraser Reports, Selections 1944–1968.* Toronto: Macmillan of Canada, 1969.

Freeman, Barbara M. *Beyond Bylines: Media Workers and Women's Rights in Canada.* Waterloo, ON: Wilfrid Laurier University Press, 2011.

———. "Ferguson, Catherine (Kathleen Blake) (Willis; Watkins; Coleman)." *In Dictionary of Canadian Biography*, vol. 14. Toronto and Laval: University of Toronto Press / Presses de l'Université Laval, 2003. biographi.ca/en/bio/ferguson_catherine_14E.html.

———. *The Satellite Sex: The Media and Women's Issues in English Canada, 1966–1971.* Waterloo, ON: Wilfrid Laurier University Press, 2001.

Gaudreault, Amédée. *Trente Ans de Journalisme: Souvenirs, Portraits et Anecdotes.* Montreal: Éditions Méridien, 1991.

Gibson, Frederick, and Barbara Robertson, eds. *Ottawa at War: The Grant Dexter Memoranda, 1939–1945.* Winnipeg: Manitoba Record Society, 1994.

Gossage, Patrick. *Close to Charisma: My Years Between the Press and Pierre Elliott Trudeau.* Toronto: McClelland and Stewart, 1986.

Graham, Ron. *All the King's Men: Politics Among the Ruins.* Toronto: Macfarlane, Walter and Ross, 1995.

Gray, John. *Paul Martin: The Power of Ambition.* Toronto: Key Porter Books, 2003.

Greenspon, Edward, and Anthony Wilson-Smith. *Double Vision: The Inside Story of the Liberals in Power.* Toronto: Doubleday Canada, 1996.

Gregg, Allan. "1984 in 2012 — The Assault on Reason." Notes for an address to Carleton School of Public Affairs, 2012. allangregg.com/1984-in-2012-%e2%80%93-the-assault-on-reason/

Gwyn, Richard. *Nationalism Without Walls: The Unbearable Lightness of Being Canadian.* Toronto: McClelland and Stewart, 1995.

———. *Northern Magus: Trudeau and Canadians.* Toronto: McClelland and Stewart, 1980.

Gwyn, Sandra. *The Private Capital: Ambition and Love in the Age of Macdonald and Laurier.* Toronto: McClelland and Stewart, 1984.

Halton, David. *Dispatches from the Front: The Life of Matthew Halton, Canada's Voice at War.* Toronto: McClelland and Stewart, 2014.

Harte, Walter Blackburn. "Canadian Journalists and Journalism." *New England Magazine* 5, no. 4, 1891.

Hendra, Peter. "Rogue Reporter." *Ryerson Review of Journalism*, Spring 1988. rrj.ca/rogue-reporter.

Hillmer, Norman, ed. *Pearson: The Unlikely Gladiator.* Montreal: McGill-Queen's University Press, 1999.

Hoff, George. "Douglas Fisher: Politician and Journalist, 1957–2006." Master's thesis, Carleton University, 2009. douglasfisher.ca/wp-content/uploads/MA-thesis-re-Douglas-Fisher.pdf.

Hutchison, Bruce. *The Far Side of the Street.* Toronto: Macmillan of Canada, 1976.

———. *The Unknown Country: Canada and Her People.* Toronto: Oxford University Press, 2010. First published 1942.

Jobber, Barbara. "The Man Who Flipped Off Trudeau." *Ryerson Review of Journalism,* Spring 2009. rrj.ca/the-man-who-flipped-off-trudeau.

Kay, Linda. *The Sweet Sixteen: The Journey that Inspired the Canadian Women's Press Club.* Montreal: McGill-Queen's University Press, 2012.

Kesterton, W.H. *A History of Journalism in Canada*. Ottawa and Toronto: Carleton University Press/McClelland and Stewart, 1970.

Lang, Marjory. "Lipsett, Genevieve Elsie, Alice (Skinner)." *In Dictionary of Canadian Biography*, vol. 16. Toronto and Laval: University of Toronto Press / Presses de l'Université Laval, 2003. biographi.ca/en/bio/lipsett_genevieve_elsie_alice_16E.html.

———. *Women Who Made the News: Female Journalists in Canada, 1880–1945*. Montreal: McGill-Queen's University Press, 1999.

Lang, Marjory, and Linda Hale. "Women of *The World* and Other Dailies: The Lives and Times of Vancouver Newspaperwomen in the First Quarter of the Century." *BC Studies* 85, Spring 1990.

Lavoie, Luc. *En Première Ligne: Le Parcours atypique d'un Communicateur*. Montreal: Éditions de l'Homme, 2018.

Levine, Allan. *King: William Lyon Mackenzie King: A Life Guided by the Hand of Destiny*. Vancouver: Douglas and McIntyre, 2011.

———. *Scrum Wars: The Prime Ministers and the Media*. Toronto: Dundurn Press, 1993.

Litt, Paul. *Elusive Destiny: The Political Vocation of John Napier Turner*. Vancouver: University of British Columbia Press, 2011.

Lynch, Charles. *The Lynch Mob: Stringing Up Our Prime Ministers*. Toronto: Key Porter Books, 1988.

———. *You Can't Print THAT!: Memoirs of a Political Voyeur*. Edmonton: Hurtig, 1983.

MacDonald, L. Ian. *Mulroney: The Making of the Prime Minister*. Toronto: McClelland and Stewart, 1984.

MacKenzie, David. *Arthur Irwin: A Biography*. Toronto: University of Toronto Press, 1993.

Magurn, A.J. "The Ottawa Correspondent." *Massey's Magazine*, May 1897.

Mansbridge, Peter. *Peter Mansbridge One on One: Favourite Conversations and the Stories Behind Them*. Toronto: Random House, 2009.

Martin, Lawrence. *Iron Man: The Defiant Reign of Jean Chrétien*. Toronto: Viking Canada, 2003.

Martin, Paul. *Hell or High Water: My Life In and Out of Politics*. Toronto: McClelland and Stewart, 2008.

McIntosh, Dave. *Ottawa Unbuttoned, or Who's Running This Country Anyway?* Toronto: General Publishing, 1988.

Meisel, John. *The Canadian General Election of 1957.* Toronto: University of Toronto Press, 1962.

Mount, Nick. *When Canadian Literature Moved to New York.* Toronto: University of Toronto Press, 2005.

Mulroney, Brian. *Memoirs.* Toronto: McClelland and Stewart, 2007.

Newman, Peter C. *The Distemper of Our Times: Canadian Politics in Transition: 1963–1968.* Toronto: McClelland and Stewart, 1968.

———. *Here Be Dragons: Telling Tales of People, Passion and Power.* Toronto: McClelland and Stewart, 2004.

———. *Renegade in Power: The Diefenbaker Years.* Toronto: McClelland and Stewart, 1963.

———. *The Secret Mulroney Tapes: Unguarded Confessions of a Prime Minister.* Toronto: Random House, 2005.

———. *Sometimes a Great Nation.* Toronto: McClelland and Stewart, 1988.

Nichols, Marjorie, with Jane O'Hara. *Mark My Words: The Memoirs of a Very Political Reporter.* Vancouver: Douglas and McIntyre, 1992.

O'Leary, Grattan. *Recollections of People, Press and Politics.* Toronto: University of Toronto Press, 1977.

Oliver, Craig. *Oliver's Twist: The Life and Times of an Unapologetic Newshound.* Toronto: Penguin Canada, 2011.

Pearson, Lester B. *Mike: The Memoirs of the Right Honourable Lester Pearson.* Vol. 3, *1957–1968*, edited by John A. Munro and Alex I. Inglis. Toronto: University of Toronto Press, 1975.

Poling, Jim, Sr. *Waking Nanabijou: Uncovering a Secret Past.* Toronto: Dundurn Press, 2007.

Radwanski, George. *Trudeau.* Toronto: Macmillan of Canada, 1979.

Rae, Bob. *What's Happened to Politics?* Toronto: Simon & Schuster, 2015.

Robinson, Judith. *This Is on the House.* Toronto: McClelland and Stewart, 1957.

Russell, Nick. *Morals and the Media: Ethics in Canadian Journalism,* 2nd ed. Vancouver: University of British Columbia Press, 2006.

Rutherford, Paul. *When Television Was Young: Primetime Canada, 1952–1967.* Toronto: University of Toronto Press, 1990.

Sawatsky, John. *Mulroney: The Politics of Ambition.* Toronto: Macfarlane, Walter and Ross, 1991.

Sharp, Mitchell. *Which Reminds Me…: A Memoir.* Toronto: University of Toronto Press, 1994.

Simpson, Jeffrey. *Discipline of Power: The Conservative Interlude and the Liberal Restoration.* Toronto: Macmillan of Canada, 1980.

———. *The Friendly Dictatorship.* Rev. ed. Toronto: McClelland and Stewart, 2002.

Skelton, Oscar. *Life and Letters of Wilfrid Laurier.* Ottawa and Toronto: Carleton University Press/McClelland and Stewart, 1966.

Small, Doug. "The Power and Jurisdiction of the Parliamentary Press Gallery." Research Paper, Carleton University School of Journalism, 1977.

Smith, Denis. *Gentle Patriot: A Political Biography of Walter Gordon.* Edmonton: Hurtig, 1973.

———. *Rogue Tory: The Life and Legend of John G. Diefenbaker.* Toronto: Macfarlane, Walter and Ross, 1995.

Sotiron, Minko. *From Politics to Profit: The Commercialization of Canadian Daily Newspapers, 1890–1920.* Montreal: McGill-Queen's University Press, 2005.

Stevens, Geoffrey. *The Player: The Life and Times of Dalton Camp.* Toronto: Key Porter Books, 2003.

Sullivan, Martin. *Mandate '68: The Year of Pierre Elliott Trudeau.* Toronto: Doubleday Canada, 1968.

Tetley, William. *The October Crisis, 1970.* Montreal: McGill-Queen's University Press, 2007.

Trudeau, Margaret. *Consequences.* Toronto: Seal Books, 1982.

Trudeau, Pierre. *Memoirs.* Toronto: McClelland and Stewart, 1993.

Van Dusen, Tom. *Inside the Tent: Forty-Five Years on Parliament Hill.* Toronto: General Publishing, 1998.

Vastel, Michel. *The Outsider: The Life of Pierre Elliott Trudeau.* Toronto: Macmillan of Canada, 1990.

Waddell, Christopher. "Berry'd Alive: The Media, Technology, and the Death of Political Coverage." In *How Canadians Communicate IV: Media and Politics,* edited by David Taras and Christopher Waddell. Edmonton: Athabasca University Press, 2012.

Wade, Mason. *The French Canadians.* Vol. 2, *1911–1967.* Rev. ed. Toronto: Macmillan of Canada, 1968.

Waite, P.B. *In Search of R.B. Bennett.* Montreal: McGill-Queen's University Press, 2012.

———. *The Man from Halifax: Sir John Thompson, Prime Minister.* Toronto: University of Toronto Press, 1985.

Wells, Paul. *The Longer I'm Prime Minister: Stephen Harper and Canada, 2006–*. Toronto: Vintage Canada, 2013.

Westell, Anthony. *The Inside Story: A Life in Journalism*. Toronto: Dundurn Press, 2002.

Whittington, Les. *Spinning History: A Witness to Harper's Canada and 21st Century Choices*. Ottawa: Hill Times, 2005.

Willison, John. *Reminiscences, Political and Personal*. Toronto: McClelland and Stewart, 1919.

Zolf, Larry. *Dance of the Dialectic*. Toronto: James, Lewis and Samuel, 1973.

IMAGE CREDITS

INDEX

Book Credits
Acquiring Editor: Scott Fraser
Developmental Editor: Dominic Farrell
Project Editor: Elena Radic
Copy Editor: Cy Strom
Proofreader: Ashley Hisson
Indexer: Sergey Lobachev

Cover Designer: Laura Boyle
Interior Designer: Courtney Horner

Publicist: Elham Ali

Dundurn
Publisher: J. Kirk Howard
Vice-President: Carl A. Brand
Editorial Director: Kathryn Lane
Artistic Director: Laura Boyle
Director of Sales and Marketing: Synora Van Drine
Publicity Manager: Michelle Melski

Editorial: Allison Hirst, Dominic Farrell,
Jenny McWha, Rachel Spence, Elena Radic
Marketing and Publicity: Kendra Martin, Kathryn Bassett, Elham Ali

dundurn.com   dundurnpress
@dundurnpress   dundurnpress
dundurnpress   info@dundurn.com

FIND US ON NETGALLEY & GOODREADS TOO!

DUNDURN